Lake Powell Tales

Lake Powell Tales

◆

An Anthology of Adventure

Edited by
Tiffany Mapel

Hadley! Someday, I will bring you, Matt, + Abby to Powell, and we'll all have fun in the Sun and splash in the waves! Love, Tiff

iUniverse, Inc.
New York Lincoln Shanghai

Lake Powell Tales
An Anthology of Adventure

Copyright © 2007 by Tiffany Mapel

iUniverse books may be ordered through booksellers or by contacting:

iUniverse
2021 Pine Lake Road, Suite 100
Lincoln, NE 68512
www.iuniverse.com
1-800-Authors (1-800-288-4677)

Because of the dynamic nature of the Internet, any Web addresses or links contained in this book may have changed since publication and may no longer be valid.

The views expressed in this work are solely those of the author and do not necessarily reflect the views of the publisher, and the publisher hereby disclaims any responsibility for them.

ISBN: 978-0-595-45126-5 (pbk)
ISBN: 978-0-595-89439-0 (ebk)

Printed in the United States of America

Contents

"Life is pretty dry without a boat."

—seen on a billboard

Foreword

This book is dedicated to all who have experienced and have a passion for Lake Powell. The stories herein are a collective work of various authors focusing on memories of Lake Powell; real life adventures that span the decades. Lake Powell is an amazing place—it has the power to draw you to it, relentlessly as some can attest—and will always keep you coming back for more. She can be kind to you with perfect weather and water once, and another time eat you up and spit you out in the worst storm ever. No matter what happens, you always come back. Lake Powell has that mysterious, tantalizing quality. It is never the same lake twice; you couldn't see the whole lake at every water level during one lifetime. Resplendently clad in swirling sandstone of every rosy hue, underneath a sapphire sky with waters so pure—it is the best dose of color therapy for which one could ever wish. She is without a doubt America's most scenic lake. Humans, by nature, are drawn to water. So come with us, experience majestic Lake Powell, and rejuvenate your soul in her waters.

—TM

Broad peaceful lake,
Mysteriously vast at twilight;
Sacred hush,
Glimmering waters open to the sky.

—Everett Ruess, 1933

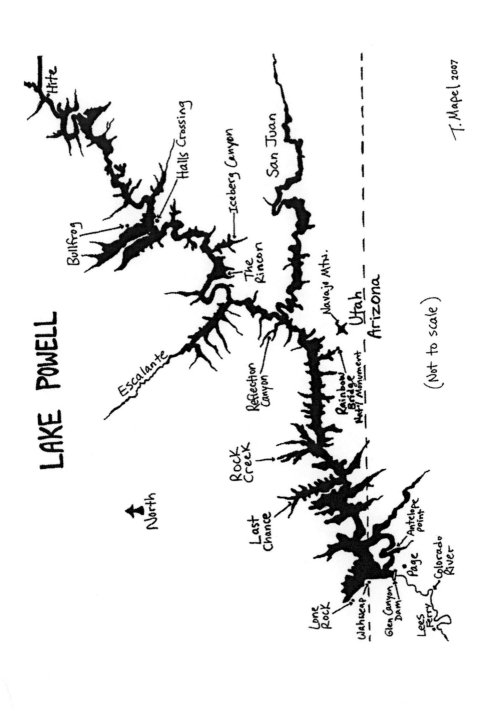

LAKE POWELL

North

Hite

Halls Crossing

Bullfrog

Iceberg Canyon

The Rincon

San Juan

Escalante

Reflection Canyon

Navajo Mtn.

Rainbow Bridge Nat'l Monument

Utah
Arizona

Rock Creek

Last Chance

Page

Antelope Point

Colorado River

Lone Rock

Wahweap

Glen Canyon Dam

Lees Ferry

(Not to scale)

T. Mapel 2007

History of Lake Powell

By Tiffany Mapel

"Already the storage of these waters has begun; the people are constructing reservoirs, and will continue the process until all the streams of the arid region are wholly utilized in this manner, so that no waste water runs to the sea."

—Major John Wesley Powell, Aug. 1889

Lake Powell lies in scenic, sandstone Glen Canyon, located in south central Utah and north central Arizona. It was named after Major John Wesley Powell, a one-armed Civil War veteran, geologist, and explorer. For millennia, the Colorado River had faithfully flowed southwest, cutting through ancient layers of sandstone, mudstone, limestone, and shale, and drained into the Gulf of California. The Colorado River was deemed the most treacherous waterway in the northern hemisphere.

On May 24th, 1869, Major Powell took his first run down the Colorado with four rowboats, and a crew of nine. It was undoubtedly during "high tide" of spring runoff, so it was likely a wild ride. He started at Green River City, Wyoming, and went to the mouth of the Virgin River in Arizona near the Grand Canyon. On a second journey in May of 1871, Major Powell conducted the first scientific and geological survey of the Grand Canyon. Major Powell also helped form the U.S. Geological Survey, and was its second director in 1881.

For hundreds of years, various Native American tribes called Glen Canyon home. Two predominant groups were the Fremont and Anasazi cultures. The Fremonts were hunters and gatherers, so were more nomadic. The Anasazi were primarily farmers, irrigating and growing squash, beans, corn, and other crops. They lived in pit houses, and preferred dwellings off the canyon floors that were also protected by alcoves in the sandstone walls. "Anasazi" is a Navajo word, meaning "the ancient ones." Both cultures left behind plentiful ruins and petroglyphs (etched into rock) and pictographs (painted on the rock), ancient art depicting their lives.

The first known white explorers happened upon Glen Canyon in 1776, the very year our nation was born. Two Franciscan priests intended to set up a trade route, linking Santa Fe, New Mexico to Monterey, California. Silvestre Velez de Escalante and Francisco Atanasio Dominguez set off from Santa Fe with a small party of explorers and horses. Throughout the fall and early winter of 1776, the party explored Glen Canyon, noted the harsh environment, and looked for the easiest and safest place to cross the raging river. At times, they had to cut stairs into the steep sandstone, so that their horses could navigate the precarious canyon. The historic "Crossing of the Fathers" took place on a slow, shallow portion of the river, currently underwater at Lake Powell's Padre Bay. Other people who came to know Glen Canyon were homesteaders, ranchers, miners, and various river runners from the early 1900's to when Glen Canyon Dam was born in 1963.

In 1922, the western United States wanted to ensure they had water and electricity for the future. The Colorado River Pact was signed, and it was decided that the Colorado River be dammed not only for flood control, but also for its wealth of resources: water supply, electricity, and later, recreation. Then-President Dwight Eisenhower authorized the construction of Glen Canyon Dam in 1956.

The site for Glen Canyon Dam was chosen soon afterward. It was to be built in a narrow, deep canyon, with strong walls and no faults. The location also had the added bonus of being next to Wahweap Creek, which had a generous supply of rock aggregate to aid in dam construction. Glen Canyon Dam was on its way.

On October 1st, 1956, the first blast started clearing tunnels for water diversion. On February 11th, 1959, water was diverted through the tunnels so dam construction could begin. Later that year, the bridge was completed, allowing trucks to deliver equipment and materials for the dam, and also for the new town of Page, Arizona.

Concrete placement started around the clock on June 17th, 1960. The last bucket of concrete was poured on September 13th, 1963. Over 5 million cubic yards of concrete make up Glen Canyon Dam. The Dam is 710 feet high, with the surface elevation of the water at full pool being approximately 3700 feet above sea level. Construction of the Dam cost $155 million, and 18 lives were lost in the process. From 1963 to 1966, turbines and generators were installed for hydroelectricity.

Upon completion of Glen Canyon Dam on September 13th, 1963, the Colorado River began to back up, no longer being diverted through the tunnels. Lake Powell was born. As the lake filled over the years, minor seismic activity in the area occurred as the ground shifted beneath the increasing weight of the water. It took 17 years for the lake to rise to the high water mark, on June 22nd, 1980. However, in the spring of 1983, unusually heavy snows fed the runoff, and the lake crested to 3708.4 feet. This was just seven feet below the top of Glen Canyon Dam. The water came perilously close to topping the dam, but luckily it never did. As a result, dam operators were better able to gauge water releases, and plan for future high-water emergencies. In 1964, Glen Canyon Dam was voted Outstanding Engineering Achievement of the year by the American Society of Civil Engineers. On September 22nd, 1966, Glen Canyon Dam was dedicated by Ladybird Johnson.

Lake Powell is 140 miles long from Glen Canyon Dam to Hite Marina, with 96 major side canyons. The deepest part of the lake is around 560 feet. Lake Powell has plenty of shoreline, and lies amidst the stunning sandstone of the Colorado Plateau, a geologic feature that covers the Four Corners region. Lake Powell is the second largest man-made lake in the U.S.; only Lake Mead, located 300 miles downstream from Lake Powell on the borders of Arizona and Nevada, is bigger.

Lake Powell and its surrounding area were designated as Glen Canyon National Recreation Area (GCNRA) in 1972, and GCNRA is governed under the National Park Service. The total area of GCNRA is about 1,250,000 acres, and Lake Powell takes up only 13% of the Recreation Area. Visitation numbers from one to three million people each year. Water-based and backcountry recreation opportunities include: boating, swimming, water sports, scuba diving, kayaking, fishing, hiking, camping, canyoneering, and 4-wheeling on designated roads and trails.

Lake Powell is just one part of the Colorado River Storage Project (CRSP), and is the premier storage reservoir for the Upper Basin states that use the Colorado River: Colorado, Wyoming, Utah, and New Mexico. Because of the CRSP and the various reservoirs and dams along the Colorado River, over 30 million people in the west benefit from the stored water and clean, renewable hydroelectricity from the dams.

Geezer Tales

By Pete Klocki

"All Americans believe that they are born fishermen. For a man to admit to a distaste for fishing would be like denouncing mother-love and hating moonlight."

—John Steinbeck

Art Greene, as some will remember, was the driving force behind getting the Wahweap developments under way and putting Lake Powell into the public's conscious as the original concessionaire. The first and only time I ever met the man, well, no, that's not quite right—I didn't actually "meet" him, in the formal sense, but rather, I was there, and I was a co-victim of one of his practical jokes. At any rate, it was sometime in the 1950's, probably '53 or '54, because I was still in High School and dumb as a box of rocks.

We—and that would be my Dad, myself, and a couple of my Dad's adult friends—used to hunt deer on the North Kaibab on a fairly regular basis back in the '50s. It was a grueling trip in those days because Hwy-89 north of Flagstaff was a narrow, nasty little road, and I-17 was still just a gleam in President Eisenhower's eye. In order to get to Jacob Lake from Phoenix, it was necessary to motor out Grand Avenue and continue to Wickenburg, climb Yarnell Hill to get to Prescott, take 89 over Mingus Mountain and on through Oak Creek Canyon to Flagstaff. In a 1948 wood-side Pontiac station wagon you MIGHT make Jacobs Lake in fourteen hours on a good day without flats or breakdowns. Standard procedure for these trips was to grind it out with driver changes and thermos bottles of coffee and limp sandwiches in a single mad, non-stop-except-for-fuel-dash to Jacobs Lake Lodge, where we would crash before proceeding deep into the woods the following day to set up camp.

On one such trip, we just couldn't git 'er done and shortly after crossing the river we pulled in at Cliff Dwellers. We had roared out of Phoenix around

4:00am and by the time we crossed the river the sun had set and we were all pretty well done in. So, we opted for a hot meal and a bed at Cliff Dwellers instead of Jacobs Lake, and that's when the fun began. The Art Greene family owned and operated the place and had built much of the stone lodge and out buildings that still exist today. The whole enterprise was a family staffed affair, with Art's wife, Ethyl, and two or three daughters doing the cooking and table service, while one of Art's sons operated a river tour business. It appeared that Art's main job was to hover over tables and promote the area, his business interests, and himself. And he was a natural born genius of a pitch-man!

As soon as our dinner was served, Art came over to our table and went to work. It started well enough, with the typical intro-phase: "Where you boys from? Deer huntin', huh? I know where the big bucks hang out, boys," and so on.

I'll guess Art was in his 50's then—maybe a little older. It was hard to tell because his face betrayed a life of outdoor exposure and hard miles. He had a sort of bulldog look about him with a knobby chin on a square jaw. But there was also a mischievous eye twinkle that was hard to ignore.

After he got past the "intro-phase," he got down to business. Literally. Because that was what Art was all about. He was apparently into everything and anything connected to acquiring wealth and was anxious to share his expertise and methods with anyone who would listen. None of this had anything to do with patting himself on the back or bragging about his accomplishments or anything like that, however. What he was actually doing was *trolling* for possible investment partners, or failing that, to sell whatever he had available to sell. Which was considerable.

So, he starts explaining how you could make decent money operating a Reservation trading post, filing a uranium mining claim, operating a tourist lodge, a guide service, and any number of other schemes he had in mind, or had already done and proven to be lucrative. He is throwing around terms completely foreign to a teenager's ears, like "investment return, recapture, extending credit to compound your net," and on and on and on.

I had no idea what Art Greene was talking about, and to be perfectly candid about it, I don't think my Dad did either, because all he did was nod his head once in a while and continue to chew. So Art can see he's getting nowhere with this, and he's basically wasting his time with this bunch of blockheads. And with that read on the situation, Art drifts over to another table and starts all over again on a fresh audience. But apparently he didn't fare too well at the other table either, because after our dinner plates were cleared and we hovered over coffee cups, he returned to our table with a whole new strategy.

Now, let's see. Where were we? Oh, right … pie and coffee time.

Before I move on with this though, I need to paint a word picture of the dining room seating and table arrangements. It's relevant to the story. I should probably tell you something about my Dad at this juncture as well. I'll start with him. My Dad had, what we would call today, some "issues." In a nutshell, he was a very proud individual, took no guff from any man, was quicker to fight than argue, and, at the same time, was just a tad self-conscious about what he perceived to be certain personal shortcomings. Here's what that was all about: To begin with, he had very little formal education, having been kicked out of High School without graduating because he had been caught shooting craps in a basement boiler room. He came from a very poor immigrant family that tried to scrape out a living on a small farm back in Ohio and that had limited command of the English language. Dad was always sensitive about his European-sounding surname and the connection it made with his humble roots. On top of this, he had bad lungs and never enjoyed good health. This resulted in being rejected by the Army when he tried to enlist at the outbreak of WWII. And that was a tough pill for him to swallow because just about every other able-bodied male in our family had gone off and bulled their way through the war, while he was left behind.

And if all of that were not enough, Dad had only recently founded a small construction contracting company and he was having a tough time making a go of it. Money was short almost all the time. None of this made him what you might consider a fun guy to be around.

Knowing a little about him now, you might better understand why Art Greene was not terribly high on Dad's list of favorite people. Dad had already formed an opinion of Art based on the previous conversation that sounded to my Dad's ear like so much pretentious bragging and horn tooting. So when Art came back later to talk with us again, I was relieved that the conversation took a much different turn this time. But wait. I can't go there yet. I have to tell you about the table position.

Our table was more or less at the center of the small dining room; a pretty rough affair, as I remember it, with stone floors and walls, hard, straight-backed chairs and tables that seemed to stand too high and were covered over with red and white checked linoleum table cloths. My Dad and I sat next to each other on one side of our table, while across the table from us were his two pals; a fellow named Chick Scussel, and the other, Al DeRosa.

There was another table against the window wall, behind my Dad's back, that he could not look directly at. Another party had left and the Greene girls had cleared it off. Art had picked up some napkins and a fist full of silverware and was moving in our direction on his way to do a fresh set-up on that table.

Meanwhile, we are all engrossed with pie and coffee and hunter's tales of mule deer bucks with rack spreads so wide they couldn't fit through a three-foot door and such as that. I don't remember what kind of pie I had, but whatever it was, I had wolfed it down in typical teenage fashion and was already eyeing the other plates for possible scraps. I distinctly remember, however, that Dad had cherry pie. And, he didn't like it.

So Art breezes by on the way to that other table behind us, and says: "How 'bout that pie, boys. Pretty good, huh?" Everyone had something favorable to say, except, old Dad. And he pipes up and says: "Well, you could have put some cherries in it! It's all just red cornstarch!" So Art comes right over. He doesn't get that other table set-up done. He just dumps the napkins and silverware in a heap, and comes over and tells Dad not to eat that damned cherry pie. He says he will bring out a piece of apple pie that is guaranteed to please, instead. And he did. Then he asked Dad how the apple pie was, and Dad allowed that it was much better, but it could be even further improved if it was heated just a bit and had a dollop of vanilla ice cream along side it.

Al and Chic just rolled their eyes and shook their heads. I could have crawled under the table. But Art Greene just lets this slide right off his back. "You're right, by golly," he says. And he goes back to the kitchen again and a minute or two later returns with another piece of apple pie that is heated and has a big pile of ice cream melting all over it. Right then and there, I decided that Art Greene, for whatever fault my Dad had found in him, was a pretty righteous, stand-up kind of guy. Though a little embarrassing, that whole thing had turned out to be quite a bonanza for me. I polished off both unfinished pieces of Dad's pies—the rubber cherry, as well as the cold apple.

So things settle down after the pie episode and Art goes back to the set-up job on the other table, which is well within earshot, and strikes up a new conversation just like nothing had happened. He starts talking about the river that runs through Glen Canyon, which none of us had even heard of before, and about Major John Powell's expeditions and how Art used to take tourists down the river to see the wonders of it all, but had since turned that job over to his son, because Art had bigger fish to fry and really didn't have time to do those trips the right way anymore.

Suddenly, Art changed the subject, asking an odd question of us. (Bear with me on the spelling here). He asks if any of us had ever heard of "Tseh Na-ni-a-go atin?" Well, none of us had, of course, and we pretty much sat there with blank stares on our faces. And for my part, I guessed he was talking about something to eat—some sort of Navajo dessert maybe. So I think it was Chic who replied that, "No, we've never heard of that. What is it?"

"That's Navajo for Rainbow Bridge," Art answered, and immediately launched into this fantastic description of a natural stone arch that spanned a live creek full of snowmelt that ran down from Navajo Mountain. It soared so high in the air that you could fit the Westward Ho Hotel under it and still have room to fly a B-29 between the hotel roof and the underside of the arch.

Under his breath, my Dad mutters, "bull-puckey." Art does not stop there. He goes on to speak of other such wonders hidden away within the mysterious confines of Glen Canyon that test the imagination and defy description. He speaks of huge grottos that have never seen the sun that lie under towering canyon walls and that have snow-white sand floors containing pools of spring-fed water so still and clear that you must first step in them before you realize they are there. He went on about hanging gardens of fern and wildflower that grow from the rock along fault lines that weep pure, cold water. And ancient Indian ruins that look as though the inhabitants had left just last Wednesday, and of mule deer that share the river with big horn sheep, and beaver dams on the tributary creeks, and all manner of other wildlife and wild things that only the privileged few have seen.

I'm going nuts. I'm hooked. I want to go there and see such things. Again, Dad mutters, "bull-puckey." Art Greene continued to regale us with marvelous descriptions of the Canyon in a most colorful manner. I am mesmerized. Dad is concentrating on his pie. He says nothing. And if I had to guess, he probably didn't believe a word Art was saying. I ask a couple of stupid questions that Art patiently answers, and then, Art sets the hook.

"There's only a couple of different ways you can get to Rainbow Bridge," he tells us. "You can't drive a car to it. You can only get there by horseback, on foot, or by boat. If you go overland, you have to come from the south across the Reservation, over Navajo Mountain, and then down along the creek on a pretty tough trail. It's pretty hard to do on foot. Round trip you are looking at around forty miles as the crow flies. But the trail sure don't go like the crow flies. It's likely closer to sixty, maybe seventy trail miles. You can't hardly do it on foot because it takes so dang long and you can't pack enough supplies to last you. Takes a good man at least a week to make that round trip. And it ain't something you want to try in summer either. Can't haul enough water and you can't drink the creek. Sheep and goats foul it too bad. Now, you can hire a Navajo guide and pay to use his horses. Do it in maybe four days if you push it. But even then, it's better done in winter than summer."

"What about boats?" someone asked. "You mentioned something about a boat." It was time for Art to reel us in.

"Right," Art said. "Well, there's a couple of different ways to go about that, too." Art was grinning from ear to ear, horn-rimmed glasses bouncing on his little nose as he spoke. "My son runs those tours and you can pretty much customize them any way you like. You can choose to make a power boat run up the river from Lee's Crossing (as Art called it) to Bridge Canyon and power boat back down again. Or, you can go up to Hite's Crossing and put in and float the river down to Lee's and take out there."

Now we are firing questions at him—but not Dad. We are asking stuff like, "How long do these trips take? How much does it cost? What's included, and what must be brought along? Do you just go to see the bridge, or do you get to see some of the other stuff too?"—That sort of thing.

Art tells us we can make the float trip down from Hite in as little as six days if you are really in a hurry, but that's no way to do it. You miss too much. That kind of trip should take at least two weeks to do it right, and even at that you just scratch the surface. The power boat trip was the better option for those in a hurry. That could be done in five days and still allow some time for side trips. As far as what was required to bring along, all that was necessary was your own smokes, your toothbrush, booze, if so inclined, and a bedroll. Everything else was furnished.

I can't remember the exact dollar costs for these trips, but at the time, they were WAY out of my range. They were priced per-person, per-river day and the unit cost was something like a hundred and some odd bucks per. And this was in the 50's when three bucks an hour was considered to be a living wage. So, depending on how you wanted to go about it, you could be looking at anywhere between eight hundred to two thousand dollars per person.

And now for the practical joke part. While talking to us about the wonders of Glen Canyon, Art had taken up a standing position directly behind my Dad and was standing over him while Dad scarfed down his pie and ice cream, oblivious to the whole pitch. My Dad had a big, bulky, parka-like canvas coat draped over the back of his chair, and Art's hands were resting on the coat's shoulders as he spoke. He had finished the table-set up job and had a few leftover pieces of silverware in his left hand, the one nearest me. Somewhere during the boat-trip talk, Art's hand came down and he slipped that silverware into Dad's coat pocket. Hunched over his pie, Dad didn't see this. I did. I was twisted around on my seat to face Art because I hung on every word he said and couldn't miss the sly maneuver. And of course, both Chick and Al saw this happen too.

Art gave us a big wink, and put a fingertip to pursed lips. At that moment, the three of us became co-conspirators in whatever play Art had in mind. So Art winds up his pitch about the boat trips and asks if any of us might be interested in an adventure like that, and I of course start babbling about saving up the money so maybe I could do it in a year or two, or some such as that. Art pulls out a stack of business cards and starts passing them out and I took a half dozen or so in case I lost one. I really wanted to DO THIS!

We finally got coffeed out and Art drifted away again. We figured out who owes what for dinner and leave crumpled bills on the table and get up to leave for the room we had booked in one of the little stone bungalow units. We have to go outside to get our stuff out of the car and make our way to the room. Coats are pulled on and we start for the door.

Art intercepts us there. "If I don't see you boys again in the morning before you leave out of here, have a great hunt and stop in on your way home and tell me all about it." As he says this, Art slips an arm around Dad's shoulder and adds: "And when you come back, bring my silverware back along with you."

Dad shoots him a look and asks, "What the *&%*#@ are you talking about?"

Art pats Dad's coat pocket to make the silverware rattle a little. "Your son slipped this in your coat pocket during dinner," he says. "But that's okay. I just figured your kit must be light. Just bring it back with you when you're done with it."

I don't think the joke came off in a way Art intended it to. But in any case, it hit Dad pretty hard. He's a proud man, remember. One of those types who believes your word is your bond. He's also hit a rough financial patch and does all he can to hide this from the world. And then there is the European thing. And now he's thinking he has a common thief for a son.

Art has a wide grin going, Chic is laughing out loud, and Al is absolutely cracking up. My Dad's face has gone beet red; he's looking at me with fire in his eyes. Having seen that look before, I took several prudent and precautionary backward steps, and shook my head violently. "UH-UH!! I DID NO SUCH THING!!" says I. So now, not only am I a common thief, I'm a liar as well, he reasons, as he prepares to separate my head from my neck.

Art jumps in to rescue me just in time and explains it was all a joke, and admits to planting the contraband silverware himself. Dad fails to see any of the humor attached to this joke gone bad, and says so, in somewhat profane terms, while pulling the silverware out of his pocket and flinging it to the stone floor with a clatter you could have heard in Kanab. All in all, it was a pretty bad scene. Art apologized profusely and admitted it had gone badly, adding that he had pulled it off at least a hundred times before without muffing it as badly as he did this night, and as a peace offering, Art offered to give us a free breakfast in the morning.

Dad wasn't buying any of that and he stormed out the door with the three of us in tow. I was trailing behind and as I reached the door, I sort of shrugged and said again that I wanted to take that boat trip in a year or two. Art laughed and said something like he was looking forward to it and he would make sure I was well taken care of. Pretty decent, I thought.

When we got out to the car, Dad already had the engine running and told us all to get in, right now. Chic, or maybe Al, protested immediately. "What about the room?" The short answer was, "To hell with the room!" And we roared off into the night throwing a shower of gravel off spinning wheels, headed for Jacob Lake, which didn't pan out so well either. By the time we got there the place was closed up and dark. A couple of dozen other hunters had probably beat us to it and the place was filled up.

On the way to Jacob Lake, I broke the stone-silence in the car by mentioning how much I would really like to float that river through Glen Canyon. (Told you I was a dumb kid). Dad looked over at me and said, "You must be nuts! I wouldn't float ACROSS a river with that guy, let alone DOWN one."

We slept in the car that night and suffered mightily for it. Condensation froze on the windows and sometime in the night my right cheek became welded to the steel door-sill. But the days passed and all of us managed to take decent bucks and the episode at Cliff Dwellers was largely forgotten. We had our campfire stories and laughs and poker games and shares of Christian Brothers Brandy and burnt steaks and half cooked beans and deer liver and onions and had a high old time. And when it was time to go home after a week or so, we piled three skinned out and tarp-wrapped deer on the roof and squeezed a fourth one behind the back seat and started down the road.

At Cliff Dwellers, we sped right past without a word spoken, my Dad staring straight ahead, two white-knuckled hands on the wheel. We hunted the Kaibab a couple of more times after that, but we never did stop at Art Greene's place again. But each time we drove by, the notion of floating Glen Canyon popped into my head again. I was still convinced that I would do that yet, if only I could scrape together the money. I never did. The opportunity slipped away and was lost forever. I graduated from High School in the summer of '55, and I joined the Air Force the following February. When discharged in 1960, I learned that a bridge had been thrown over the river and a huge dam was under construction at the foot of Glen Canyon. The town of Page had been built and Art Greene was indeed frying bigger fish.

◆   ◆   ◆

Discovery Years

The highways and byways of life take many a twist and turn. Some of those turns take us up dead-end alleys while others lead to remarkable and unexpected discoveries. The discovery of Lake Powell was at the end of one such alley for me. The journey began as the result of a casual conversation late one summer night in 1961 that had nothing to do with fishing or boating. But that's getting ahead of the story. Let me back up just a bit.

I had enlisted in the Air Force, completed basic training at Parks AFB near San Francisco, and had gone on to electronic warfare school at Keesler Field down in Biloxi, Mississippi, and was back home in Phoenix on a delay-enroute before moving on to my first duty station in Condon, Oregon. It was early July, 1956 and a terrible air tragedy had occurred above the Grand Canyon. Two commercial airliners, a UAL DC-7, and a TWA Super Connie had collided with horrible loss of life and the wreckage was scattered both within and upon the surrounding rim country of the canyon.

A story about the tragedy in the Phoenix newspapers made small mention of Art Greene, who, among others, had been interviewed by a reporter. I don't remember much about that article, except that Art had something to say about people finding and carrying off parts of the wreckage that had fallen on the Navajo Reservation, and that this might hamper findings of the accident investigation.

The name, Art Greene, of course caught my eye and rang a bell for me, reminding me of the silverware fiasco at Cliff Dwellers back in '53. And that in turn reminded me that I still had a river float through Glen Canyon stored in my mental agenda of future things to do with myself. I had completely forgotten all about that.

Over the next four years, though, Glen Canyon eased from my mind and was again forgotten. I was completely immersed in the Cold War hysteria of the day and was fairly well convinced that a Soviet bomber stream loaded with 19,000-

pound nukes would pop up on the radar screen's outer range rings at any minute. Curt LeMay made sure I took that whole thing pretty seriously. "SLEEP WELL AMERICA—YOUR AIR FORCE IS AWAKE," is the rah-rah motto we lived by.

The Air Force had me all over the place, which wasn't all bad. During off-duty hours it gave me the chance to hunt Roosevelt elk, blacktail deer, stubble field geese, pheasants and rock hens, and to fish the John Day River and other water-ways in Oregon for Cuts and Steelhead, and other exotics that an Arizona boy would never have otherwise experienced. I didn't have any such opportunities in Korea or Taiwan, but back stateside and stuck on Santa Rosa Island, I had oppor-tunities to fish saltwater species and hunt feral hogs, that were grand adventures every time out.

That reminds me of something that deserves a side-bar: One of the mess cooks on Santa Rosa was an Italian kid who introduced us to "Cioppino," a seafood stew that made you want to smack your Grandmamma down. It was an Italian version of French Bouillabaisse that was, in my view, entirely superior. The kid's name was Louie, and whatever we caught we brought to him for inclusion in the Cioppino pot. Didn't matter what it was. Abalone pried off the rocks at low tide, snapper, pinto, bass, barracuda, whatever. Everything went into a huge steam kettle in a corner of the kitchen that was in a perpetual state of simmer and added to almost daily. It was sort of like a seafood stockpot that just got better and better as time went on. I've had Cioppino in fine Italian restaurants but have never found anything to rival Airman Louie's masterpiece.

I was discharged in February, 1960, after marrying a tall blond girl in '57 that had an extraordinary talent for making girl babies, so, it was time to move on and make a serious living that would support an expanding family. Dad's company had by now become successful and I jumped in as an estimator and project manager. That kept me hopping and in the air almost constantly, traveling between projects in West Texas, Arizona, and Southern California. And during this period, Glen Canyon remained completely obliterated from my mind by a fog of capitalistic confusion. But I still found time to fish. You couldn't take that away from me. And on weekends, if I wasn't after "bows" up on the Rim Lakes or in a variety of White Mountain streams, I was chasing bass and crappie on the desert lakes around Phoenix.

I had a fishing buddy, called him "Slim." Big guy. Six-three, happy-go-lucky type from "Bama." We were on Saguaro Lake one night, catfishing after a good bass day, and passing idle conversation while anchored over a proven catfish hole, waiting for something good to happen.

We were after serious fish. Flatheads or channel cats, either one, but nothing under ten pounds would be allowed in the boat. We had bought a couple dozen of the biggest waterdogs we could find, and augmented these with palm-sized bluegills caught earlier in the evening and added to the bait bucket. Slim had hand-picked the dogs from a bubbling bait tank at a small East Valley bait & tackle shop. They were beyond just "bait." Some looked large enough to produce decent fillets. We tail-hooked these and fished them a foot off the bottom with only a large split-shot to keep them down, but still allow them to swim freely.

"Y'all want big cats, ya don't mess with chicken guts and such," Slim advised. "They want live bait. And they want bait big enough to make it worth their time to fool with."

It was Slim's favorite hole and I felt honored to be let in on its location. He had a lot of time invested in that hole. He would regularly stop at a valley egg ranch and pick up old dead laying hens, allow them to ripen in the sun for a few days, then stuff six or eight of them in a burlap sack half filled with rocks, and go salt the hole with them about twice a month. Catfish were not exactly my thing, but Slim promised that I would be hooked once I tied into a REAL fish, and he was doing everything he could to make sure that happened. We quit bass and bait fishing around sundown and headed up-lake to the river end and at the designated spot, he put down a very light anchor on a short rope; just enough ground tackle to keep the boat in place as long as a wind didn't come up, but not so much that a big flathead couldn't drag it around.

"Y'all need that little bit extra load on 'em to help get one 'long side the boat," he said, while pointing to faded ribbons of engineer's tape hanging from trees on opposite shores that marked the hole. "We dead on it now," he said. "This the spot. Now when you hook up, you lemme know. I'll take all the slack out the anchor rope and let the fish pull us around. You snag one in the 30-pound or better range and you'll see what I'm talkin' 'bout. That sucker will take off for the dam and there ain't squat you can do to change his mind. But the boat will slow him up some."

Alrighty then. Sounded good to me. But it didn't go well. The hours passed without so much as a nudge. Eight o'clock. Nine. Ten. Nothing. My bluegill would make a little run and I would see the line move and get all excited, take up slack, lower the rod tip, tense up, and get ready to slam a hook-set that would cross a hippo's eyes.

"Nah," Slim would say. "That ain't him. That's not how they do. Big flathead come swimmin' by 'bout ten mile an hour and he's just gonna nab your bait as he's passin' and never slow down or look right nor left. Then it's Katie bar the door."

Eleven o'clock. Midnight. Two o'clock and I'm thinking we should just pack it in. The sandwiches were long gone, so was the beer, I was down to a half pack of smokes, I had maybe a cup of cold coffee left in the thermos and my butt was getting sore.

"Nah," Slim said. "Not just yet. Won't be long now. They should be coming back any minute."

"Coming back? What the hell does that mean? Coming back? Coming back from where?"

"From the dam," Slim drawled. "The big ones go down to the dam to turn around. Takes 'em a while to make the round trip. What is it? 'Bout eight, nine miles ain't it?"

It was pitch dark, so I couldn't see his face. But I know he was doing all he could to keep from busting out laughing, because I could feel the boat shaking. So, while waiting for the big cats to come back from the dam, we started chatting about this, that, and the other. Slim was a drywall contractor at a time when the construction industry was transitioning away from interior wet plaster toward gypsum wallboard and he was something of a pioneer in the field. He was pretty enthusiastic about the potential for these relatively new materials that allowed completion times approaching one-third the time that a conventional three-coat plaster job would require.

"Y'all ought to look into it, Pete. Get in on the ground floor. I'm tellin' ya, it's the future, man."

I didn't say anything. Not because I wasn't interested, but because I was just seconds away from falling dead asleep.

"I just finished a motel job up in Page in four weeks," he continued. "Plaster would have taken almost the whole summer. Made good money, too. Nobody wanted to go up there and even bid on it. Could just about name any price and get all the work you want." That woke me up. Anytime a construction estimator hears about a door of opportunity hanging ajar, his ears tend to come to life.

"Where's Page?" I asked. "Never heard of Page. Is that in Arizona?"

"Yeah. It's up there on the Utah line next to that big old dam they buildin'. Brand new little town ya ought to see what all's goin' on up there. Started from scratch out the middle a noplace. It's mainly to have a place for the guys and their families that's workin' on the dam. But it's gone on past that now. It's a reg'ler little boom town."

"What dam? Where exactly are you talking about?"

"Well, shoot, Pete! Y'all just blow in from the moon or sumpin'? They buildin' a dam on the Colorado River just up a ways from the Grand Canyon. Been workin' on it a year or so already. Ain't never seen nothin' like it. Built a new highway up to it, throwed a big high bridge over the canyon in somethin' like three months, threw this little town together in a few months. Its sumpin.' Never seen stuff go together so fast. And there ain't no end in sight. There's this Art Greene guy up there that's gonna build this big old resort with hotels and stuff and a marina on the lake and I don't know what all. I'm tryin' to get in on some of that stuff."

"Art Greene? Did you say Art Greene?"

"Yeah. Art Greene. Good old boy. Talk yer dang leg off, but he's got deep pockets and big ideas."

"And there's going to be a lake?" I asked.

"Well … yeah. That's gen'rly what happens when you dam up a river," Slim drawled. "The lake supposed to fill up Glen Canyon. The whole thing. Make a lake a coupl'a hundred miles long they say."

It was around 4:00am now. I was wide awake and fumbling for a smoke. GLEN CANYON!! FLOODED!! My mind was racing with the implications. About the time I got that cigarette lit, my line went tight and started cutting the water in the direction of the dam. But I was so caught up in the whole idea of a flooded Glen Canyon that I didn't even notice it until Slim let out a whoop.

"HERE YA GO, PETE! KEEP THAT ROD TIP UP. AIN'T NO NEED TO WORRY 'BOUT SETTIN' NO HOOK! YER BLUEGILL'S ALREADY IN HIS BELLY! JUST STAY WITH HIM. THIS WHAT WE COME FOR!"

It all came back to me in a flood of tangled recollections and thoughts. THE GLEN CANYON FLOAT TRIP! I had completely forgotten how the notion had grabbed my imagination during that Art Greene encounter at Cliff Dwellers years ago. But now Slim is telling me of a great new dam on the river that will flood the canyon with a huge lake. So now what? Was there still time to make such a trip before it was too late? Or, did it even matter? It suddenly occurred to me that I might not even need Art Greene's services. If a lake was forming, why couldn't I just use my own boat to explore Glen Canyon?

What became abundantly clear, however, was that I needed to get up there and check this all out for myself. I needed more information than Slim could provide. But I felt better. I could see the possibilities of a whole new world of adventure waiting in the wings. Plenty to think about. But that would have to wait. For the moment, I had my hands full.

The power of the fish was amazing. Far more than anything I had expected. Slim fished for these things with a stout, stubby, blue-water trolling rod, mounting a Penn Senator and I thought that had to be overkill, with maybe just a little show-time involved here to impress a catfish novice. But now I understood. That stuff was for real. I was under-gunned and in trouble from the get-go. We didn't have graphite rods in those days, and the hollow-core fiberglass buggy whips I used for bass and crappie just weren't enough stick for this sort of thing.

The fish slammed the rod down on the gunwale before I knew what was going on and I thought for sure the rod would break. But it didn't, and when the fish spun the boat around I was able to raise the rod again and get the flex working against the brute. Slim is sitting in the back of the boat, yelling encouragement and instruction like a sideline basketball coach.

"USE THE WHOLE ROD, PETE! KEEP YER HANDS DOWN ON THE CORK! DON'T BE GRABBIN' YER ROD HALF WAY UP LIKE THAT. YOU'LL BUST IT SURE! LET HIM RUN FER NOW. YOU CAN'T TURN HIM ANYWAY! NOT YET. KEEP THAT TIP UP, DAMN IT! YOU KNOW BETTER'N THAT! KEEP THE LOAD ON THE ROD, NOT THE LINE!"

I hate pressure like that. If I lost this fish I knew I'd get over it. It certainly wouldn't be the first time I'd lost a heart breaker. But Slim was so into the whole thing that I knew losing the fish would bum him out for a month!

My reel was one of those old Shakespeare level-winds with a free-spool bait clicker but no drag mechanism. A thumb on the spool served as a drag, and when the fish peeled the line, the clicker sounded like a machine gun. Spooled onto this midget was a couple of hundred yards of 20lb mono, that early stuff that had all the fishing attributes of electrical cable. It didn't just have "memory," it had an archive. And when you clamped your thumb down on that stuff it gave you a third degree burn in seconds.

I was in the bow of the boat and Slim was aft, with the anchor line trailing off a stern quarter. He started the engine, leaving it to idle in gear, and pulled up the anchor. He could see I was in trouble with this fish and made ready to chase it if need be, but for the time being he would just allow the fish to pull the boat along. Yep. This was fun, alright. Slim just might have something here, I was thinking.

On that first big boat-dragging run, the fish managed to peel a hundred yards off the reel and it got me to thinking about a time back on Santa Rosa Island. I had been jigging a spoon off the end of the pier and had somehow managed to snag a passing harbor seal in the side. That thing ran off a whole spool of 80lb braid on me and when the end came, rod, reel, and all just flew out into the Pacific.

I could see the possibility of a repeat as I watched the spool shrink behind this gator or whatever it was I was tied into. But after about fifteen minutes or so, I could sense the fish tiring, and I was actually able to gain a crank or two on it every now and then.

Slim sees this and says, "Hold on a minute, Pete. Here's what we'll do. Take yer line a turn or two 'round yer reel handle to lock it up and hold yer rod straight up. I'll slip into reverse here and idle back some. I think we can turn him around. And when I tell ya, free up yer line and drop the rod and reel like hell. That ought to put some line back on yer reel."

We did that. Twice. And it worked great. And in another ten minutes or so I had the fish on its side alongside the boat, and I was anxious to look it over. It had to be a fifty-pound fish! Slim held the Coleman lantern out over the water at arm's length. "Well, shoot," he said. "The way y'all was carryin' on with that weenie tackle you got, thought sure you had a keeper. This ain't much more than bait, Pete."

"WHAT?!?!"

Slim reached down into the water, stuck his fist in the cat's gallon-paint-can-sized mouth, grabbed something important, and hauled it in. It wasn't a flathead. It was a channel cat, and by Slim's rusty old Langley "DeLiar" it missed the ten-pound mark by a smidgeon.

"Might just as well turn him loose," Slim said. "Need to get back to the hole."

"WELL, I DON'T THINK SO! This is the only fish we have to show for a whole night's work!"

"There's gonna be others."

Well, maybe, maybe not I'm thinking. I decided to keep the nasty thing until something better came along to replace it. So I ran the wire of a chain stringer snap through the cat's lower lip and eased him back into the water. (I'm saying "him" because I don't know how to tell a girl catfish from a boy catfish).

With the excitement over for a while, we started talking about Page again and I was peppering Slim with all sorts of questions. All the while, this catfish is jerking on that stringer. Chunk, chunk, chunk, chunk, chunk ...

Eventually we were talked out, rotten-mouthed, and sandy eyed; the eastern sky had taken on a blush and we both fell dead asleep to the world. We had re-anchored over the hole and the boat was maybe twenty feet off and under a cut-bank. While we slept, a half-dozen wild burros came down to the water and apparently they objected to our presence. Standing on the cut-bank right over our heads, one of them let out an ear-splitting bray that obliterated that dawn's velvety silence and damn near drove both of us overboard. There are any number of lousy ways to be roused from a sound sleep but this easily has to rank among the top five.

I told Slim to fire up his old Evinrude and get me out of there. I had enough fun for one night and I wanted to get home and go to work on figuring out how to get myself up to this new little town of Page as fast as I could. As Slim yanked on the starter rope, I reached over the side to pull up my one and only catfish, and found an empty chain. The snap hook had pulled open and the wire was straight as an arrow. My almost-keeper catfish was gone. Headed for the dam to turn around, no doubt.

Back home a couple of hours later on a Sunday morning, I gave another friend a phone call. Ronnie Roth was his name (now deceased). Ronnie was a project manager at the time for the Henry C. Beck Construction Company out of Dallas, Texas that we did a lot of sub-contract work for. He was an excellent pilot and we often flew together in rented or club aircraft of various types to and from construction projects in other states that we were both involved in. He had only recently picked up a really nice, low-time Cessna 310D and I knew he was anxious to get some time in it. I got him on the phone and asked if he had ever heard of Page, or the new dam. "Yeah, sure," was the reply. "Why?"

"Well, I just found out about it this morning and I'm curious about it."

"THIS MORNING?! What, do you lead a sheltered life or something? They started pouring concrete on that thing over a year ago. You need to pick up a newspaper once in awhile. You want to fly up there with me and take a look at it?"

"Funny you should ask," said I. And the next weekend found Ronnie and I winging it for the dam site, the town of Page, and whatever else there was to see. Even though it was a weekend day, the level of activity below us was astounding. At the dam site, workers crawled all over the place like hundreds of little black ants. Equipment churned up clouds of dust everywhere—above the canyon rim on the west side, at the concrete batch-plant, in the river both above and below the dam, at the Wahweap hotel/marina site, and in Page itself. And even from a thousand feet above the surface the pace of activity seemed nothing less than frantic.

The dam itself appeared to be about one-third complete in height and was a tangle of activity, people, and equipment. The river both above and below the dam appeared to be flowing in a normal fashion without any restriction or disruption of any kind. From the air this seemed to be an impossibility. The river on the upstream side just stopped dead at a huge earthen cofferdam above the new, concrete dam site, and then picked up again on the downstream side beyond a several hundred yard long earthen pad as though the dam didn't even exist. What you could not detect from the air, of course, was that the river was flowing through a great diversion tunnel to make this not an optical illusion, but rather a well-planned feat of hydro-engineering.

Out at what would become the resort/marina complex, dust clouds were rising from a large cut-and-fill project and a few buildings were starting to take shape. Not enough was done yet to provide any insight into what it might eventually look like upon completion, but you could tell even then that whatever it was, it was going to be on a fairly large scale. But looking at it from the air, you had to wonder why they picked the site that they did. It was a LONG way from water, and was bordered on the east by a deep, snaky canyon that looked like it offered no access to its bottom. But of course there was no lake yet, and the Colorado River was several miles south of the site. To the innocent eye, and mine surely was, it was difficult, if not impossible, to imagine a lake large enough to back water that far up that canyon. (The canyon of course, was Wahweap Creek).

Orbiting Page itself, it was easy to see that the town was still a work in progress. Streets were laid out and most were paved, and the loop of Lake Powell Boulevard was prominently visible. But what struck me was the amount of open undeveloped land along both sides of the main drag. Only a couple of buildings were up back along the north side of "Church Row" and the site of the now existing Page High School was a huge graded field, empty except for three or four tin-roofed temporary buildings clustered along the apex of the curve. Only one of the shopping center parking lots was visible. I forget which one. But I think it was the one that houses the Dam Bar & Grill, True Value Hardware, etc. No more than a hundred residential rooftops were scattered about on the north side, and most of those were single-wide mobile homes. To the south, where the industrial area along Border Street exists today, there was nothing but sage and sand; and to the east the Navajo Generating Plant had not yet been built.

After seeing all there was to see in the neighborhood, both of us were very anxious to head up the river and get a look at fabled Glen Canyon. But it was not to be. It was not a good day to fly. Towering-Q with anvil tops and black, sinister, lightning flashing bases were all over the place, making our flight an aerial slalom course as we dodged cells. Photography was almost impossible. Shooting through the distortion of plexiglas and trying to hold a camera still in the turbulence made it a futile effort. Two rolls of film would eventually yield nothing worth printing.

So, as prudence would dictate, we banked away from Page and headed for Phoenix on one of the wildest flights I've ever experienced. A line of thunderstorms stretched across the horizon from Williams to Winslow and we had to fly over the Grand Canyon on a line to Seligman in order to skirt around it. I thought we were going to lose it a couple of times in the turbulence over the Canyon but somehow the wings stayed on and we bulled our way through it, fighting headwinds, up and down drafts, shears, and cloud-to-cloud lightning flashes that were blinding. We chewed up the gas pretty good too, and dropped in at Prescott's Ernest Love Field to top off the gas tanks and empty the bladders. (mmmhhmm, boy that felt good!) Pretty weird to be able to recall how good something like THAT felt, forty-six years later. Must have been a doozy.

On the ground at Phoenix Sky Harbor where Ronnie hangared the 310 in those days, we decided we would take another crack at it later that fall after the monsoon season played out, and decided we would rent and use a different aircraft for the next trip—something that would fly slower and had a window that could open to permit better photography. Didn't happen. We were both too busy with work and time slipped away. The calendar would roll into 1963 before we ever got around to another aerial exploration. But it was worth the wait …

It was late spring, 1963, before Ronnie and I were able to fly up to Page again. Too much was going on in our lives to allow another flight sooner than that. So, this was some twenty months later and as we came in low over the dam the scene below looked so dramatically different it was hard to believe it was the same site. The dam was just about topped out. Even more significantly, the cofferdam on the upstream side had water over it. The Colorado River was now lapping at the dam's upstream face. Lake Powell had been born!

The drama of that moment was spoiled to some extent by the mess of driftwood debris and flotsam trapped behind the dam. It was a huge raft of floating detritus stretched solid from one canyon wall to the other and extending upstream some three or four hundred yards. But aside from that minor distraction the spectacle below was breathtaking. The dam itself was a beautiful thing to behold. From a builder's point of view, anyway, because I doubt that any card-carrying Sierra Club member would have agreed with that assessment. When talking about a chunk of concrete of such magnitude, it seems hard to justify the word that best describes it, but nothing else seems to fit. From the air, the dam actually looked "graceful."

A lot of other folks must have been wowed by it too, because the airspace over and around the dam swarmed with civil traffic. Light aircraft were everywhere: above, below us, off either wing. Neither of us felt comfortable with being part of that flying circus, and it's hard to appreciate what's happening on the ground when its necessary to keep one's eyes peeled for the traffic around you. And when you have a wing down flying a three-sixty, you have no idea what's under your belly. So, we took a quick turn over Page and widened it out to include Wahweap, and then at long last, headed up the river. After ten years of wondering, I was at last to see Glen Canyon with my own eyes and perhaps discover what it was about the place that inspired Art Greene and others to set up shop in this desolation so far removed from civilization.

The town of Page seemed to have changed only marginally. Some in-filling had taken place but it was obvious there was a long way yet to go. The same might be said for the resort-marina at Wahweap, but here, great progress was in evidence. The big round-roofed building that houses the restaurant was built and one of the hotel buildings was complete and functional, and a second one looked like it soon would be too. The finished building was the one on the left that connects to the main lobby and the gift shop.

Considerable work was underway at the marina as well and the big ramp's fill and grade work appeared complete, but not yet paved. To the south of it, a smaller secondary ramp looked about ready to go but there was no water backed up to it yet. Art Greene was indeed a busy boy. It was only a matter of time now before it all came together with rising water and it was obvious he intended to be ready for it when it did.

Wahweap Canyon still snaked its way to the river but its bottom was now painted with a sliver of green almost as far upstream as the location of today's Stateline Ramp site. It looked like the water would surely need to rise at least a hundred feet or more before it would spill over onto Wahweap Canyon's lower rims and make Art's temporary ramp functional.

We banked right and away from Wahweap to head up river and would have passed almost directly over the Castle Rock Cut, except of course there was no such thing, nor was it obvious that there ever would be. It was all featureless desert below as we continued the turn toward the south over what is now Antelope Island.

It was hard to keep track of where the river actually was. It was buried deep in a sheer-walled canyon that twisted snake-like in a northeasterly direction and you had to be almost directly above it at times to see the water. I'm guessing the lake level was probably at or near the 3400-foot mark, or about 200 feet below the current level, so it still looked more like a river in a canyon than a lake. The river was just somewhat wider once you flew beyond the narrows and the canyon opened up some. And when it did that, in the vicinity of Gunsight, we dropped down to about 200 feet above the surface and just flew the twists and turns of the river. We were in the 310 again. We had tried to rent a nice little Cessna 140A that had opening windows but it just didn't work out. So we were still handicapped by the 310's speed but we weren't complaining. We spent the next hour—an entire hour—oohing and aahing, as we flew up, down, over, and across every canyon between Gunsight and the San Juan River.

What did we see? I wish I had the verbal capacity to tell you. If I took a stab at it you would think right off that I was full of more crap than a Christmas turkey. The few photos I have are small, faded, and fuzzy. I knew little about photography then, and not much more now, and I regret that deeply. To realize what I saw that day will never again be seen in the same way by human eyes is a pretty heavy thing to carry around with you. You can try to talk about it, but it just doesn't work. How do you describe the sense of overwhelming awe you experience when confronted by towering, patina coated sheer-wall cliffs hundreds of feet in height? Or amphitheaters of such scale they would swallow a C-17? Or bright green cottonwood forests along canyon bottoms in a land of barren rock, and do it justice? Can't be done. No more than we can describe Lake Powell today to someone who has never experienced it before. Tell them in language you and I may be comfortable and familiar with, and they will look at you like you just fell out of a tree.

Ronnie and I never found Rainbow Bridge that day. To be perfectly honest, I think I had forgotten all about it. I think we were too caught up in everything else there was to see and probably blew right by Forbidding Canyon without even realizing it. We didn't have anything in the way of a map, except sectionals that only showed the river in small scale and without any detail or place names. And since neither of us had ever seen this chunk of America before, we really didn't know where we were if we strayed too far from the river. Something would catch our eye that deserved a second look, either because of its beauty, or, because it just seemed impossible and a second look was required to make sure what we had seen was real. We would add power, pull up, do a one-eighty and go back for seconds, sometimes even thirds. You do that a few times and you can really get yourself gummed up. Somewhere along the way we lost track of which river we were flying and discovered after a while that the river below us was not the Colorado. We were flying up the San Juan and didn't even realize it until the country opened up and the spectacle of Monument Valley began to grow off the right wing.

"Something doesn't seem right," Ronnie mumbled. "I think we got lost."

I looked at the gyro and nodded my head. "One-one-oh. Yeah. We're lost. Let's go home," I said.

I rummaged through the chart bag for a sectional that would do the trick and that's when I found out we had turned up the San Juan shortly after passing

Navajo Mountain. We had been at this for an hour, flying S-turns and eights about a point, criss-crossing the river time and again to soak up all the eye-candy we could and thinking we were doing a fair job of covering all there was to see in Glen Canyon. And now, to discover we had seen only HALF of it came as something of a shock and disappointment. It is a somewhat humbling experience to discover you are not nearly as smart as you think you are. And it went a long way to point out how vast the country is and how insignificant we humans are. Both of us had been so mesmerized that we had forgotten all about pilotage. And with fuel dwindling, the country could easily have had us for lunch.

Flying through Monument Valley at low altitude was quite a revelation for me. I was amazed to discover that all that stuff I had seen in western movies was actually for real! I had always assumed that all those impossible stone formations and giant sand dunes were fake movie sets. But no, it was the real deal, not a "reel" deal. It had the flocks of sheep and the dogs and the Navajo herders wearing purple, mud-roofed hogans, and the whole ball of wax. We didn't want to be rude or make life difficult for the sheep dogs, so we pulled up to maintain at least 1500 feet above the surface. That was just about right, and a fair compromise. We still had plenty of visual detail and I don't think we ruined anybody's day. We might have been lost, but at least we were not irresponsible.

I gave Ronnie a bearing for Flagstaff where we would have to drop in for fuel at the Pulliam discount tire, hair salon, and convenience mart before continuing on to Phoenix. I had seen what I wanted to see, but had mixed feelings. It was nothing like what Art Greene had described ten years before, nor what my imagination had supposed. It was better. Better by a hundred fold. And that posed a new problem. Looking at Glen Canyon from two hundred feet above the river and ripping by at 180 miles per is an exhilarating experience without a doubt. But I remembered something Art Greene had told me way back then: "You need to take two weeks to do it right." I needed a boat—a serious boat.

After that memorable flight in '63, Ronnie and I often talked about making a follow-up trip to see what we had missed above the San Juan junction, with a thought of continuing on up the Green to see Flaming Gorge Dam which was also under construction at about the same time. But the opportunity never came about. The same problem plagued us that still exists for many of us today. We were just too busy making a living. Life is cruel that way, but maybe there is good reason. It makes the good times that much more precious and appreciated. And perhaps it was fortunate that we didn't do another flight for another reason. After we got home and started bragging to other pilot friends, we discovered we were mere lightweights. A lot of these other guys had not only flown Glen Canyon, they had also seen and flown UNDER Rainbow Bridge! I know what would have happened if we had made a third flight. Yup. We would have done the same thing and probably would have killed ourselves in the process.

It would be mid-summer of 1964 before I would see Lake Powell again, but in the meantime, we somehow managed. Ronnie and I were both tied up on the same two Southern California projects at the same time—one in downtown Los Angeles and the other a high-rise condo project on Point La Jolla. Another La Jolla project was waiting in the wings so we decided to rent and share a small house in Pacific Beach, near San Diego's Mission Bay. I had bought a very basic 1962 Falcon sedan for surface transportation and we were running the wheels off of it dashing back and forth between L.A. and San Diego.

On the weekends when we did not fly back to Phoenix for one reason or another, we would often rent a boat at Mission Bay and try our luck chasing Yellowtail. Our favorite rental was a 25-foot "Trojan" cruiser that had the speed and range necessary to get us out to Yellowtail waters. But we struck out more often than not, contenting ourselves with Bonito, King Mackerel, and 'Cudas instead. We didn't care. ANY fish is better than TV! And besides, do you remember what TV had to offer in the 60's?

Many mornings we would check out the Trojan at dawn with a thick, wet fog and a strong ocean scent hanging in still air, idle over to the bait dock for a couple of scoops of anchovies, and then pick our way out—under the bridge and past the breakwater, turn north, and motor cautiously up the coast through murk with no more than thirty yard's visibility. Navigating by compass alone, and listening for the sound of the surf to make sure we were not in too close, we would grope our way up to Point La Jolla and drop anchor on the outer edge of the kelp beds. We would bottom fish there until the sun came up and burned off the fog. And once we could see where we were going, we would haul anchor and beat cheeks for the big water with a sharp eye for wheeling gulls.

That was all well and good as far as it went, but I could not shake Lake Powell from my mind. I had to make that happen somehow. But I had a couple of hurdles to clear first, and a proper boat was at the top of that list.

I finally got a boat—it had been a high school graduation gift to me from my Uncle, a master carpenter and cabinet-maker. He had hand-built the boat from marine-grade spruce plywood for bottom and sides, with mahogany upper works, and exposed, delicately shaped white oak frames that displayed his impeccable joinery, all finished to glass-like perfection in marine spar varnish—a beautiful little thing. It had classic sea-skiff lines with hard chine rails and a semi-V bottom. But it was only fourteen feet long, had a very narrow beam, and was modestly powered with a 30-horsepower Evinrude outboard. It was a beautiful boat to look at, and may have served me well on the desert lakes near Phoenix, but clearly, this would not do for Lake Powell.

I needed something with more power, greater carrying capacity, and longer range if I hoped to do the sort of boating on Lake Powell that I had in mind. I wanted to see all the things that Art Greene had planted in my mind back in '53 that you really can't see from an airplane, and I had visions of 200+ mile long round-trips spanning several days at a time. Well, you know how this works. The first order of business is to convince your wife that such needs are not frivolous extravagances that one can easily do without, but are, rather, NECESSITIES that promote family health, safety, welfare and comfort.

I was not having a great deal of success with this. But, ah, the Lord works in mysterious ways. I was running up lake at Saguaro one night with old Slim. We were on another catfish mission again and it was my turn to bring the boat. It was pitch dark, we are chatting back and forth, distracted, running way too fast for the conditions, and, well, what do you know? Ran the boat right out of the lake and thirty feet up onto dry ground! The boat thudded along and came to a grinding stop and pitched both of us out into the desert, with engine kicked up, prop in the air, and twirling at about 8,000 revs. Neither of us was badly hurt. That's the only way I can prove that the Lord had a hand in this, because by all rights we should have been dead. Slim had a raw scrape on his chin and I had a Cholla Cactus pad stuck under one armpit, but aside from that, we were good as new, if not for the shakes.

I managed to find the kill switch and took the engine off the transom to lighten the load, and we man-handled the boat back to the water. Surprisingly, it would still float, the only visible damage by flashlight being a patch of fractured plywood between two ribs on the starboard side about midship—it was not holed through. The plywood was pushed upward with entwined strands of splintered wood sticking up an inch or so, but that was the worst of it. It leaked alright. But it was more of a fast seep than a running flow and it looked like it would be manageable with occasional bailing. So we clamped the engine back on and gingerly made our way back to the launch ramp in the dark. Slim felt badly for me, telling me again and again how sorry he was that I had ruined my pretty little boat. He was sure though, that it could be fixed easy enough since none of the oak ribs or stringers had been broken.

Slim was a great guy, a good friend, fun to be with, warm, generous to a fault, always there and ready with a favor or help if called upon. A guy wants to take care of a friend like that. Let him know how much you appreciate that kind of loyalty and friendship. I gave him the boat. Well now, a guy without a boat is like a guy with shoes but no socks—peanut butter with no jam, cookies but no milk, a rod without a reel. Add your favorite and take it from there. You know what I'm talking about.

I took a lot of heat from Patty for my stupidity, but I was smart enough to keep my mouth shut and merely nod in agreement.

"Yeah, you're right Patty. Uh-huh. Dumb. But what are we going to do now?" Bottom line here, I HAD NO BOAT! I was not a whole person. I am not going to be a fun guy to be around. I'm a victim! I'm borderline suicidal!

I found what I was looking for within a couple of weeks. Good thing too. If it had taken much longer I would have lost what remnants of rational behavior I still possessed. It was another wooden boat, but I had to have it. Glass boats of the day were still a little on the cheesy side unless you laid out serious bucks for something like a Larson, Tom Sawyer, Aristocraft or something like that.

The replacement boat. P. Klocki photo

The boat I had my eye on was a wide-beam 16-footer with a modified-V bottom going to zero deadrise at the transom, and had a nicely flared bow, a pretty,

Philippine Mahogany deck, two nice side-by-side seats, a windshield, plenty of open floor space, two built-in ten gallon saddle tanks, forward controls and a steering wheel, and a forty-horse Johnson hanging on it. The guy selling it said it would run about 25 miles per hour and he wanted five hundred bucks for it.

Now, I may not be the brightest crayon in the box, but I'm not a total loss, either. I told the guy that we needed to take it out for a test run and that I wanted MY WIFE TO COME ALONG. There was a method at work here. Anytime a guy wants to buy a boat, as anyone knows, the first thing that has to happen is to sell it to the wife. The trick in this is to make the whole thing her idea. If you can pull that off, it's a slam-dunk. You should remember this if you have an eye on a new Ranger, guys. So, a few days later the three of us ran out to Lake Pleasant and put the boat in the water. The guy turns a key and fires up the Johnson.

"Oh. It has an electric starter?" Patty asks.

"Yeah," I answered, adding a little shoulder shrug. "But I don't know how important THAT is."

"Well, it's better than you yanking on that rope all the time, isn't it?" she says.

"Uh … yeah. I suppose. But now I have to worry about a battery."

The guy opens the throttle and we blaze along at 25mph as he had promised. "I like this windshield," Patty says. "My hair doesn't blow around so bad."

"Uh … yeah. I guess that's good. But you could just wear a hat, couldn't you?"

The guy crossed a couple of boat wakes at speed and the flared bow threw spray out to either side but not a drop came inside the boat. "Wow," Patty says. "You sure couldn't do THAT with the old boat!"

"Well … no. That's true. But all you had to do was slow down if you wanted to stay dry."

Patty asked the guy if she could take a turn at the wheel. (OH, thank you, sweet Jesus! Thank you, thank you, thank you!) I could not talk her out of it no matter how hard I tried. She FORCED me to buy that boat. I knew better, and we really couldn't afford it. But I loved my wife dearly. I loved her so much I had even bought her a poodle! I just didn't know how to say no to her. So, what's a guy to do? Huh? You tell me.

♦   ♦   ♦

1964

Nineteen sixty-four was an interesting year that would see Barry Goldwater's Presidential bid go down in flames, Nikita Khrushchev would be deposed, the Chi-Coms announced to the world that they were nuke capable, the Beatles came to America, and the Tonkin Gulf Resolution would open the door to combat operations in Vietnam. And for me, the ten-year-old dream of putting a boat in the water to explore Glen Canyon would finally happen in June. After being talked into buying the boat Patty wanted, one more logistical problem had to be dealt with first though—how to get the boat from Phoenix to Lake Powell.

It was hot enough in June to melt the copper dome on the Capital building and if Patty was to be involved in this adventure, an air-conditioned vehicle was a must. A couple of young guy types could make this trip in T-shirts and opened windows with no problem, but ladies are too delicate for such hardships.

I had a couple of boy-toy vehicles: a Willys 4x4 Utility Wagon and a '56 Ford pickup that I refused to part with, but neither were equipped with air. The Jeep's 6-cylinder engine wasn't up to the tow-task to begin with, so it wasn't even in the running. A few months earlier, Cal Worthington and his dog Spot had convinced me that I needed a new, 1964 Ford Falcon Sprint, a snappy little car with a fairly strong little V-8 and four-on-the-floor, so I bought one from Ralph Williams instead. It had an after-market under dash AC unit that would freeze your knee-caps in short order. Problem solved! Just crawl under that sucker, drill a couple of holes in the frame rails and hang a hitch on that puppy. Now you can drag a boat in air-conditioned comfort.

Well, I was still in my twenties. Sometimes I was guilty of forging ahead without thinking through unintended consequences. It was a wooden boat, fairly heavy, and the same was true of the trailer, a back-yard fabrication that utilized steel members that may have been salvaged from a dismantled ore smelter. All told, with full fuel and everything we thought we needed for a week on the lake, the tow package probably weighed around 2200 pounds. And that proved to be far more than the Sprint's COOLING SYSTEM would handle.

We pulled out of Phoenix at dawn and pointed the Sprint's nose north. It started out well enough. Most of I-17 was more or less complete to give us a straight shot to Flagstaff, which was a big improvement over the goat paths of yesteryear despite detours for construction still in progress. It was still cool when we topped Sunset Point, the car had enough snort, and everything looked green to go.

The first hint of trouble arose as we climbed out of the Verde Valley on Seventeen Mile hill. Just past the Stoneman Lake turnoff the temp gauge needle swung to "H." I didn't want to spook Patty so I just pulled off onto the shoulder and shut down the engine without saying why. I just suggested we take a break, eat a sandwich or something, and go visit the bushes. Good plan. So we are sitting there munching boiled eggs and Patty asks, "What's that moaning sound?"

I shrugged my shoulders. "I dunno. Maybe it's just the way the breeze sings through the Juniper." Remarkably, that was accepted as a legit explanation, although the auditory connection between a venting radiator and the breeze in the trees was a pretty long stretch.

Back on the road, I switched off the air and ran the rest of the hill in 3rd gear at a leisurely pace, rolling down the windows and enjoying the rush of naturally cooled air as we neared the 6,000 foot mark, and reminding Patty what a treat it was for a couple of flat-land desert rats to be able to do that. All the while I kept one eye on the temp gauge and breathed a sigh of relief once we topped out and got into the pines. Coolant temp had slipped back down into the normal range and it was staying there.

I-17 south of Flagstaff had a few unfinished gaps in it, and the I-40 by-pass south of the city still had a long way to go. You had to drive through Flagstaff proper, which we did. We continued on, picking up Hwy-89 northbound again, and all was well. Descending the north side of the mountains, it became necessary to turn on the AC again in the vicinity of Grey Mountain. No problem. Temp stayed normal. But this was all down hill, of course. Once over the Little Colorado River at Cameron, however, a gradual climb comes back into play, and the temp needle started to slide toward bad news. By the time we reached the Tuba City junction the radiator was venting again and I had to pull over and stop. The outside air temp was about as hot as it would have been in Phoenix and sitting in the car under a bright sun waiting for the radiator to regurgitate its contents was not high on the list of fun things to do.

I had a gallon jug of water in the trunk and when it was safe to do so I dumped the whole gallon into the radiator. It took it all! Not a good sign. The car had a pitifully small radiator and I doubt the system capacity would have exceeded 12 quarts by much. We were in big trouble and I couldn't keep this from Patty any longer. I told her we would have to run without AC if we were to have any hope of reaching Page. We took off again and that gallon of water got us to within five miles of the Gap. This time I pulled off near some green growth off the east side of the highway that suggested a stock pond. Could it be? It was. They are long gone now, but in '64 there used to be three stock ponds alongside the highway, between Hamblin Wash and the pavement. East of the wash, at the foot of the cliffs, there was a spring and a small home that housed a Navajo family.

Patty volunteered to go down to one of the ponds and fill the emergency water jug so we wouldn't have to use any of the fresh drinking water we had for the trip. And as she started back with a jug of brown water, I noticed four or five small children emerging from the Navajo dwelling and they were kicking up dust as they ran down the two-track that led to the highway. She handed me the jug, and as I poured muddy water into the radiator I pointed out the approaching kids. "Where did they come from?" she asked.

I don't know why I do things like this. Lord, I know it ain't right. But sometimes I just can't pass up an opportunity. Now, Patty had never seen this country before and had very limited knowledge of the Navajo people. She was just a touch on the innocent side, and, I would have to say, somewhat vulnerable when it comes to practical jokes.

"I don't know where they came from," I said, with a faked frown and a subtle sense of urgency added to my voice. "From that little house over there, maybe," I added, pointing. "And we might be in trouble for stealing their water! We might be in for it! Angry Navajos are not somebody you want to mess with! They kill Hopis for less than that!" (Isn't that terrible? Now that ain't right, right there. I'm ashamed of myself).

"OH, MY GOD, PETER! LET'S GET OUT OF HERE!"

But it was too late to make a run for it. They were on us and we were surrounded with no way out! And John Wayne, Randolph Scott, or Glen Ford were nowhere in sight! The kids were no older than twelve or thirteen with outstretched palms covered with silver baubles and fetishes available at about two-bits apiece, on average, and they of course had no interest whatsoever in a pilfered gallon of muddy water. I made the most of it.

"Buy all of it, Patty, and give them some apples and peaches too. If we keep them happy maybe we can get out of here okay before the folks show up!" (Lord, forgive me and be with the little fisherpeople in New Guinea).

Up the road, we stopped at the Gap to fill the jug with clean water again. And then once more at the Chevron station that used to be at Bitter Springs. When we topped "Big Cut," we used up the spare water for the last time. On the downgrade toward Page, we made that last sweeping turn and a little sliver of blue came into view. Not much, but just enough to give it away.

"HOLY COW! LOOK AT THAT! A LAKE!"

I really didn't expect to see a *lake*-lake. Not from ten miles out anyway. I don't know what I was expecting, exactly, but it was no doubt something less. After all, when Ronnie and I flew over it, it was only a fat river in a canyon. And it just didn't seem that long ago. It was still a fat river, and the slice of blue didn't look anything like what you see today, but just the same, it was an inspiring sight.

"Man, this is exciting," I said, on the downgrade to Page.

Patty nodded. "Yeah," she said. "It is. But I'll tell you something right now. If you want me to come up here again with you in the future, you are going to have to figure out a better way to tow the boat. This doesn't cut it, and I'm not going to put up with blast-furnace heat on the road again. If I'm going to sweat my butt off, I can stay home and do that with a lot less hassle. You need a big, air-conditioned truck!" (Thank you Lord for many small favors. I promise to make it right with you).

All of Page was up on the hill. If there was anything down along the highway back then, I don't have any memory of it. Where Days Inn, Jack-In-The-Box, and the Shell station stand today, dust devils danced on the sand, and there were no visible clues that a golf course might someday skirt the pavement. Up the hill, in town, the main commercial core was already filling in with small shops and motels and Stix Market was THE place to go for local boating and fishing advice, tackle, and live bait.

We had brought along all that we needed and then some, so there was no reason to linger in Page, other than to check progress to see how the little town was coming along, and to make a quick stop at Stix for a little local contact. So, we completed the loop back down to 89 and headed for Wahweap. Crossing over the bridge, hundreds of feet above the river below, cannot be done for the first time without stopping for a long reality check. The visitor center on the west rim had not been built yet, but there was ample space to park so we walked back out to the center of the bridge and ooohed and ahhhed for half an hour, running back and forth across the bridge to look first at the dam and then to the river downstream and back again.

I had seen the dam and the bridge from the air before, so I had a fair idea of what to expect, but this took me by surprise just the same. I don't think one can truly appreciate the dam's scale without standing over it at the bridge center to look down at turbulent water ejecting far below without the faintest sound of it reaching your ears, or spotting tiny ant-like workmen going about their workday, or to smell the river's scent on a wayward updraft of dancing air. You get none of that zipping over it in an airplane. The dam was topped out and essentially complete now, as was the power house at the dam's base, although water was not running through the turbines yet. It seemed that all that remained of this grand project before it could be called done was to clean up the site.

We could have easily spent another fascinating hour or so on the bridge, but the clock was ticking and we were running way behind. We had left Phoenix at four in the morning and it was already three in the afternoon. And you will love this part: I still had in mind to put the boat in the water and run all the way up to Rainbow Bridge yet that day!

Well, like I said, I was in my twenties—and as green as any other first-time Pilgrim. But in my defense, I was further handicapped by the map I based my near-term planning on. This was not a map you pay money for. It was an 8x10 letter-sized sheet that was free for the taking from a rack at the Stix store, with the entire lake portrayed on one side of the sheet as a squiggly blue line with a few of the more prominent canyons and other place-names spelled out in red, type-written letter. And since Rainbow Bridge was only three inches away from Wahweap, well, it looked doable to me.

The junction of Lakeshore Drive and Hwy-89 was configured a bit differently than it is today, and of course there was no entry station either, but otherwise, Lakeshore Drive from the highway to Wahweap was essentially the same, except that it had that old, coarse-aggregate "Gummint" paving that made a Falcon Sprint sound like an eighteen wheeler rolling over the road.

Big changes had taken place at Wahweap since the flyover. Two of the hotel buildings were complete and in use, a gas station sat at the top of the hill, and a well stocked marine store and repair facility was across the pavement from it. The pizza place wasn't there and neither was that fancy restroom atop the hill. And as for the ramp, the rough grade for today's 1,000-foot long ramp was there, and served as a big parking lot, but it was still a long way from water or being functional.

About half way down the ramp's grade an interim launch ramp road peeled off to the south and wound its way down to the marina area. It was paved almost, but not quite, all the way to the water. The pavement ended just about where it really mattered, and at that point you had a 90-degree turn onto wet sand that took you the final thirty yards to your destination. Floating a boat off the trailer and then pulling out an empty trailer usually went well enough, but retrieving a boat and dragging it out on that sand ramp was an exercise in patient humility. If you could pull it off without getting stuck, the gallery of eager onlookers would take off their caps and cheer you all the way up the hill.

I got the trailer lined up straight and eased the rig into the water to pull off my patented one-man launch technique. I had observed this once when around age twelve and it stuck with me ever since, and I use it yet today. Goes like this: you tie one end of a FLOATING 50-foot rope to the boat's bow eye, tie a loop in the other end, and drop the loop over the trailer's winch stand. Next, you start laying loose coils of the rope on the boat's foredeck until you have taken up all the slack and nothing is going to drag on the ground. Following that, you back the rig into the water and as the boat starts to float off, you tap the brakes. The trailer stops and the boat keeps going, the coils flopping into the water one by one until the boat pulls the line tight and its rearward motion stops. At that point you have an option to either pull forward and drag the boat to the ramp where it grounds, or, you can stop short, get out, retrieve the looped end and walk the boat to a courtesy dock if one is available, or if not, to some other location out of harm's way. Works beautifully every time and for any size of boat.

That was the plan that day, and it was a work in progress—except it was not working. Patty stood by my open window to tell me the boat had not budged. I would need to back up farther. So I did. And it still would not float. Eventually the Sprint's exhaust pipes sounded like gas bubbles in a bathtub and I noticed my feet were getting wet as water flooded over the door-sills onto the floor.

It pains me greatly to see other guys herniating themselves trying to shove a boat off a trailer when the damned thing is nowhere close to being ready to float. I hate that. But that's exactly how it wound up. That boat was not about to float before I had the Sprint submerged up to the door handles.

When I decided to make this first trip to Powell I planned it like you would plan any such trip into the great unknown: be prepared for any contingency. I didn't know what to expect. I looked upon the whole thing like a great exploration worthy of a Magellan or Drake, Lewis and Clark, Major Powell, or old, what's his name.

Our non-perishable rations of Spam and canned beans alone would have fed a platoon of Marines for a week. Three 48-quart metal-sided Coleman coolers stored our perishables with 120 pounds of wet ice and four pounds of dry ice. Two crates held our black-iron Dutch oven, our nesting aluminum pot and pan set, an iron grill, a Coleman stove, plastic plates, bowls, silverware, all manner of cooking utensils, and whatever else from our home kitchen that we could think of. And together with this, were two sleeping bags in case June turned cold, a huge duffel bag crammed with enough clothing to outfit us for a wedding in case we ran across one, a smaller hard case with our toiletry articles, an 8x10 canvas tent with poles, a shovel, saw, axe, folding chairs and a neat little folding table, a porta-potty, a half dozen Coleman two gallon water jugs, two Stanley thermos bottles and six bags of charcoal in case we couldn't find any driftwood for a cook fire, a Coleman lantern, three gallons of Coleman fuel, three flashlights and a dozen spare batteries, one 80-pound female Labrador, a case each of Coors, 7-UP, Coke, and Pepsi, two quarts of cheap bourbon, an outsized tackle box, four rods, and a ten pound bag of Purina dog chow. The only thing we didn't bring was the poodle. It didn't know how to swim otherwise I'm sure we would have found room for it.

It's little wonder the damned boat wouldn't float off the trailer! It was carrying over a thousand pounds of cargo and we were not even in it yet! Eventually, standing belt-buckle deep in Lake Powell, I managed to shove the hulk off the trailer.

"Something doesn't look right," Patty said. "It looks like it's sinking. Did you put the transom plug in?"

Yeah, yeah, yeah. What am I, stupid or something? Of course I had put the plug in. That wasn't the problem. The boat was over-grossed and it was only showing about two-thirds its normal freeboard. I got the rig parked, walked back down to the boat in squishy shoes, hopped in, and rubbed my palms together.

"All-righty, then. This is it, Pal," I said to Patty. "After all these years. Can't believe it's finally going to happen."

I fired up the Johnson and idled out past the marina docks. Art Greene had made a lot of progress on the marina since the last flyover. The main walkway dock stretched east about half as long as it is today, and there were three or four slip docks that sprouted off the south side. All in all, I would guess there were around 100 rental slips available and about half of them were vacant, and maybe as many as twenty rental houseboats took up part of those. The marina store was right about where it is now, but it was a lot smaller. On the north side of the main walkway dock there were no slips at all. The fuel dock was attached to it about halfway out and all of the rest served as courtesy docking.

Turning south beyond the marina, we lined up on the channel of Wahweap Creek and headed for the Colorado River. Lining up on the channel required no particular navigating skills because you really didn't have an option. The channel resembled something akin to an irrigation canal as it slithered south in a series of S-turns. I opened the throttle once clear of the marina wakeless zone, my head spinning with anticipation, and wondering how in the world I had gotten so lucky.

"What's wrong with the boat?" Patty asked. "How come it won't go?"

I had the hammer down, wide open, the tach was showing something like 2500 revs and the boat wallowed like a crippled goose. It would not come up on plane. Nowhere close to it. We were hull down and pushing a bow wave that would have made the Mayflower proud. And it was probably pushing six o'clock by now, too. It was June. The sun still high with lots of daylight left, but I knew we would have to abort for the day. This wouldn't cut it. With a ten mile per top speed, a trip to Rainbow that day was not in the cards. We would have to lighten the boat somehow.

I came up with a plan. "Tell you what, Patty. Here's what we'll do. We will continue on like this until we get down to the river, then turn up lake, and as soon as we spot a beach we will call it a day, set up base camp, and unload some of this crap."

I was starting to feel better about myself. It had been a bad day for me. The Sprint's cooling problems couldn't be blamed on anybody else but me. Launching the boat like a Gibboni with a dozen guys watching me make a fool out of myself didn't help either. But I had just exercised a prudent command decision, putting my wife's welfare and safety ahead of my burning need to get up that damned river. That was a sign of maturity.

At the river junction I turned left, gingerly, because I had already discovered that when heeled over in a turn the boat was in no hurry to right itself. Starting up the Narrows for the first time was somewhat intimidating. The lake level was probably about 150 feet lower than it is right now and boating through can best be imagined by comparing the visual experience of starting out on an upstream run from Lee's Ferry, with towering cliffs to either side. If there was a difference, it would be that there are numerous beaches along the river downstream from the dam. There were NO beaches in the Narrows in 1964. Of course there are not many today, either, but at least you can find a few patches of sand in the vicinity of Antelope Point. In 1964 those few beaches passed by 100 feet or more above your line of sight.

On and on we plodded, passing a little white, floating sign that bobbed on the water in front of a small slit in the canyon wall. "Antelope Canyon," the sign read. And after what seemed like an hour, another sign. "Navajo Canyon," this one proclaimed. Splendid. That one was on my free map. "Look, Patty," I said, stabbing the wrinkled sheet with a finger. "This is where we are!"

"Whoopee," she says. "So where's a beach? I gotta whiz."

Daylight was beginning to fade as we passed our third floating sign close to the north wall in front of another slit in the rock—"Warm Creek." It was a narrow, uninviting gash that from all outward appearances probably didn't have much to offer besides a sheer-walled dead end, so we didn't bother with it. Since departing Wahweap, we had seen a few passing boats headed in the opposite direction. No more than a dozen in the space of two hours, and while we were outbound, all of these were inbound. All of the boats were emblazoned by a large, circular logo displaying "Canyon Tours, Inc," the Art Greene subsidiary that hauled paying Pilgrim guests on up-lake excursions.

The boats Art Greene used back then came in several different sizes and configurations. Your basic low-dollar-twirl-around-Wahweap and down-to-the-dam-and-back rigs were smaller aluminum logged pontoon deck boats with candy striped surrey tops and were about 20 feet in length. These accommodated six to eight Pilgrims.

A step up from that class was a similar pontoon deck boat that was a stretch version utilizing multiple logs welded together end-for-end for an overall length of something like 40 or 45 feet. It had the same 8-foot beam width and this example could haul a whole mob of Pilgrims. Provided they behaved themselves, that is, and stayed put on their bench seats. They were apparently reluctant to do that however, because when thus seated, the surrey top interfered with their views of the rising canyon walls.

A problem would then arise if someone standing at the bow spotted a soaring raven or some interesting rock formation high above and pointed upwards while shouting, "LOOK! LOOK AT THAT!" Whereupon all the other Pilgrims would jump up and rush to the bow in order to see what it was that had captured the first Pilgrim's attention. When this happened, the bow would submerge and water would flood the foredeck and the boat would look somewhat like a submarine initiating a crash-dive.

No great harm would come of this, except to soak the Pilgrim's shoes, because the vessel was apparently designed to automatically correct such problems. As the bows went down, so too did the stern rise. So much so, that the outboard motor would lift out of the water with a "ringy-ding-ding-ding" and forward motion would momentarily cease, thereby arresting the dive. Very clever. And at the same time, all the Pilgrims would rush back toward the stern to avoid the perceived danger, the boat would right itself, and all would be well again until the next time a soaring raven was encountered. This remarkably entertaining boat was dedicated to cruises up and down the Narrows with side trips into Navajo Canyon.

For long-range tours, to Rainbow Bridge, for example, V-bottom runabouts in a variety of lengths from 16 to 24 feet were utilized. Some of these were outboard powered while the larger ones were inboard-equipped. The 24-footers could seat about a dozen passengers and for larger groups these boats would double and triple up to run nose-to-tail with full loads of happy folks waving and shouting as they passed to make sure they were seen to be having the times of their lives.

As we continued up lake however, the passing of these boats dwindled and as darkness settled over Lake Powell we found ourselves entirely alone. I couldn't see squat. There was no moon and I had no clear idea of where I was or even if I was still headed in the right direction. Somewhere along the way, the river must have turned because I very nearly ran smack into the north canyon wall before I realized it was there. I cut power to a fast idle and crept along, staying within a couple of boat lengths of the rock so I could keep track of things, while Patty played a flashlight beam along the water's edge. We went along this way, looking for a place to make landfall, until, when nearly nine o'clock, we ran out of lake, arriving at a narrow dead end.

"Well, heck," Patty said. "This lake isn't nearly as big as you said it was."

I killed the engine and tossed out the anchor into three feet of driftwood-choked water. "I think we are lost," I mumbled. "How about rummaging around for one of those jugs of 'Early Times' and popping open a 7-UP, huh? I'm about whipped."

Old Blue, our wonderfully tolerant and patient Labrador, wagged her tail to let us know she was approaching her limits, but never so much as whined or whimpered in complaint. I gave her a hi-on hand thrust and she leaped out into the night, grateful that it turned out to be water that she landed on. Her favorite. And so, our first ever day on Lake Powell drew to a close. Somehow, I had managed to squirrel our way to the end of Gunsight Canyon in the darkness and had no idea that I had done so. I didn't know where I was and I didn't really care. There would be no cushy camp. We would sleep in our seats with what padding we could scrounge together and call it good.

While alone together in unknown surroundings and bathed in silence so profound you could feel its weight, we looked up to a sky carpeted and ablaze with more stars than we thought could possibly be crammed into the heavens. Then somewhere along the way, we fell dead asleep. Good thing, too. We already had three daughters.

I woke up to day-two with a pile-driving headache behind eyes pasted shut with salt grit and a taste in my mouth that can't be described without giving offense. It was light but the sun had yet to break the horizon. On either side, about forty yards away, wind weathered sandstone rose some twenty feet above the boat, but directly ahead, the country opened to a plain of sparsely vegetated rolling hills of sand and rock below rising canyon walls of immense proportion. In the distance off to my right a bit and some half-mile ahead, a towering butte rose to dominate the scene. After consulting my free map, I decided it must be "Gunsight Butte."

The boat was surrounded by a raft of driftwood floating on stained water; the impression of my surroundings left something to be desired. That's being kind. Actually the place was pretty ugly. Patty was not in the boat. Neither was the dog. I had no idea where they might have gone but I could worry about that later. In the meantime I had creature comforts to attend to.

Anchored in three feet of water about thirty feet from the nearest dry land, there was nothing else to do but scramble over the side and hop into the drift-wood and wade to shore in surprisingly cold water. Making my way up the thread of a dry creek bed I reached higher ground quickly and found Patty and the dog sitting on a Volkswagen-sized slab of sandstone. Joining them, I turned to face a grand panorama of surreal formations of sand, rock and sky that stretched to the horizon in all directions.

There is something humbling about a Lake Powell dawn. In that moment just before sunrise when the blues and lavenders give way to reds and yellows, your sense of humility peaks. So overwhelming is the beauty surrounding you that the insignificance of your own existence smacks you in the face. There is this enormous urge to thank someone, anyone, Him, Her, or otherwise, for putting you here, at this moment, at this place.

Looking south from our vantage point to the expanse of the Navajo Nation beyond the river, the dark and silent shapes of buttes and mesas and castles of stone seemed as sleeping giants awaiting the sun's warmth to kindle their day. And in the foreground, the river, passive and inviting, fat and lazy, its power masked by a mirror-like surface unruffled in the calm of dawn's still air.

I climbed higher for a better look. Once out of and above the rims of Gunsight Canyon I was better able to understand how and where I had gone wrong during the night. Hugging the north shoreline I had just blundered into the dead end. It was also easy to see why we had not been able to find a beach or some other suitable landfall. There weren't any. And there would be none, at least not in this neck of the woods, until the lake had risen another fifty feet or so.

From my high point I could easily see the great horseshoe bend in the river that would in time disappear to form Padre Bay. Traveling up-lake from the dam, the sheer walled confines of the Narrows ended here and the country to either side of the river opened to allow its spread. But that spread was not yet sufficient to overtop and submerge the canyon's slick rock second rim. The canyon descends from the mesa tops to the bottom of the river's bed in a series of steps. From top to bottom you can plainly see four such steps in most places, perhaps more in others. In mid-June, 1964, the lake had only begun to lap the second step. It would be necessary to overcome it before the water once again touched sand.

I had not expected or foreseen anything like that. Flying up the river the previous year, sandy riverbanks were the common norm and this was how my mind's eye had still envisioned it. But those sand banks were now submerged and gone—only to be replaced by smooth rock. But while this condition might have been immediately disappointing, I could also see the incredible potential once the lake rose above that lower rim of smooth rock. When it did, an entirely different world would greet Lake Powell boaters. The expanse of sand beaches would then be virtually limitless in all but the narrowest of canyons.

The lake was rising that June at a fairly steady inch-per-day or more rate. You could tell that in another year, two at the most, the rock versus sand condition would be completely reversed. But in the meantime, I had to figure out how to find a suitable base camp and it seemed apparent that it would not be found anywhere around the Gunsight-Padre Creek area. We needed to continue up-lake to find a different geological regime.

The sun broke over the spine of Kane Point—the long, narrow plateau that separates Padre and Last Chance Canyons that is called "Gooseneck Point" on some contemporary maps. And with the sun the cool morning air vanished along with the muted colors of dawn. It was time to move on.

As I stood up to leave, an arrow of rising dust in the distance caught my eye. It was the plume left in the wake of a motor vehicle, a pickup with a tin boat sticking out over the tailgate, charging along some track on higher ground that I could not see from where I stood. It was making pretty good time so I guessed whatever road it was on must have been a pretty good one. I watched for a while as the dust plume continued on, skirting the lake's north shore on easy ground above the slick rock rims, making a mental note to check out that road at some point in the future. But I never did. And by 1966 it was under water and forever lost.

It struck me as odd though, that looking down on the water's mirror-like surface there was not so much as a ripple to betray a boat's passage, while in the vast emptiness behind us, a token of civilization was roaring by at 35 miles per hour. In a land of such amazing contrast, that incongruity should not have surprised me, but it did.

Before abandoning the high ground, I marked those prominent terrain features that I could identify on that stupid little map I had. Lacking pencil or pen, I used a knife point to poke small holes into Padre and Gunsight Buttes, and into the end of the short, skinny little blue line that represented the end of Gunsight Canyon. At best, this told me where I had been and where I was and gave some scale of reference but didn't give much of a clue as to what lay ahead as we proceeded up lake. But I figured that if I could find and identify the next map feature called "Gregory Butte," I would be in the hunt.

We pushed the driftwood aside and jumped in for a much needed bath, struggling to cope with thermal shock, loaded the dog, downed a shot of orange juice and choked down a doughnut, and fired up the Johnson. I would have killed for a cup of coffee but there wasn't time to dig out the Coleman stove and the fixin's necessary to make that happen. We put up the bimini hoping to arrest our sunburns at the tolerable point that they had reached, and squirmed out of Gunsight Canyon. We turned left at the canyon mouth, opened the throttle, and resumed the barge-like pace in search of whatever surprises day-2 had in store for us.

We passed the inlet of Padre Creek on our left, then turned south around Padre Point which at the time was probably a good half mile north of Padre Butte itself, and headed directly toward the mouth of "Face Canyon." Before pulling out of Gunsight I fiddled with the trim set-up on the engine. This was well before the advent of such goodies as power trim & tilt and a trim adjustment was strictly a manual affair that required the reverse-lock to be released and the engine tilted full up in order to change the pin hole setting for the tilt stop rod. I moved to the next highest pin hole to tilt the engine up a bit when running. This would have the effect of raising the bow somewhat, which I hoped would eliminate the big bow wave and possibly give us a little more speed.

When you do this job, it's necessary to re-engage the reverse-lock when you lower the engine back down to its run position. If you forget to do that, the engine pulls itself out of the water as soon as you shift to reverse. And, of course, being borderline stupid, I forgot to do that. So, as soon as I shifted to reverse in order to back out of the notch we were in, the prop slung bits of driftwood splinters and chunks all over the place. Day-2 would be a "Boating 101" lesson from start to finish. The next lesson on the menu popped up about five minutes later.

The tilt adjustment helped very little as far as speed went, but it did have the positive effect of making steering easier. Lifting the bow made the boat less likely to seek its own course and made it track better. What I did not immediately realize however, because I did not bother to look back, was that the wake left behind our boat was huge with the boat configured bow-high. As we rounded Padre Point I saw a small boat close to the south shore. It was a little 12-foot tin boat and some guy was fishing in the back of a small cove from it. I thought this might be an opportunity to learn something about not only fishing conditions but perhaps some insight regarding up-lake camp sites, so I wheeled over and headed for the little cove.

As I approached, the guy in the tin boat started waving his arms and making all sorts of odd motions I couldn't put purpose to. Patty thought the guy must have been in some sort of distress, so as we got closer I just kept the throttle pegged in order to get there as quickly as possible. And the closer we got, the more frantic the guy's waving became.

With about thirty yards to go before I ran him over, I shut the power down to idle and the boat almost immediately pitched up stern-first as the following wave washed under us and rolled on. The wave was easily three feet high and when it reached the tin boat it very nearly turned the guy over. I was absolutely mortified. I had no idea we had that kind of a wake following us. I immediately shouted an apology but it likely was not heard as the guy shouted back at me: "YOU EVER LOOK BEHIND YOU TO SEE WHAT YOU'RE DOIN' TO THE LAKE? WHAT THE HELL'S WRONG WITH YOU, YOUNG FELLER! YER RE-ARRANGING THE LANDSCAPE!"

I told him I saw him waving and thought he might be in trouble so I figured I'd best come over for a look.

"I was waving you DOWN, damn it! I was tryin' to get you to slow down. Next time I see you go by I'm just gonna lay down in the damned boat so you can't see me."

The guy's name was Jake something-or-other. About in his mid-sixties I would guess, and one of the few people I've ever met that actually made me look good. The color and condition of the skin on his face made it look like something you could make a saddle out of, and a mop of lead-colored hair stuck out from under a beat up straw hat to resemble stuffing leaking out of a pillow. He settled down some after I finally got my apology out and I ventured a few questions, the first of which was, "You from around here?"

"Ain't NOBODY from around here. Look around you boy."

Since that didn't go well, I asked next how the fishing was.

"It was pretty good 'till you showed up to damn near knock me over." And with that he pulled up a rope stringer that had about a half dozen small bass on it. None were over twelve inches long.

"Well, that's pretty decent," I said. "Do you ever catch any bigger than that?"

Now, that's a pretty stupid question to ask a guy showing off a stringer of fish to a stranger. But Jake pretty much just let it slip by.

"Oh, sure," he said. "But I don't keep nuthin' that don't fit a fryin' pan."

Okay. I guess I had that coming. So I moved on and asked him if he knew of any decent campsites up the lake.

"Don't know nuthin' 'bout up the lake. Ain't lost nothin' up there and ain't never been. Catch all the damned fish I want right here. I just put the boat in over there and come over here to fish 'cause it keeps me out the wind."

We said goodbye and resumed our journey. Jake was not exactly a treasure chest of information, although it might have been different if I had not been so stupid when I came in on the crest of a tidal wave. So, that was the second lesson. Take a look behind once in awhile to see what affect your wake is having on others. I've kept it in mind for forty-three years.

As we continued on toward Face Canyon, the breeze came up. It wasn't a big deal. Not a Monsoon Chubasco or anything like that, just a stiff breeze of about 15mph, but enough to raise a few small whitecaps. With the bow-high condition, spray was flying out to either side and the breeze didn't present much of a problem, except to cut our speed even further. As we passed Face Canyon and made the looping turn to the north, Gregory Butte came into view in the distance and I started to feel pretty chipper about my navigating skills. And also about this time, a trio of "Canyon Tours" boats came by running up-lake at a fair clip.

When we made the turn, the breeze was now on our stern and our speed picked up a bit. There were a few moments when I thought the boat might actually get up on plane but that was overly optimistic. If I had been able to change the engine trim it might have made it, but of course there was no way to do that without coming to a dead stop, and I didn't want to do that.

There was a chance that I could ride the smooth-water tongue of the tour boat wakes, and besides that, I assumed those boats were headed for Rainbow Bridge and might serve as a free guide service. We slipped by Gregory Butte and everything was going hunky-dory. The tour boats had outrun us but they were still visible in the distance and now it seemed that we were actually gaining on them. In a few minutes, that suspicion was confirmed. Not only were we gaining, but it appeared that the three boats had stopped dead in the water. The place where they had stopped looked interesting. The huge, sheer canyon walls to either side of the channel marked yet another geological regime and I supposed the boats had stopped in order for the tour guides to talk about it with the Pilgrims.

As we caught up with them, I remembered about the wake thing and slowed down to a fast idle long before I probably needed to, but I had taken the pledge to be a good citizen and I didn't want to make anybody else mad at me. As we drew nearer, we could see that box lunches had been passed out and all the folks were chatting, chewing, and waving as we pulled up along side the last tour boat.

I shouted over to the boat skipper that I had no idea the canyon closed in on the river like this.

"Oh, this isn't the river," he shouted back. "You are in Last Chance Canyon."

Did I mention something about navigating skills? Mm-hmm …

I thanked the tour boat skipper for that timely update, poked another hole in my free map, then did a one-eighty and got out of there as fast as our 16-foot LST would go. Patty never said a word. Neither did I. Blue's tail was doing a wag-thump on the side of the boat but she never said a mumbling word either.

Back out in the river channel, we were soon overtaken by another sixteen—a Larson, as I recall—with two nice folks in it. As they passed they waved us down and we pulled up alongside. The guy wanted to know if everything was alright with us. "You look a little low in the water," the guy said.

I was starting to think that finding a suitable campsite was much less important than finding a place to hide. Out here in front of God and everybody, I should have been flying the "I'M STUPID" flag. I explained that we were overloaded, under powered, and under educated, but we had high hopes for the future. They told us they were on their way to Rainbow Bridge and this was already their third time on the lake.

"Don't feel bad," the guy said. "We did exactly the same on our first trip. It takes awhile to figure out you only need half the stuff you carry along."

We sat there bobbing in the middle of the lake for a good fifteen minutes chatting back and forth and the guy was a wealth of information. He advised that I should take a look at Rock Creek for a decent campsite. There were several small sand dune islands that were ideal spots, and it was just a few miles further up lake. And while I'm picking the guy's data-base, Patty is chatting with the guy's wife and the next thing you know they are swapping tomatoes for oranges and coffee for canned beans.

Soon we were joined by yet another boat, this one coming down lake, and it pulled over to raft up with us. This was a couple who had been all the way up to Oak Canyon and were now homeward bound. They had spare ice they would no longer need and asked if either of us could use some. Over the next couple of years, Patty and I realized that this was the norm. Early Lake Powell boaters were remarkable people. It became almost standard operating procedure to hail every passing boat and swap information, groceries, and well wishes. I think there was something of a pioneering spirit at work here. Like wagon trains headed across the prairies of old, people relied upon each other and took comfort from the human contact in a wild country. And a wild country it was. If you saw more than a dozen boats over the course of a single day you would consider it busy. So given that scant volume of traffic, it was hardly an imposition to stop and exchange news of experiences and discoveries. On the contrary, it was something you looked forward to. It was a very different era.

Rock Creek was easy to find. Another of those little floating signs said this was the place. But the sign was hardly necessary. You really couldn't miss it or confuse it with some other feature—like Friendship Cove, for example. As you passed "Friendship," you really were not even aware that it was there. Water had not yet backed into it, so it was just another wide spot in the canyon. Rock Creek was at the apex of a great river bend that looped around a string of river-run gravel bars in an S-turn. As you entered the "S," your bow was headed directly toward Rock Creek, and even a bozo with a free map full of holes could have figured it out.

Rock Creek Bay today covers a wide plain of undulating dunes and gravel bars that was then bisected by the cut of Rock Creek's channel. As the lake began backing up onto this plain those dunes and bars became small islands and on that first trip there were probably dozens of such islands to choose from in selecting a campsite. I picked a soft one about thirty yards in diameter and almost perfectly round. It was probably very near the center of the mouth of the wide bay of today, and about a half mile from the three-shouldered cliffs to either side of the bay. Another island next to ours, separated from us by ankle deep water and about forty yards away, was a bar of bowling ball sized river-run. I couldn't tell if this was a gravel bar washed down from Rock Creek or one connected with the river. I guessed it came from Rock Creek because looking up the nearby thread of the creek, the gut of it was paved over with about the same sized rock.

The flat top of the dune I picked for our camp rose about four feet above lake level and the gravel bar was slightly lower than that. It looked like a great setup and I eased up to our little island and nosed up onto the sand. Blue was airborne and hit the beach running before I could kill the engine and get out to tie us off. We were home and Blue's job was to check it out. After a three-minute squat in the sand to empty her tanks, she was off to run laps around our domain. She liked it. She was especially fond of the idea of having yet another island so close by that allowed even further exploration as soon as she had sniffed everything there was to sniff on our little island.

The next order of business was to unload the boat and set up camp. The tent came out first. That was sixty pounds right there. Once it was set up I went back to the unloading business and started moving stuff from the boat to the tent, but I wasn't allowed to go INSIDE the tent, because my tennis shoes were wet and I would have tracked sand into the tent. Patty does not allow sand inside the tent! She solves the sand problem with a painter's drop cloth and a bucket of water.

The drop cloth was not one of those cheap plastic jobs. Oh, no—it was the genuine article: a 12x12 heavy white cotton duck affair that itself weighed twenty pounds. She spread this in front of the tent so that you were obliged to walk on twelve feet of clean material before entering the tent. And, to make sure the drop cloth stays sand-free as well, you were instructed to dip one foot and then the other in the water bucket to rinse off any sand that may have collected on your shoes. This makes it somewhat difficult to transport a fifty-pound ice chest from the boat to the tent's interior while standing on one foot and dipping the other, but I go along with it. On the water I am Captain. On land she is the Sergeant Major. And Blue is the Corporal.

Corporals give Sergeant Majors fits. Blue thinks the water bucket is a pretty silly idea. There is a whole lake full of water to drink from. Who needs a bucket? But it does not take Blue long to figure out the drill. After being chased off the drop cloth twice, she learns to stand next to the bucket and wait for Patty to dip each of Blue's four paws in the bucket before entering human territory. I just shrug and try to explain the order of rank and commensurate privilege. "At least you aren't the poodle," I tell her. "Your fuzz-ball cousin is really going to be in trouble."

I make several trips from boat to tent, unloading from the port side where I can stand in only a foot of water. The water on the other side of the boat has a hole in it and is about belt-buckle deep. (Keep this in mind as the story moves on. It has bearing). It takes an hour, maybe a little more, to get camp set up and organized. It looks good. The ice chests are inside the tent to keep them shaded although it's twenty degrees hotter inside the tent than out, the folding chairs and table are set up, fire ring is built, the grill set up, the Coleman gizmos are fueled and pumped up, the lantern is hung on a sheep herder's hook pole, and so on. You know. You've done all this.

The sun is about to set on the upper west rim of Rock Creek Canyon, and Patty asks what I think we should fix for supper. "How 'bout we burn those steaks," I answer. She says, no. The ground meat spoils quicker. We should just grill some burgers. I'm wondering why she even asks if she already knows the answer. But I don't want to get provocative here. I don't say anything. I just set about to get a cook fire going. Because the quicker I get that chore done, the quicker I can break out a rod and test the water before it gets too dark.

There is ample driftwood all over the place, but it's all in the water. Won't burn. So I dump an entire ten-pound bag of charcoal in the ring and ask her where the lighter fluid is. She says she has no idea. That's my department. Well … I have no recollection whatsoever of putting a can of lighter fluid in our kit when packing, so I figure I'm out of luck. But not to worry. I'll just splash a little of our spare boat gas on the charcoal like the Boy Scouts do and the problem is solved. That will get it going, all right. And then it comes to me—I don't remember loading any spare gas either! I immediately stop what I'm doing and run to the boat, the shallow side. I jump in and grab my handy little dip stick and shove it into the port fuel tank, the one we had been running on since leaving Wahweap. And the stick comes out with maybe a half inch of wet on its tip. We are in serious trouble. We have burned up 10 gallons of fuel. Exactly HALF of our total capacity. I don't say anything about this to Patty just yet. I have to think about what this means for awhile before I throw it out there.

I dash a cup full of Coleman fuel on the charcoal and light it off. Then I sit down to sulk in silence and contemplate my stupidity. I am flat on my butt on the sand, leaning back on stiff arms, hands flat on the ground, and a sudden dull pain erupts in the palm of my left hand. It's one of those deep, sick kinds of pain. Kind of like those you get when you step on a nail and it goes through your shoe. Not a sharp sting, but on a 1 to 10 scale it goes from five to a nine in five seconds flat.

I pick up my palm to look at it, and as I do, a scorpion scuttles off across the sand with its tail stuck straight up in the air proud as you please. Excellent. Great way to cap off my day. Man, if ever there was a Lake Powell "Pilgrim," I was it. The scorpion sting wasn't a big deal. Some are worse than others. There is a little-bitty variety that lives down in the guts of Grand Canyon that can put a real hurt on you, but this wasn't one of those. It was just your run-of-the-mill two-incher with no particular claim to fame. It gave me a lump in the middle of my palm about marble-size and it hurt about the same as a yellow jacket sting. But a little medicinal spirits took care of it pretty quick. That would be the Jack Daniels. I always kept a fifth on hand in my kit for emergency treatment. Early Times was for drinkin', Jack Daniels was for healing.

What I did not realize at the time, and would not for some time after as well, was that rising water was flooding virgin ground and scorpions and all manner of crawly things were being driven from their lairs and were trying to reach high ground. This most certainly applied to mice, too. And every time one would high tail it across open ground, Blue would be on it like stink and scarf those things down like candy.

I was completely bummed out. With luck, we might have enough gas to get back to Wahweap but I can't even count on that. What little wind we had encountered on the trip up lake had been at our backs for the most part, and that meant we would be bucking it on the way home. A trip to Rainbow was definitely out, and even worse, I couldn't use the boat for fishing unless I felt like paddling.

I sat there in a funk and broke open the tackle box to see if inspiration lurked there within. And that tackle box was part of my problem too. It was one of those ridiculously huge hip-roof things that clam-shelled open to reveal FOUR fold-out trays on EACH side, and had a belly deep enough to hide an engine block in. Stupid. And it probably weighed thirty pounds. So I made myself a promise right then and there to downsize. After all, four of every pattern and color of artificials known to man was probably over the top.

I tied on something for top-water as the light was fading fast: a fat, black "Hula-Popper" as I recall, and started flinging it at every patch of water I could reach while sitting dead on my butt in the sand. It had a white rubber skirt and my standard drill was to just let it sit there after a cast and not twitch it until the ripples had disappeared. This worked well because it allowed me to take a snort off the JD jug between casts. It was a win-win situation. One good fish would wipe away all the gloom. And if nothing smacked the plug, the JD would work a similar magic. Couldn't lose.

"Your dog is sick," Patty said.

I always found that "your dog" business mildly irritating. Whenever MY dog did something good, she was just good old Blue. But if she barfed on the carpet, she was MY DOG. Like her poodle was just three good tricks short of sainthood, or something. Blue wasn't really what you would call sick. She was just unloading. She had done this plenty of times down on Horseshoe Lake on duck hunts when she over indulged on field mice. After wolfing down a dozen or so, she would just spit them out, one after another, like some kind of sausage machine. When she ate them, she never put a tooth mark on them. Just gulped them down whole. And they came out exactly the same way, whole, in one piece, except they were hairless and snow white. It was pretty disgusting to watch, but if you've been there before you knew it wasn't anything to get excited over. And as soon as she got rid of one load, she would go right back to work cleaning up any mouse that moved. It wasn't all bad. On a forty-foot island, I figured she would have the whole place cleaned out by morning.

I threw that Hula-Popper till dark without so much as a flash, got myself half-ripped, burnt the burgers, cleaned up, and was ready to call it a bad day. Patty thinks it's too hot to sleep in the tent and she's right. So she suggests we just roll out the sleeping bags onto the drop cloth and sleep on top of them. Any other time I might have agreed with her as a fine idea, but by the light of the Coleman lantern you could see scorpions cruising the sand under the lantern waiting for moths to come fluttering down. So we rolled the bags out on the floor of the boat instead. Blue curled up on the front portside seat, and we settled in for the night, glorying in quiet solitude under a sky, once again, ablaze with stars, and it seemed a shame to close one's eyes and shut out the spectacle, but both of us were whipped and in minutes we were sawing logs.

I can't remember exactly what time it was, but I think it was fairly late. Ten o'clock, eleven, maybe. Patty thinks not. Her recollection is that it happened right after we dozed off. But in any case, she shook me awake from a sound sleep and asked me if I heard anything. Has that ever happened to you? Somebody wakes you up from a deep sleep to ask if you hear something? I mean what kind of a question is that? Of course you don't HEAR something.

"No, I don't hear anything," I tell her. "Why?"

She says she hears a motor. I tell her it's a dream.

"NO, damn it! I hear a motor, I tell you!"

Now in order to get your arms around this I must first explain that we are completely ALONE in Rock Creek Canyon. We have not seen another soul since late afternoon. It's like being shipwrecked on a deserted island. And the notion of a boat being out there somewhere in the middle of the night just doesn't seem to square with reality. "I don't hear anything," I repeated. "If you heard an engine maybe it was an airplane passing overhead."

"I didn't 'HEARD' an engine. I hear it now. Look at 'your dog,' she hears it too."

MY dog's ears are rotating like a doe-deer's, a pretty good tip-off that something is going on.

"THERE! Can you hear that? My God, are you stone deaf?"

I could hear it now. It was faint. And it would come and go as thermals played with the sound. But there was no mistaking it. It was an outboard motor running at low speed somewhere in the distance.

"Yeah," I said. "It's a boat alright. Some guy must be lost out there somewhere."

"That's terrible," Patty said. "I can't imagine what it would be like to be lost out here in a barren wilderness like this."

"Sure you can. We were lost last night, remember?"

"We should turn on a light or something," she says.

"We should go back to sleep," I answered. "What's turning on a light going to do for the guy? How do we know where he wants to go? Turning on a light might mess him up. Go to sleep."

Getting back to sleep was impossible. You could not ignore the sound that was drawing nearer with each passing minute. And then, stretched out flat on the boat's floor, I saw a flash of dim light pass through the darkness over my head, momentarily reflecting off the boat's bright-works. That did it. I sat straight up to see what was going on and to my amazement immediately saw the white bow of a small runabout not more than thirty yards away. A fat lady was standing up in the boat and playing a dim flashlight over our campsite.

"HELLO?" she called out. "CAN YOU HELP US? WE ARE LOST!"

"Told you," Patty said.

I called back to the approaching boat and told the lady she was in Rock Creek and that the main channel was directly behind them. I assumed the guy driving the boat would be satisfied with that pearl of information and turn about to head for deep water. He did nothing of the kind, but rather continued idling toward us until he at last grounded on the sand right next to us on our starboard side. The two boats were separated by no more than ten feet and the lady continued on in conversational tones.

"Oh, thank goodness. I'm Rowena (such and such). My husband, Woodrow, and I have been to Rainbow Bridge today and the time got away from us. Ha-ha. We thought we could make it back to Wahweap, ha-ha, before nightfall but we misjudged badly. Ha-ha. You are the first people we have seen since about six o'clock. Do you mind if we just stay here with you the rest of the night? Ha-ha."

Rowena is doing all the talking. Woodrow just sits there staring straight ahead. Then this tea-cup dog of theirs jumps up and starts to growl at us. It's one of those cute but useless little "chee-wa-wa" things, and it's got the lip-curl working to demonstrate half-inch long fangs. Well, this gets Blue's attention and she moves to the starboard seat, puts her front paws on the gunwale and gets the arched neck thing going. The chee-wa-wa sees this and launches into that yip-yip-yip-yip business. And of course Blue responds with a single, black-night shattering WOOF! The chee-wa-wa disappears somewhere within the confines of their boat.

"Oh, my," says Rowena. "Is that dog as dangerous as it looks?"

"Oh, hell no. Blue is everybody's friend. She's not going to bother your ... whatever that thing is. But you know, if it troubles you, there are dozens of these little islands around in here. You could find one of your own nearby I would think."

"Oh, no. We aren't going anywhere else in the dark. We will stay right here with you, if you don't mind. We have been wandering around in the dark quite enough, thank you. We saw the glow of your lantern earlier but then you turned it out. Ha-ha. So we just headed in your general direction and hoped for the best. Ha-ha."

Their boat started to drift away from shore and Woodrow gets out a paddle to bring it back. "Can you get that bow line?" he asks Rowena. She is an excellent crew member. Without a word or second of hesitation, Rowena steps over the side of their boat, directly into that hole in the water I mentioned earlier, loses her footing, and goes in up to her eyes.

"PETER! HELP HER!" Patty shouts.

But I'm not quite sure what I can do for her. The water is only three feet deep or so, she's not going to drown or anything. And while I'm running options through my mind, Rowena finds her footing and comes thrashing out onto the shore. For some odd reason, Blue thinks this has something to do with play time and leaps out of our boat to join in the fun. Rowena is not amused by a large black dog licking her kneecaps and insists that I 'CALL OFF MY DOG!' Blue can take a hint. She knows when she's not wanted. So she resumes her favorite activity and starts running around chasing mice. The chee-wa-wa sees this and decides this could be a fun game to learn, and leaps off their boat to go play with Blue.

The two dogs do the arched-neck, one paw in the air, stiff-backed nose-sniff routine, and decide to become immediate friends. Blue takes off running laps around the island with the chee-wa-wa hard on her heels. They are kicking up sand, spinning around to reverse directions, yipping and woofing, and having a high old time as dogs can do. Rowena is freaked out. She's pretty sure her chee-wa-wa is going to get hurt, so she takes off to chase after the dogs and the whole thing takes on the air of some kind of a circus routine involving the fat lady and a pair of clown dogs.

In the meantime, Woodrow stands up in his boat and he's hollering at Rowena to get the bow line because the boat is drifting off again. Rowena catches up to the chee-wa-wa and snatches it up from the jaws of death just in the nick of time, and remarkably, tosses the damn thing through the dark of night out to Woodrow who is supposed to catch it, but doesn't even see it coming. The chee-wa-wa lands with a thump somewhere inside the boat and that was all we saw of the chee-wa-wa for the night.

Rowena gets the boat tied off, climbs back into their boat and without another word, retires for the night. It was not a good night. There is a lot of whispering going on in the dark. Patty thinks these people must be up to something. It's all just too "convenient" that these people managed to find the only camp for miles around in the middle of the night. Over in the neighbor's boat, I can hear

Rowena hiss something about our "pet buffalo." And later, it turns out that Rowena could out-snore Woodrow hands down, no contest.

I came to at early light with sandy eyes and rotten-mouth trying to identify the sound that woke me up. It sounded something like gravel falling into a tin washtub. So I sat up for a look around and spotted old Woodrow standing in his boat and peeing over the side. The guy was good for two quarts and obviously didn't have any plumbing problems. I don't want to interrupt a performance like that, so I politely wait before asking, in low tones to avoid disturbing Rowena, if old Woodrow just might possibly have some spare gas he'd be willing to sell.

"None I can spare," he mumbles. End of conversation. No, 'Why? You short? You in trouble?' Nothing like that. Okay. So maybe the guy has gasoline troubles of his own. I don't dwell on it. Instead, I hop out of the boat and walk up to the tent to fire up the Coleman stove and cook a pot of coffee. Blue, of course, hops out with me.

I'm being super quiet so I don't louse up anybody's morning. But things can happen. I'm fumbling around trying to do too many things at the same time and I manage to drop a tin coffee percolator on the stov''s wire grate. The clattering racket shatters the dawn, and down at the boats I hear old fat Rowena mumble: "My GOD! What now?!" Well, "what now" happens in a pretty quick chain of events. While I am fumbling around with the coffee pot, Blue has waded over to the gravel bar and all of a sudden she starts that flat, mono-toned WOOF WOOF WOOF WOOF. I've heard it before and know exactly what it means—SNAKE! And I look over there and sure enough, she's standing on spread out, stiff legs, with her tail ram-rod straight and the hair on her ruff all bristled up.

From the boat, Rowena calls out: "CAN YOU PLEASE DO SOMETHING WITH THAT DAMNED DOG?!" I don't even bother to look her way. I'm splashing over to the gravel bar at as close to a run as I could manage. Blue is snake-savvy and probably won't do anything stupid, but stuff can happen. It's a small snake. A little rattler about eighteen inches long, and you had to be almost on top of it before you could see it. At the "LEAVE IT" command, Blue stops barking and backs off. And now I have to figure out what to do about this. I won't normally kill a snake if it doesn't pose a threat, but this was an odd situation. They can and will swim, and in this close proximity to people and two dogs I decided not to take a chance. I dropped a large rock on it and that was that.

Meanwhile, fat Rowena is standing up in her boat, with that chee-wa-wa in her arms, and she's hollering to me: "THAT DOG OF YOURS NEEDS TO BE ON A LEASH!" You know, a guy has limits, and some are more tolerant than others. I guess I fit somewhere in between. I didn't say anything to her. Me and Blue splashed back over to our little island and I just walked down to her boat, untied the bow line, tossed the loose end up onto the bow, and pushed their boat off the sand. As might be expected, old Woody stands up, and he's a tad on the surly side.

"WHAT THE HELL DO YOU THINK YOU'RE DOING?!"

I raised my right hand in my best aloha wave. "You folks are leaving, ha ha. Just thought I'd help you on your way." Blue helped out with a parting, WOOF, and I think that sealed the deal. Woodrow fired his outboard and off they went in a cloud of blue smoke. Later, after their boat was no more than a speck carving a wake toward Gregory Butte, I broke the bad news to Patty. We would have to abort the trip. There really wasn't much choice. We couldn't go any further up the lake. I had just enough gas left to get back to Wahweap if we were lucky, and our present surroundings didn't have much to offer aside from scenic beauty. The place was lousy with scorpions, centipedes, and mice, and the snake thing had pretty much done it for me. If there was one, there was a fair chance it had a cousin and I wasn't about to give up the best Lab I ever had to a snake bite miles away from the nearest Vet. I didn't have gas to spare for fishing and you can only toss a "Hellbender" so many times from the bank before that gets old.

So, we packed it in. And that ended our very first trip to Lake Powell. We made it back to Wahweap just before sundown with nothing but vapor left in the fuel tank, but good enough. Sure. It was a big disappointment. A huge one. But that only served to sharpen our appetites. We knew we had just barely scratched the surface. We had to see it all! And that June of '64 trip was just the beginning. We made three or four more trips during that year, with each better than the last, and inching our way just a bit further up lake each time. We took our time and did quite a bit of hiking and exploring that might be likened to turning the pages of a really good book. You hate to put it down. And like a good book, the excitement and anticipation grew as you approached the end pages. Each new discovery topped the last one. And waiting at the end, was Rainbow Bridge.

◆   ◆   ◆

A lot of water has gone down the river since 1964, and over the course of 43 years the changes we have seen in not just the lake itself, but in equipment, boats, motors, tow-vehicles, facilities, conveniences and the fishery are amazing. Much of what we take for granted today as the norm simply did not exist in 1964. Here are just a few examples of what we cheerfully went without and didn't even know we were deprived: Zip-lock bags, bottled water, deep-cycle 12V batteries, electric trolling motors, power-trim and tilt, water shoes, reliable catalytic heaters, outboards over 100-hp, modern sonar electronics, and VHF radios for EVERY-BODY!

Sixteen-foot boats were common on the lake, largely, I think, because outboard engines weren't big enough to power anything much larger, and inboards were considered somewhat exotic. We used the lessons learned from our first trip to make life easier and longer-range explorations possible. Lesson number one was to shed the excess weight, supplies, and equipment that added nothing but grief to our travels. The first to go was that big, 60-pound tent, replaced with a flyweight backpack model that tipped the scales at just nine pounds including the bag it came in. Next were the three ice chests. If you could forego multiple whole heads of iceberg lettuce and whole celery stalks, you discovered you could get along quite nicely with a single cooler. And if you lived in a T-shirt and cut-off jeans, it was hardly necessary to bring along half the clothes you owned. I learned, too, that weight and space thus saved allowed for spare gasoline. And even more to the point, pared weight permitted the boat to get on plane at speeds that effectively doubled gas mileage.

Our last trip to Powell in 1964 came at about mid-October, which provided perhaps the best lesson of all. October is THE prime month at Lake Powell. At least that's the way we see it. Water temps are still pleasant for bathing, the Monsoon Chubascos have passed, and the fish are on the prowl to bulk up for winter. The lake had risen to nearly 3500msl (mean sea level) by the time we quit Powell for that year, which opened up a great many more beach and campsite options too. The following spring and summer would be the time for grand explorations and access to places not yet readily available to boaters. So, yes, while there was a sense of loss as Glen Canyon began to flood, so too were new opportunities for discovery available to anyone who could get their hands on a boat. There was enormous value in that. You might compare it to trading off an old car that had served you well and you mourned its loss, but the smell of new upholstery soon replaced the gloom.

Frankly, I think we have a much better lake to enjoy today than we did in 1964. Many will not agree with that assessment. But for the most part, those who would advocate draining our lake are generally younger folks who envision a fantasy of what they THINK Glen Canyon used to look like. I won't even engage in conversation with somebody of such mindset that's less than seventy years old, because if they didn't see it with their own eyes they really don't know what they are talking about.

Rising waters flooding virgin ground at Powell created some problems that today's boaters need no longer worry about. You rarely encounter scorpions below the lake's high-water mark nowadays. It seems once dislodged from their hunting grounds they are reluctant to return as lake levels fall again. Oh, sure, you will stumble across one now and then lurking under some rock you overturn. But in '64 there were literally armies of them fleeing to higher ground. We don't see snakes in numbers we saw back then either. This, I suspect, has less to do with higher water levels than with increased human shoreline activity and noise that serves to drive them further inland.

Another hazard common in the late '60s and into the early '70s were collapsing sand dunes and rock spalls. It still happens now and then, but nothing like on the scale witnessed in those first-water days. This was not a hazard to be taken lightly. You had to be pretty picky about campsites at the foot of big dunes rising along otherwise sheer-walled cliffs. Water lapping at the base of these dunes would penetrate and saturate the dune bottoms and when the sand's load bearing limits were thus compromised, the whole shebang would come crashing down in a thunderous rush and a fog of dust. I'm talking about dunes as high as a ten-story building and several hundred feet wide at the base. They would just disappear before your eyes in a matter of seconds. You need only see that happen once to figure out what your chances might be if camped at the bottom of one of those collapses. At times the threatened dunes gave ample warning signs if one paid attention. Fresh, sharp-edged fissures, especially at the contact zone between sand and cliff face were pretty good tip-offs that something was up. So were little unexplained puffs of dust rising in still air.

Another significant change over the years was the gradual reduction in driftwood. Some driftwood comes down each year during the spring runoff floods, but the volume hardly resembles or replaces the quantities of driftwood we used to have. I guess folks just gathered and burned it all up over the years, and there's both good and bad to be found in that. Water-logged trees floating stump-up just below the surface used to rip lower units off of boats at an appalling rate. That would be a rare occurrence today, and we can be grateful for that. On the other hand, finding wood for a cheerful campfire is quite a chore today. But what I miss most about driftwood is the floating rafts of it we used to find at the backs of canyon coves that were genuine hog-farms! Bass would hang out in the shade under those rafts and any bait heavy enough to break through would trigger a strike right now! It was heaven.

So, yes, a lot of changes, a lot of lessons. Although they were the rare exception among people of those days, old Woodrow and fat Rowena taught us a valuable lesson as well. After that first trip, we started bringing both, his and hers, dogs. If campsite privacy mattered to you, there was no better way to guarantee that than to have it guarded by an obnoxious poodle!

◆   ◆   ◆

As the calendar rolled into 1965, each new trip on rising waters presented a new face and character for Lake Powell. We were launching our old wooden boat off pavement now at Art Greene's temporary ramp, and the Rainbow floating marina in Forbidding Canyon was now complete and fully operational, though not without a few small problems. A quality fishery had exploded and I don't use that term loosely. I had been blessed with the opportunity to fish a lot of different water around the western United States and I had never experienced anything quite like this. The variety and quality of the fish was astounding. And best of all, most of the fish were remarkably stupid. They would eat just about anything dangled in front of them no matter how badly presented.

Rising water provided easy boat access to places one's imagination could not have foreseen. Water caves, grottos, and amphitheaters never failed to leave you breathless in discovery, as did riparian forests of cottonwood and willow trees at natural artesian springs and along tributary creeks, their beds stepped with beaver dams and small ponds that drew wildlife of all species like magnets. Seemingly barren and hostile, the country was home to deer, big cats, raccoons, porcupines, badgers, coyotes, bobcat, fox, and even an occasional bighorn.

Nineteen sixty-five was the first year during which we experienced the white "bathtub" ring at water's edge. It had not occurred to us that the lake would do anything other than to continue rising. In our defense, I would remind you that we were still quite young and not entirely aware of how the world worked yet. Most certainly we were naïve to the dam's operation and purpose. The normal seasonal drawdown and fluctuation was still something of a mystery to us.

Our top priority was to at last discover Rainbow Bridge, and we did that in 1965, hiking the trail from just inside the narrow passage at the junction of Forbidding and Rainbow Bridge Canyons. It was a pretty stiff hike then and we were lucky to be able to function on young legs. The installation of Rainbow Marina was a mixed blessing. On the one hand it solved our fuel duration problems with that old boat, but the downside was the volume of boat traffic it drew into Forbidding Canyon. Folks were churning the canyon with wake-wave action whether or not they intended to visit Rainbow Bridge, and from 1965 on, the volume of that traffic steadily increased. But that was of course during the height of the boating seasons between May and September. After Labor Day, the canyon was virtually deserted.

For this and a number of other reasons, the month of October turned out to be our favorite time on the lake. Still is. The summer Monsoon Chubascos were well past, and the weather was generally perfect with still air, bright sky, and shirtsleeve days. Cool nights allowed serious sleep and the water temperature still permitted perfect bathing conditions. But best of all, fish were into serious foraging activity in order to bulk up for the coming winter.

The operation of the floating marina over the winter months paints a picture of sharp contrast between eras. In the 60's the marina store closed around the first week of November, depending on traffic volume and visitation, and the folks who ran the place during the busy season deserted the place. The gas pumps, however, were left running and unlocked! There was a steel lock-box with a money slot provided and you were on the honor system to pay for whatever gas you drew.

It was up to the individual to determine whether or not you wanted to beat Art Greene out of a few bucks. Remarkably, very few did. Patty became fairly good friends with the lady that ran the place and she learned that upon opening in spring, the count came out on the plus side more often than not. That speaks volumes about the evolution of our society but speaks even more loudly about the man, Art Greene, whose faith in the goodness of human nature went far beyond my own. How do you suppose it would turn out if the pumps were left open at Dangling Rope Marina over the winter months today?

Hiking the trail and seeing Rainbow Bridge for the first time made quite an impact on us. I probably don't have to tell you what that was like, you no doubt have vivid recollections of your own surrounding the first time you rounded the canyon bend to catch a glimpse of the arch in the distance. There is that first flutter of excitement as you realize you are about to complete your pilgrimage, immediately followed by mild disappointment because it doesn't seem quite as large and spectacular as you had been told to expect. But of course you are still quite some distance at that point of first visual contact and as you continue on the trail the specter grows ever larger until at last, standing in the shadow of the great arch, the enormity of it all comes to your senses in a rush and you somehow begin to doubt the accuracy of your own vision.

Often times in the 60's, and especially during the off-season months, you could sit beneath the bridge for hours on end, watching soaring ravens dance the canyon's air, their calls echoing off the cliffs to add an aura of the surreal, and not see another human visitor the entire time. *THAT* is the way to experience Rainbow Bridge, and it can still be done today if you arrive at first light or linger beyond sundown. To be alone with your God in that canyon is an opportunity to discover far more than nature's beauty. It is also an opportunity to plumb the depths of your soul and discover something about yourself as well.

Once we had finally discovered Rainbow Bridge, our journeys to Lake Powell fell into a new routine. We made it a point to visit, explore, and fish at least one new canyon with every trip. Typically, we would establish a base camp at the campsite of our previous trip and then go from there. Some highlights during this period included: the discovery of Hole-In-The-Roof at Rock Creek, the captive deer herd in Dangling Rope Canyon, the ruins and rock art in Reflection Canyon, Elf's Den in Llewellyn Gulch, dinosaur tracks, petrified wood forests, fossilized remains in the upper San Juan, the beaver colonies in upper Oak, Reflection, and other canyons, and, two and a half million crazy crappies in Wilson Creek and a herd of arm-long Rainbow Trout in Wahweap Bay.

Which reminds me, it's about time for some fish stories. I'll come back to our discoveries later. When I do, I won't focus on the myriad examples of eye-candy that are above the current water level and still available for all to see. That would be redundant, somewhat pointless, and would defeat the original purpose of describing what is now lost beneath our keels so all can experience in some small way what Lake Powell was like in the early years.

Somewhere along the way I discovered Lake Powell was full of Rainbow Trout. It must have been around 1967 or 1968. You may have heard that trout fingerlings and older trout were air-dropped in Wahweap Bay in the past. That was for real, and National Geographic featured a story on it and also a belly-view of one such drop. We were at the ramp at Wahweap loading the boat and getting ready to shove off for yet another up-lake adventure when a bunch of people started shouting and pointing at a low flying aircraft making its way south to north from the dam toward Castle Rock. "Here it comes, here it comes!" they were shouting.

I didn't quite know what to expect. Apparently all these folks knew something I didn't. The plane was either a C-46 or C-47, can't remember which, and as it descended to about 600–800 feet above the surface, the gear and flaps came down and it looked for all the world like the guy was on some kind of final approach to a disaster. Frozen in place, I grabbed Patty's arm and told her to watch this because there was about to be one hell of a crash. A few seconds later a silvery plume erupted from the plane's belly and the shimmering cloud drifted down to the water's surface with a three hundred yard long splash. At that point, the gear and flaps were retracted, the pilot added power and the plane rose to bank sharply to the west. The bystanders started whooping and cheering and I still didn't know what was going on or what I had just seen. So I asked some guy what that was all about and he told me the Fish and Wildlife Service had just dumped five thousand Rainbow Trout into the lake, and apparently it was not the first time either. You learn something every day if you manage to wake up. This was the first I heard or knew anything about trout being in the lake.

"Oh yeah," the guy said. "There's some dandy fish in there. Ten-, twelve-pounders are pretty common."

Yeah. Right, I'm thinking. I've got a couple of good fish tales of my own.

After getting the boat off the trailer, Patty and I motored out to the drop zone to see how the whole thing had turned out. For the life of me I couldn't see this as a cost effective way to plant five thousand trout. I couldn't understand how trout could hit the water at 150 miles an hour or more and survive. Seems to me that backing a hatchery truck up to the water's edge and opening a gate valve was the better way to go. But what do I know? At the drop zone we found about a dozen, no more than that, five inch trout floating on the surface, and a few of those were still making an effort to right themselves and swim off. That was incredible. I wouldn't have thought that to be possible. But that being as it may, I started to get serious about trout fishing in Lake Powell after that. This shift in focus from bass to trout eventually led to some big boat changes also. I'll get into that later.

You could fish the "'bows" year-round, but technique had to vary with the season. During the majority of the time, trolling flashy iron at slow speed and at depths to reach cold water worked just fine. But at winter's end, a special situation developed. Around the end of February and into about mid-March the trout went to shallow water in upper Wahweap to attempt to spawn. Wayne Gustaveson, the Biologist for the Utah Division of Wildlife Resources for Lake Powell, tells us these spawns failed but nobody told the trout it was a hopeless situation. They went at it with great vigor and determination. At such times the fish were remarkably easy to catch. In fact it almost bordered on the criminal. Just about any son-in-law that could turn a reel handle in the right direction could catch these things. And I'm not talking about hatchery trout either. These were serious fish. When the guy at the ramp told me ten- and twelve-pound or better fish were common, he was right on the mark.

When I first got into fishing the spawn I used a 6-wt fly rod and used to throw big elk hair minnows that I tied myself, way back when I thought that was something I wanted to do. I gave that up many years ago however, when I discovered it was cheaper and easier to buy flies that were far better than whatever I could produce. Half the time my own flies would come apart after two or three false casts. But I soon gave up on the fly rod altogether anyway. There were too many problems with it. First off, the big cows would have their noses to the bank in water often times so shallow you could see the dorsal fin and top of the tail waving at the surface. Putting the fly in that two feet of water between their noses and the water's edge with any consistency was beyond my capability. My casting accuracy just wasn't up to that challenge. Besides that, putting a ten-pound trout in the boat with that rod and 6-lb leader material required more patience, time, and finesse than I was willing to devote. So I switched to bass tackle and had a lot more fun. That's what we used during the summer months anyway when trolling, so what's the diff?

The main problem with fishing the spawn though was the weather. For some reason it just seemed to be a lot colder in February and March back then than it is now. I don't know that it is true, but it just seemed that way. And fishing from an open boat could be downright brutal if there was no opportunity to take a break and warm up now and then. You would be all jammed up in winter clothing that limited easy movement and even at that, no matter how much rag you piled on, sooner or later the cold would seep through and you would have to call it a day.

That's largely what led me to give up on our old wooden boat and get into something I could close up with a tight fitting camper-back. Thus equipped, a guy could stop now and then, zip up, and light off a propane cat-heater or a Coleman lantern and thaw out your fingers once and awhile. I needed more boat anyway. Our three daughters had attained the age and the interest and we stopped leaving them behind on our multiple lake trips. I had upgraded from that original 40hp Johnson to a 65hp Merc to make that possible but the boat still wasn't big enough to make a trip for five feasible.

So, I bought a bigger boat. It was terrible. It was an eighteen-foot Dorset that was supposed to be, according to the manufacturer and the dealer, a *cabin cruiser*. Get real. There is no such thing as a "cabin cruiser" that is just eighteen feet long. But never mind that for now. The boat did have a good camper-back canvas set that met the original goal of all-weather capability. And we used the boat in exactly the way I had envisioned. Fish for an hour, knock the ice out of the guides, retire to the so-called cabin, fire up some heat, sip a little Early Times and regroup. As soon as you stopped shivering you could go back out and try it again.

The Dorset. P. Klocki photo

My dear old Dad was not a fresh-water guy. He kept a little boat up at Coos Bay in Oregon, and venturing out for Salmon was his thing. He had a sixteen-foot Larson with twin 35hp outboards on it and it also had a snug-fitting camper back. He gave it a cute little catchy name too. He called it, "For Pete's Sake." Pretty clever, I thought. I was needling him to bring that boat back down to Arizona to get in on some of this fantastic trout action but he wouldn't do it. He went one better instead—he offered to go halves with me on a Powell boat that made more sense than that stupid Dorset. I was always complaining about how big a mistake I had made in buying it and he was offering a solution.

His idea was to snag us a slip at Wahweap and buy and keep a bigger boat there. Well, I went along with it, but I decided to keep the Dorset anyway. I still fished the Arizona desert lakes a lot when there wasn't enough time for a Powell trip and I didn't want to give that up. I needed at least three days for a decent trout hunt at Powell but I could be fishing Bartlett, Pleasant, or Saguaro in an hour and a half.

The IMP. P. Klocki photo

The boat we bought was a twenty-three foot IMP Inca and it offered quite a bit more in creature comfort, but it too was still a long way from perfect. The problem with small cruiser types is that the manufacturers, in my opinion anyway, try to cram in too much livability. The inevitable result is that you have a bunch of miniaturized features that look okay but don't really work all that well and head, deck, and elbow space is left wanting. The IMP was like that. With twin 6-cylinder in-line Chevy engines the engine cover stretched across the aft cockpit from wall-to-wall. It was a big, plushy, padded lounge type thingy that was essentially useless to fishermen. So you were denied the transom, and fishing from either side was as good as it gets unless you felt like fishing on your knees. The interior was the same. It had a cute little two-burner alcohol stove that was good enough to make a grilled cheese sandwich but that was about all. The head *looked* like a stand-up head until you tried it. It would accommodate your average dwarf but anybody over five feet tall was in trouble. Gauchos to either side of a small table and the cabin converted to fairly comfortable V-berths but you could never figure out which end to put your head at. Two guys had the option of either breathing in each other's ears or playing toe-tag. But again, for winter all-weather fishing the boat worked fairly well in much the same and better ways than my Dorset did.

So, one fine weekend toward the end of February, me and the old man decided to go hunt cow rainbows in upper Wahweap. This would be his first, and, unfortunately, last such adventure. No, no. He didn't die or something. Nothing like that, although he should have, it's just that he got soured out on the whole deal.

◆　　　◆　　　◆

We were ready to set out fairly early to hit the Wahweap spawning grounds despite a nasty weather forecast and a wall-hung el-cheapo barometer that was showing pressure down around 27 inches. That's like *hurricane pressure*! But I pretty much wrote that off as bogus data from a flawed instrument. The air pressure couldn't possibly be that low. But nonetheless, first light revealed a sky the color of wet lead that was weeping cold drizzle and the thermometer read something like 35 degrees.

"Whaddaya think?" the old man asks. "Should we just hang out in the slip and play a little gin? Drink a little whiskey maybe? See if the weather clears?"

"Nah, the fish don't care how miserable it is. They're makin' babies and they will not be denied. Besides, there's no wind. It won't be all that bad."

So off we go, idling out of the marina area while the old man rigs up for monster 'bows. He's got one of those big old plastic Zebco reels about the size of a grapefruit screwed onto a rod that looks like it was made to support telegraph wires and he's tying on about five pounds of metal to stiff, fat mono that had memory dating back to Camelot's heyday. He's got cowbells and Ford fenders and all sorts of crap strung out all over the aft deck and a huge, chrome Z-Ray tied to the business end. I didn't even know they made Z-Rays that big. It was bigger than a buck-knife and weighed about the same.

"*What, exactly*, do you intend to do with that mess?" I asked. "How do you propose to fling that load of scrap metal out of the boat?"

"Ain't gonna, I'm gonna troll with it."

"No, no. We aren't going to troll. The spawn is on. We are going to bait-cast in shallow water."

"Thought you said you troll for these things?"

"Later, in summer, not now," I said.

But he wanted to troll. And he had a pretty good argument. "Look," he said, "I want *MY* engine shut off. You can do whatever you want with your engine."

Ah, geez, how do you deal with something like that? So we trolled. It's a big time-waster. I wanted to get to the coves and get down to business but no, we have to drag around five pounds of iron for an hour without so much as a bump. In the meanwhile, the drizzle had turned to light snow. Not a big deal, just a stray pellet now and then but it was beginning to crisp up on the cabin roof. I thought it was kind of neat in a way because this was the first time I had a legitimate excuse to turn on that cool little windshield wiper. Snick, pause ..., snick, pause ... You had time to read a page of Outdoor Life between swipes. I'm going nuts. Finally, he cranks in his scrap iron and says, "Screw this! I'm freezin', let's go back."

Uh, uh, I don't think so. I turned the boat west and rammed the throttles open. I had those poor old Chevy sixes wound up to about 4500 revs and it sounded like they were about to come through the floor. The IMP would run close to 35mph with the furnaces stoked up like that and it only took a few minutes to get to the first cove below the "Chains" area and just beyond where Aramark keeps the houseboat rental fleet today. I nosed in and shut down the engines early to drift in and grabbed my rod before the boat had stopped moving. You older guys might remember those old pointy-nosed Bomber lures that actually looked like little bombs, complete with tail fins? I had a white one with red eyes tied on and it was a killer setup. Throw that puppy right to the water's edge, or even up on the sand a few inches and drag it in and BANG! Fish on! Then it's Katie bar the door.

I used to love to hook up on those things. They would put on a heck of a show, doing a tail dance on the water like a Tarpon before taking off on a rod-bending run. It was like latching on to a silver torpedo. While I'm working this fish, the old man is dismantling his hardware store. Had it been me, I would have just whipped out a knife and cut all that junk loose and thrown it in a bucket to sort out later. But he's very meticulous in his care for this stuff, opening snaps, clipper-snipping swivels loose, and winding up these pre-rigged trashcan lids on a piece of cardboard he kept in his kit for just that purpose. You got the impression that he might actually want to try and use this stuff again some time in the future.

In the meantime my fish comes out of the water a couple of times and I get a good look at it. I can see the Bomber lure is plastered to the side of the head with both sets of trebles appearing to be stuck on pretty good, but this doesn't look so hot. It's a pretty good fish and that hookup didn't look like something you could hang your hat on. So I told the old man to get ready to give me some net work as soon as I had this cow alongside the boat. A few minutes later he jabs the net under the fish with two hands and dumps a nine-pound 'bow on the deck. Nice fish. He picks it up by the gill cover and a stream of eggs came cascading out of the vent all over the deck.

"Wow," he says. "You sure loused up *her* day."

The snow was now coming down pretty good and sometime over the last thirty minutes the temperature had fallen enough to allow it to start sticking on the slick rock and the hard parts of the boat, but not yet on the sand. A little ice crust had formed inside the line guides and I knew it would soon be too miserable to stay out much longer. So I didn't even wait to deal with the fish. I just left it flopping around on the deck while I threw that Bomber right back to the same patch of water. BANG! Two casts, two fish. Another tail dancer, and it looks about the same as the first one. Old Dad is fumbling around in his kit looking for something white to tie onto his line, and I tell him I need the net again.

We boat this one and it is an absolute clone—nine pounds on the nose for both fish. I tell the old man to never mind trying to get rigged up. I just gave him my rod and told him to go for it while I killed and gutted out the fish. We wouldn't be out here much longer and I didn't want him to miss out. So he takes my rod, rears back, and puts as much arm into the cast as a home plate catcher throwing to second base. The Bomber goes straight up into the sky and falls in the water about ten feet from the boat and my reel looks like something that nesting doves had commandeered for a bedroom. It was an old Garcia C-3 with no brakes and took some clever thumb work to control.

"How does this *&%*$ thing work?!" he says. "How come you fish with a winch? What's wrong with a good old four-dollar Zebco?"

"You fish with a winch up in Oregon," I answer. "What's the problem?"

"Yeah, but I don't *cast* with it! We just troll like civilized people do. Watching you fish is like watching a tennis match."

He's standing there shivering, snow sticking to his shoulders and on his little, black Greek Fisherman's cap and he's picking at this mess and getting nowhere with it.

"To hell with it," says he. "Let's get out of here. It's turning into a regular *&*^%$# blizzard. We can try this again tomorrow."

He didn't get an argument out of me. My teeth were chattering and my wet hands were starting to sting. I'd had enough too. So I fired up the engines, eased us out of the cove and headed for the marina at a modest speed to accommodate the visibility. That was the first and only time in my life I've ever run a boat in a snowstorm and I can tell you it's a pretty weird sensation. The snow is falling straight down with zero wind but with the boat in motion it looked like it was coming at you head on, and with the rocking and pitching of the boat it was a chore to maintain orientation and equilibrium in near white-out conditions. I really don't need to ever have to do that again in order to call my life complete.

By the time we got back to the marina the stuff was coming down in big, white chicken feather sized flakes and it's snowing like a Vermont Christmas card scene. I can't tell one slip-dock from another. All the slipped boats are now the same color, white, and I have nothing recognizable to go by. It takes a half an hour of idling up and down alleyways before we find our home slip and cozy up. For all its faults, I was really happy to have that IMP that day. If nothing else, it kept a hard roof over our heads and kept us out of that weather.

The old man tied us up hard on the dock fenders, tight to the port side. This left about two feet of open water between the boat's starboard side and the finger-dock. When we left that morning we had only taken the time to boil up a pot of thick coffee and choke down a couple of donuts, so I asked the old man how he felt about me scrambling up a half dozen eggs with some raw-fried potatoes and a couple of ham steaks with red-eye gravy for some breakfast as soon as I had the camper-back zipped up.

"Scramble the whole damned dozen," he said. "Go cook. And never mind about the canvas. I'll put the rag up as soon as I scale these fish you forgot to scale. What kind of way to do is that anyway? You gotta scale these things."

He was pointing an accusatory finger at the two fish sprawled out on the deck and he had his face all screwed up into a frown like I had just done something as evil as neglecting to skin out an elk before the hide froze.

"Don't worry about it," I said. "I'll scale them when we get home. Blast 'em off with a water hose."

"WHAT? You'll ruin 'em! Ya can't hose down dead fish with warm water. You'll flat ruin 'em. Make a big mess too. I'll scale 'em right here in the water and get 'em on ice. C'mere, pilgrim, and I'll show you how easy it is to do your fish the right way."

He had this little aluminum fish scalar in his kit and he picked up one of the fish with his thumb locked on the lower jaw and his fingers shoved up under the gill cover. He then leaned over the side of the boat to submerge the fish in the water and started scraping off scales. It went pretty quick, the scales shimmering like a cloud of glitter in the water as he worked. I don't think it took more than two minutes to do a side.

"When you don't see any more glitter in the water the job is done. Just flip it over and do the other side—nothing to it, pilgrim."

With that fish done, he prepared the ice chest to receive the fish while I retired to the cabin to start peeling potatoes. He was very fussy about how he iced down fish.

"You keep 'em dry. Never, ever, let 'em wallow around in the water when they are pretty dead."

He wasn't into waxed paper or plastic wrap either, and this was the pre-zip bag era. Newspaper was his thing. This was the program: he would carefully fold multiple newsprint pages to precisely fit the bottom of the cooler and place these pages over the block ice to make a dry shelf about an inch thick. Then he would wrap a fish loosely in a single sheet of newsprint and place the wrapped fish on the shelf. This was followed by yet another inch-thick layer of folded pages on top of the fish. Thus prepared, the cooler was closed and the lid joint taped shut with masking tape, not to be opened again until arriving home.

He would bring home fish from Oregon in this manner and they would be as good as new after two days on the road, so, it must have been effective, but I thought it was a bit too complicated. I understood the insulating value of the newspaper, but the single-wrap on the fish carcass didn't do it for me. I found the paper was a pain in the butt if it stuck to the fish's sides. I would use Saran Wrap or equal instead.

"Naw," he would argue. "Makes 'em slimy."

So I go back to peeling the potatoes at the miniature galley. The cabin door is open and I see him pick up the second fish and lean over the starboard side to go to work on it. I still think this is a little silly. I don't see why it is so important to get these fish scaled in the middle of a snowstorm. The snow is now a measurable inch on the finger docks and the boat's cabin roof. The old man almost died from pneumonia when he was younger and he had bronchitis and emphysema and I don't know what all, but none of it good. And it troubled me to see him bent over the side of the boat like that with snow piling up on his back and shoulders.

That IMP had a lot of freeboard and in order for him to get a thirty-inch fish down into the water he had to stand on tip-toes and lean over as far as he could. The deck his toes were on was of course about as slick as spit on a porcelain door-knob with fish slime, fish eggs, snow, and freezing water. Out of the corner of my eye I catch movement and glance his way in time to see his legs go straight up into the air and then straight down as he disappeared over the side.

I dropped the potato and ran outside to see what I could do, fearing the worst. Fully clothed and all bound up in winter gear, hat, shoes on, can a guy swim like that? This ain't good. He's got the truck keys in his pocket. I'm leaning over the gunwale looking straight down into black water and here he comes! He breaks water like a surfacing submarine, straight up, arms flailing, blowing, snorting and spitting water, hat still on, glasses still on, and he's blubbering: "I LOST YOUR FISH!"

I had a helluva time getting him out of the water. He couldn't reach high enough to grab an edge somewhere so I reached down as far as I could, over his head, and grabbed his jacket collar and jerked him up high enough so he could grab onto something. Didn't work so hot. When I pulled up on the jacket it came up over his head and limited his arm movement. He couldn't reach up at all bound up like that. So I dropped him in order to get a better hold. Of course when I do that he goes down again, calling me some really ugly names as he goes. When he comes up again, this time I grab his wrists and he grabs mine and I get him half way up. High enough anyway, for him to hook his elbows over the gunwale. Then I reach down over his back and try to latch onto his belt, but the jacket is in the way and I can't find it. So I just grabbed him by the seat of his pants and hauled him in like a big tuna with a Melvin.

The deck might as well have been paved with ball bearings. It was impossibly slippery and he's scrambling around on leather shoe soles trying to get up and he can't. He keeps flopping and thrashing around and he's getting nowhere. If it hadn't been such a dangerous situation it would have been a real hoot. The whole thing reminded me of the time when my Labrador chewed open a plastic squeeze bottle full of bourbon left over from a river-float trip and got herself too drunk to stand up. All the while he's hollering about how he lost my fish. I'm thinking never mind the fish. He could go hypothermic on me any minute. I had to get him inside and go to work on warming him up quick. He's shaking all over like a wind-blown Aspen and his lips and fingernails are turning blue. I tried to help him to his feet but couldn't get it done, so I told him to just crawl and get inside.

I didn't lose the old man on that trip. He actually lived on to age ninety-two, not passing until 2004, despite his lousy lungs and other problems. When I got him inside I closed the cabin door, got him stripped down and toweled off, put him inside a zipped up sleeping bag and lit the cat-heater, the Coleman lantern, and turned on both stove burners. It's a wonder carbon monoxide didn't kill us but somehow we must have gotten lucky.

He quit shaking and settled down some after about a half an hour. I had shoved a thermometer in his mouth, more to shut him up than anything else because he kept on babbling about losing the fish, but his core temperature was about normal so I figured he'd live. So once he got over the shakes and warmed up a little, he decides it's time to get mad about something. He starts hollering at me for not scaling my fish in the first place. I can see where he's going with this.

Now it's MY FAULT that he went in the drink. So I need a come-back to get things evened out again. He had blubbered time and again about how sorry he was that he had lost *my fish*. So I tell him: "Look, if we don't catch anymore, I figured we could each take one of the two fish home for a nice fish dinner. I still have mine. The fish you lost was yours!"

"That's a really crappy thing to say to your old man!"

"Alright, alright, you can have that fish. We will probably catch a whole mob of 'em tomorrow anyway," I said.

"Like hell," he says. "Tomorrow we are going home! Anybody that would fish in weather like this needs professional help!"

I cooked us up that whopper three-thousand calorie breakfast and boiled another pot of 500-mile coffee and we spent the rest of that day hunkered over the little table drying out twenty dollar bills over the Coleman lantern, playing gin rummy, and drinking a little whiskey. After awhile he was able to start laughing about the whole thing and by supper time he was downright jovial. He had clipped me for about forty bucks all told and that always gave him a chuckle. A nasty little devious kind of chuckle—"Heh-heh-heh-heh." Especially when he caught me with fifteen points on a low knock. I kind of miss that nasty little laugh.

We came around in the morning to find a crystal clear, bright sky so blue you thought it might crack. I thought he might be willing to change his mind about going home but it was not to be. The air temperature of twenty-five degrees pretty much clinched it. I never could get him worked up for another winter trout trip after that. Just wasn't his thing. The guy just didn't have a sense of humor.

◆   ◆   ◆

Explorations

There were two water caves at the mouth of Rock Creek you could drive a couple of houseboats into with room to spare. Both were dark and foreboding, but one was unique. It was called "Hole-In-The-Roof." It was so called because it had one: a perfectly symmetrical house-sized hole in its roof. At mid day with the sun high in the sky a shaft of light came down through the hole and the effect on the water's surface inside the cave was neon-like, illuminating a large disc of bright emerald green surrounded by still, dark waters.

It was a wondrously beautiful sight to behold that was impossible to ignore and could not easily be left behind. Often in passing we would see a boat inside the cave that from all outward appearance seemed empty and deserted. We would not investigate however. We knew better. I suspect a lot of babies were made there.

"Hole in the Roof" at Rock Creek. P. Klocki photo

We made a point of looking for it in April of 2005 when the lake level had dropped to 3555msl but did not find it. And at that point I began to question my memory. Was it not at Rock Creek? Could I have confused its location with Last Chance? I still cannot be certain because when looking at the old photos I have I can't seem to reconcile the view with my mental image. I'm inclined to believe it is at Rock Creek but probably is exposed at much lower levels—something in the 3500–3530 range. Perhaps other geezers could add something to this mystery.

Another Lake Powell experience that stands out in my mind from those early years was the discovery of the captive deer herd in Dangling Rope Canyon. At the head of the dry creeks in Dangling Rope a short scramble is required to emerge from either creek bed in order to attain a wide, gently rolling plain of approximately one square mile or less in area. That plain, as you all know, is hemmed in by impossible, sheer-walled cliffs and at higher water there is no way out of that canyon unless you are part goat.

The first time we explored Dangling Rope (long before the marina was established) I decided to make the hike to the back walls of the canyon in hopes of discovering the origin of the name. Word was that miners or someone had left a length of rope dangling from a peg somewhere and the name stuck. I had some doubt about it because of the sheer scale involved. It seemed to me that in order to serve any useful purpose a dangling rope would have to be a pretty long son of a gun. I found out some years later that the rope part was actually true but that's not really relevant to the story. Here's what happened: Setting out at early light and coming up out of the right-hand creek bed and onto easy ground, I was startled and amazed to find myself ringed by a herd of mule deer that numbered in the area of 35 or 40 animals. Almost all were does and fawns of that spring but a couple of forkies and spikes were mixed in as well. As I came up out of the creek they were headed down to water and all of us were completely surprised and caught off guard.

It was an interesting moment. The lead doe was no more than thirty yards away with the rest of the family scattered behind her as they funneled toward the well-worn trail that led down to the creek bed. I stood motionless for several minutes while the deer did much the same except for great ears rotating like radar antennae, a hoof stomp here, a tail flicker there, but otherwise frozen in place and time. It was though these deer had no clear idea of what they were looking at and whether or not I represented a threat to them. I have no idea how long this impasse might have otherwise lasted but I decided to end it by walking very slowly, straight ahead. Incredibly, the herd separated, slowly, cautiously, as though allowing me clear passage, then closed ranks behind me as I passed through, forming a single file as they descended the trail toward water. I had to guess that their need of water overcame any concern they had over my presence.

At that point I had entirely lost interest in whether or not a length of rope dangled from the cliffs. I found the highest ground possible within a few hundred yards of their trail and just sat down to wait them out. From my vantage point I could not see down into the creek bed and began to wonder if they had another way out that would escape my view but perhaps a long half-hour later, just before the sun broke over the canyon rims, they emerged from the creek bottom on the same trail and began casually browsing across the plain as though oblivious to my presence. They were not, of course, oblivious. They knew I was there. Every now and then a doe would raise her head and twist her ears while looking straight at me. They just didn't care.

At the time, about 1965 or '66, and at the water level then attained, I don't believe that herd was trapped. I am almost certain there was a way in and out of the canyon available to them, either up-lake or down. But in later years as the water approached and eventually exceeded 3600msl I believe that any deer still remaining in the canyon would have been obliged to swim for it in order to get out. The deer are still there, or at least they were as late as 1998 when last I climbed up onto the plain, although not in anywhere near the number I had seen on that first encounter. In '98 I don't think they exceeded a dozen animals. There are a number of good reasons to explain that, with the most likely one being that nature did what was necessary in order to cull down to a number the available forage would support, whether by big cat predation or by curtailment of breeding activity.

The deer that remain no longer allow you to approach within thirty yards either. The last time I climbed up there to get a look at them they started running along the base of the cliffs at least a half mile distant as soon as I cleared the creek bottoms. Somehow, they must have learned that man is not nearly as harmless as he may appear. And by then of course, the marina and personnel housing had been installed and they no longer had the canyon to themselves.

For a number of years afterward, but still long before the marina was moved from Rainbow to Dangling Rope, if we knew we would be passing, and we usually were, Patty and I made it a habit to stop by on our way up lake to dump off a couple of bags of apples at water's edge. It was little more than a half-silly token gesture but it was something I felt I needed to do. If time permitted, we would then stop again on the home-bound leg to see if our offering had been accepted. The apples were always gone. Maybe the ravens got them, or some other critters, but I always preferred to think the deer beat everybody to the treat.

◆   ◆   ◆

As much as we enjoyed the remoteness, the adventure, and the people of the 60's, I have to admit, in retrospect, I was not all that sorry to see the decade go. The 1970's were my favorite years on the lake without a doubt. Boat accessibility to spooky places and much improved beach campsite opportunities were unsurpassed. But you had to be quick. Patty had gone off to a family reunion up in Nebraska, and I went to the lake for a long weekend by myself with only the dogs for company. The year, I believe, was 1970 or perhaps '71 because I still had the

Dorset and used it for this trip because it was faster and cheaper to run than the IMP and there was room enough for me and the dogs.

I had a very nice little 4hp Merc kicker on the boat and just ticking along at an idle so slow you could peer into the water and count prop turns, it was perfect for a run-and-gun type bass day along the shorelines. It was a warm, sunny afternoon and I was working my way up the broken rock walls on the right side of Llewellyn Gulch, pitching a deep running crank and picking up a bass now and then. Nothing special. "Tweeners," mostly. Too big for a frying pan, and too small to be a wall hanger.

The poodle was sound asleep on the cabin roof, curled up like a donut and soaking up the sun. Blue was inside, stretched out on the V-berth, sawing logs and keeping her black self *out* of the sun. There was another guy doing the same thing I was, but he was ahead of me on the same side and coming in my direction in a little tin boat. He was thrashing the water maybe a hundred yards further up the canyon. We were not yet close enough for the obligatory "Howzitgoin" and "Yaleavinsomeferme" business, but we were closing in on it, and I figured I'd just wing out toward deep water and let him have the bank as we passed.

About then I got a good hit and set the hook on a strong fish. I got it to the side of the boat and leaned way over to lip it and when I did the boat heeled over too. Far enough that the stupid poodle slid right off the roof and into the water. It was really something you would have to see to believe. The poodle stayed curled up in the same sleeping position he had been in all the way down. I don't think he woke up until he actually hit the water. Now this was a pretty weird dog. This poodle could not swim unless it waded in from shallow water and stayed upright. For some odd reason, whenever it *jumped* in, it would wind up tilting over backwards. Its butt would sink and its snout would raise up while it paddled frantically and it would just go nose over teakettle and then sink out of sight if you didn't rescue it first. And when I say it was a stupid dog, I'm not kidding. Judge for yourself. The poodle *had to know* he was a loser when he leaped into the water. You might think that after awhile he would catch on, but no. He jumped into the water on a pretty regular basis. Now that's a dumb dog.

But he was *HER* dog, and as such, I was obligated to rescue it. Now you have all seen Llewellyn Gulch, right? Deep-water canyon, rock-walled, no place to make a landfall until you get to the back of it. The only way to save the poodle is to fish it out of the water with a net. So that's what I did, scooping the little jerk up and dumping his useless, shivering little self on the deck like a drowned rat.

About this time the guy in the tin boat slides up. "Hyuk, yuk, yuk. Seen it all now, boy. Yuk, yuk, yuk. I knowed they wuz *CAT-Feesh* in the lake. But din' know they was dawg-fish too! Yuk, yuk, yuk."

Uh, huh. Laugh it off, Clyde, I'm thinking. One of these days *your* wife might ask you for one of these things. So anyway, we started talking about fishing and such. I had never been all the way up to the end of Llewellyn Gulch before and I asked him what was up there. He told me he had a houseboat anchored up at the end and it was pretty nice. Lots of shade, quiet, fish all over the place, wife and the dogs were up there taking a nap.

"But if ya ain't never been, ya need to go up there a ways and look at that big cave over on the west side. Water only needs to get up another foot before it's ruined. Couple of weeks and it will be gone."

I thanked him for the tip off and we parted company then, picking up where we left off with our bass fishing. He was beyond earshot when I thought of it, but I meant to ask him what kind of dogs he had. Just as well. He struck me as the kind of a guy who would have dogs that knew how to swim.

I found the place he was talking about easily enough. He had told me I couldn't miss it because I would see a muddy bank where spring water ran into the lake and it would be festooned with fern, wild orchid, and willow trees growing in the damp earth, and I would see a trail of mashed down vegetation that would show where a few folks had walked in to investigate. He was right. I couldn't miss it. In a canyon of hard, barren rock, it seemed like an improbable oasis of lush vegetation that stood out like a sore thumb as I nosed the boat onto the mud bank. I hopped off the boat onto the faintly visible trail and against the canyon wall ahead I could see the shape of a huge amphitheater hollowed out at the base of the cliff. But that's all I could see. I had no idea what was waiting for me.

I walked the trail of crushed fern in bright sunlight and ninety-degree air temperature, but as soon as I entered the shadows of the cliff I felt the temperature drop dramatically. I actually felt a chill. And as I broke through the jungle of riparian growth I immediately found the reason for the temperature drop. What I saw was an incredibly beautiful lost Eden of fern, ivy, and a profusion of wild flowers surrounding a perfectly round pool of gin-clear water some fifty feet in diameter covering a bottom of pure white sand. The water was motionless. Its surface was perfectly sheet-glass flat, although no light reflected from it, so that it was impossible to tell that you were actually looking at water until you touched and disturbed it.

The visual impact played with your mind. After identifying what you were actually looking at, your inner self told you it was not possible. The water was not deep. It was no more than two feet deep at the center of a perfectly shaped bowl that tapered to nothing at the water's edge. But what was impossible to ignore was the fact that the white sand bottom was absolutely flawless. There were no water striders or other aquatic insects, no water vegetation or mark of any kind that might disturb the immaculate smoothness of the sand bottom. It was as though someone had troweled a smooth putty coat of alabaster in a circular dish in the midst of a jungle.

I sat down on a cushion of wild fern and ivy and stared at the pond and its surroundings for a long time while trying to figure out and get right in my mind how any of this could be possible. A trickle of pure, clean water spilled from the bowl's eastern rim and wound its way to the lake silently in a tiny, serpentine rivulet no wider than your palm. The roof and back walls of the amphitheater, immense in size, wept cold water that dripped from ivy, fern, and orchid that lined the walls in a solid, thick mat some twenty feet high. Although mid-afternoon, and hot as blazes out on the water in the sun, the ambient temperature in the amphitheater could not have been more than 75 degrees. The entire structure functioned as a giant evaporative cooler. I stayed for a good long while taking it all in and was at once overwhelmed with the sight and saddened that I was alone and could not share this with someone. I had no camera, Patty would not be back for a couple of weeks, and by then the pond would be submerged by the rising lake waters. It hardly seemed fair. But I had no alternative but to just stay and sit and stare as long as it took to burn the scene into my memory.

I brought Patty back to the place the following year but it was too late. The pond had been inundated and then exposed again as the lake level declined during the drawdown and it looked entirely different. Almost all of the vegetation was gone except for some fast re-growth of the more hardy varieties and instead of stark white, the pond bottom was now a mysterious blackened color. And after that, it was gone forever when the lake waters swallowed it again.

Over the years we would find other similar amphitheaters with shaded, spring fed ponds, but none quite like Elf's Den. Rising waters represented a trade-off that could alternately be viewed as either a curse or a blessing. When you lost something spectacular you generally gained something else that was grand in its own right. Reflection Canyon was a fine example of this, as were Narrow Canyon, Mille Crag Bend, and Sheep Canyon at the upper extreme reaches of the lake below Cataract Canyon in later years when the lake filled to capacity.

At the back of Reflection Canyon's left fork, rising waters flooded huge cottonwood and oak trees and wiped out beaver dams and ponds, while at the same time, in the right fork, boats were now at last able to motor right up to the doorstep of what I always believed was the best naturally preserved example of Anasazi architecture in Glen Canyon. It was a single-room dwelling unit that was part of a larger canyon-wide complex of granaries and additional dwellings, all constructed on shelves within alcoves that provided overhead shelter from rain and snow. The careful selection of these sites demonstrated a level of intelligence in tune with the environmental and metrological conditions prevailing in the canyons that was impressive. I often pondered the selection process, imagining "Pueblo Pete" and "Anasazi Annie" hunkered down next to the creek, watching the shadows creep across the face of the cliffs above for hours to determine when or if sunlight might strike a rock ledge that was under consideration by the site selection committee.

Reflection Canyon Ruins, now underwater. P. Klocki photo

At day's end, they might review the entire period's results before drafting their Environmental Assessment Study for submission to the clan's elders hanging out in the oak groves: "Yep, looks good. Shaded throughout the summer day but flooded with sunlight during winter. The overhang is wide enough so that rain never hits the shelf. The floor up there is dryer than Herbie's humor. The approach along the escarpment is too steep to climb without assistance but that ain't all bad. It makes it tough for potential enemies to sneak up on us and we can confine any possible hostile approach to a string of itty-bitty toe steps that Moki Mike can peck out of the rock for us. He's got that step business down. And that way when a bad guy is forced to use those steps we can just lob a sandstone slab over the edge and send him to the happy hunting grounds. Speaking of which, have you guys seen all the deer and beaver that hang out along the creeks?"

The whole group would nod in unison and issue the final verdict. "It good. It's a go."

"Yeah, but what about the kids?" Annie might ask. "That cliff is pretty steep. If one of the kids slips or something and tumbles over the edge, it's a goner for sure. And who's gonna haul 'em up and down those steps with a water jar under one arm? I don't get a lot of help from Pueblo Pete you know. All the slug wants to do is go hunt, sleep, and make more babies."

The elders would then huddle to consider the issues raised by Annie before signing off on the deal. Their collective response might go something like this: "Haul water and baby up Moki steps woman work. It is written. Somewhere. Pete's job kill deer. Make replacement baby for one that fall. Make extra in case wolves get one. This final word on matter. Meeting now adjourned."

So that's how these things went and how the dwellings got built. Pete stacked the rocks to make the walls, carefully selecting slabs that keyed together nicely, while Annie hauled baskets of mud up from the creek bottoms to plaster the exterior wall surfaces to seal out drafts and add that special feminine decorator's touch to the place. The final dimensions and shape of the entrance doorway came about after much argument between the two. The opening that Pete had in mind was only 54 inches high and 20 inches wide. That was just barely big enough for a little guy to squeeze through and you had to bend over in order to do even that as you passed through the opening. Pete was no dummy though. He had this all worked out in his head. If a bad guy tried to get in, he would have to bend over and stick his head through the opening first. A hard smack on top of his dome would put an end to any such intrusion. And besides that, the smaller the opening the better. It would be easier for Annie to close out cold, windy weather with that reed curtain she would weave.

So Pueblo Pete steps back to admire his handiwork, but not too far because he doesn't want to fall backwards over the edge, and says: "Whaddaya think, Annie?"

She ain't goin' for it. "How am I supposed to get through that silly crack with a big basket load on my back? Dude, you want food? Make it bigger."

"How do you expect me to do that without a lintel to hold up the rock that spans the top of the opening?" Pete grumbles. "We haven't invented lintels yet."

"Hey, Bucko, work it out. That man job."

So Pete, clever rascal that he is, puzzles over this for a half day before he arrives at a compromise solution that's borderline genius. He makes the top third of the opening a full 28 inches wide while leaving the lower part at the original 20 inch width. This will allow Annie to squirm through the hole with a basket on her back while still keeping out as much cold air as possible.

Annie likes it. "Come in here and make baby, ya slug," she says. "Little Billy took a header a while ago."

◆　　　◆　　　◆

The lower ruins at Reflection Canyon's right fork were eventually inundated and forever lost. Should the lake level ever drop low enough to expose them again it's possible that some of the stone work may still be recognizable, but probably not. Annie's stucco work will most certainly be gone. An interesting aside connected with that particular ruin was that before the water reached the base of that cliff a glimpse into Anasazi life was there for all to see in an ancient "garbage dump." Apparently, Annie was a fastidious housekeeper who quite regularly tossed the garbage and discards out the door and over the lip of the ledge the place was built on to keep mice and rats happy elsewhere. If I could fault her at all, I would hazard the guess that she had a tendency to overcook the meat.

At the base of the cliff, which was actually a creek bank, remnants of Annie's discards were partially visible as shifting blow-sands uncovered them. Bits of old grey charcoal had caught my eye and given me pause. At first I thought I was looking at some sort of non-typical mineral example. But the bits turned out to be little crumbling pieces of charcoal that went to powder between thumb and finger. The pieces were very small, match-head sized particles in some cases and my thought then was that they may have resulted from a miner's camp or from some other more recent source, and I started poking around to see if I might find some sort of clue as to origin. I expected, or more properly hoped, I might find an old charred Log Cabin Syrup can, coffee can, snuff tin, broken tool piece, or something like that. That's not at all what turned up.

What I discovered was that all of the pieces were not just wood charcoal. Some of it was made up of small bone fragments and when I poked around a little at the base of Pete and Annie's cliff, I discovered that they were big into rabbits, rats, lizards, snake, mice, and birds, and not much else. What I found was a fairly large quantity of small mammal and reptilian skull fragments and bone-bits and most showed evidence of considerable charring. So I'm guessing that either Annie was a lousy cook and had a limited menu, or, she just threw the leftovers into the fire to get rid of them. I didn't find any charred corn cobs or such as that, so I have no clue what sort of side dishes she served.

It occurred to me then that I was poking around in Annie's garbage. Six hundred and fifty year old garbage! Absolutely incredible. But I suppose it seems strange to be fascinated by somebody's garbage, ancient or not. And then another thought struck me: Was pawing through ancient garbage in violation of the Antiquity Act? I don't know. Still don't. But rather than take the chance that it might be, I just pushed the talc-like sand back over the charcoal and left it to the ages. The rising lake waters soon took care of the rest and Annie's garbage is now part of Lake Powell's fish habitat.

The complex of ruins in Reflection Canyon was fairly typical of others we found over the years in that the dwelling units were often accompanied by multiple rocked-up granaries. Some of these would be in close proximity or even attached to the dwelling, while others might be cross-canyon or elsewhere, and built on weather-protected ledges of their own. In every case, they were as difficult to reach, and some even more so, than the dwellings themselves. It is difficult to imagine how a basket or pot laden with water, grain, seeds, or other foodstuffs could be managed while negotiating Mike's steps.

In most cases, Moqui steps aren't much more than shallow gouges pecked into the sandstone that offer little more than a finger or toe hold. And Mike didn't put in any extra ones that weren't absolutely necessary either. On those occasions when I tried them out for myself, I found it almost impossible to use them without the aid and assistance of BOTH hands. What impressed me was the reach often required to put a finger on the next one above while trying to maintain a toe-hold on the one below. How you would do that while carrying a basket was beyond me. So I'm guessing that Annie and her compatriots strapped the baskets or jars to their backs while negotiating these steps.

When you get into some of this sort of thing, you can't help but admire the tenacity these people displayed in their everyday life styles. It must have been a tough life, when you stopped to think about it: no Wal-Mart, Home Depot, or NAPA store. No Denny's or Dairy queen, no microwave. No pizza delivery. And it must have been a helluva hike to the video store. I'm not sure I could handle it.

The big problem that Indian ruins always presented for me was that discoveries took time away from fishing. You wake up on a crisp morning, savor the scent of it, and try to figure out what you are going to do with yourself today. Fish? Explore? Grub around in Annie's garbage dump? Try to find that beaver—the one that woke you up at 2:00am with a tail-slap on the water that sounded like a gunshot? Such decisions were often dictated by the company I kept. I was at the lake a LOT. Probably more than I should have been. Most often I was accompanied by my family: Patty and my three Muppets, who were as hooked on the place as I was. But I also did frequent solo trips and on many occasions went on just "guy trips" with one or two close friends—in the latter case, because I only *had* one or two close friends. If I was with the guys, it was an easy decision: fish first. The rest of the day would sort itself out quick enough.

Well, that leads me to another quick little fish story. Sort of. And this one takes place back when Largemouth Bass were king. They were everywhere. And they were fat as footballs and dumb as a box of rocks. Ate anything. And this little story will prove that.

I had my buddy, Jim Murphy, with me on a bass-exclusive trip. I could not use the IMP effectively for bass fishing so on this trip we had gone up the lake in the Dorset, which actually wasn't much better, but it was the best I could do. We had arrived at the Wahweap ramp late at night and ran up lake in the dark as far as the San Juan Junction before calling it quits and setting up a beach camp on the sandy stuff on the north side. The plan was to fish those local shallows in the morning, then take a run up the San Juan later. But the morning didn't start off well. When I beached the boat the night before, I had tilted up the engine, as was my then S.O.P. but left the gas line plugged in. For some reason doing so always created a problem. If you didn't unplug the gas line the engine would be flooded the following morning. I don't know why this was, it just was. Somehow, the engine would siphon fuel, even though the tanks were lower than the engine was.

The engine was one of those 135hp in-line six-cylinder Mercs with three carbs. In the morning, gas was dripping out of the open throats of all three of them and the engine would not start. This had happened to me before, so I was kicking myself for forgetting the un-plug drill. But in the past I had been able to get the engine cleared out by cranking it with a wide open neutral-throttle. That wasn't working this time and I was getting concerned about wearing down the battery or even worse, cooking the starter motor.

The good ol' bass days. P. Klocki photo

Mercury made much to-do in those days about their 50,000 volt "Thunderbolt" CD ignition system. It was supposed to throw enough flame to overcome problems like this, and with surface firing gapless spark plugs that wouldn't foul I had to wonder what was going on here. So, I'm thinking, maybe the CD system died. Maybe I'm not getting any spark. I pulled the cowl off and Jim waded into the water to get at the transom. Standing in waist-deep water he pulled the boot off the number one plug and held the lead off the plug tip about an eighth of an inch while I cranked the engine. The idea was to see if a little blue arc made it across the air gap. Well, that didn't work. He couldn't see anything in the bright daylight. Could be too that the rubber boot wouldn't allow him to get the metal terminal close enough to the plug to be able to jump the gap.

So Jim had an idea. He held his thumb over the end of the boot and told me to try it. He figured if there was any spark at all he'd feel the tingle. So I did that. Turned the key, cranked the engine, and damn near killed him. I had my head turned to watch him as I turned the engine over and it was really something to see. His face froze in an open mouth expression with arched eyebrows and eyes as big as hubcaps for a split second before his whole body leaped back and came down with a big splash as Jim felt the "tingle" of 50,000 volts while standing in water. When he started breathing again and regained his ability to speak, he advised that, yes, we were getting spark. Well, that was good news. But before I continue with this, I would like to point out that this is NOT a recommended method of testing for ignition conductivity. It can stop your heart.

So anyway, I handed Jim a socket wrench and told him that as long as he was still back there in the water and more or less functioning again, that he could just go ahead and pull all six plugs and I'd crank the engine over to blow the raw fuel out of the cylinders. He told me wasn't going to even touch that damned engine again unless I handed him the ignition key first. Couldn't blame him, I guess. After we finally got the engine started and Jim resumed normal cardio-pulmonary function, we started fishing shallow flats nearby. We were sight-fishing bedded bass in gin-clear five-foot water and it was really something. You could basically pick out your target fish and drag something under its nose for a hook-up. Nothing to it. You could see them plain as day. The boat might drift over a nest and cast a shadow and the fish would scurry off a few feet and then come right back. And these were all very nice, typical healthy spawners in the three- to five-pound range. It was bass heaven.

Jim broke out his rig and he had one of those new-fangled spinner baits tied on. I had never seen one before and I was amazed to see several more of them in his tackle box. So I started to rib him about it.

"How do you expect a bass to eat a clatter-traption like that? How are they supposed to get all that junk in their mouths?"

"Look," he said. "If a bass is dumb enough to eat a fake worm made out of rubber, believe me when I tell you, they will eat one of these in a heartbeat. Watch, I'll show you."

Jim followed this up with a pretty convincing demonstration. He pulled the spinner-bait and about ten feet of his line off the spool and cut it loose. He then tied one end of the cut length to his right index finger and tossed the bait over the side. It fluttered down to the bottom and came to rest, motionless, on the sand five feet down where it was entirely visible to both of us. Almost immediately two fat bass dashed over to have a look at the contraption. Both just stood on their noses about a foot off the bottom and watched this thing as though trying to figure out whether they should just eat it or make love to it.

Jim raised his arm a bit to take up the slack, then jerked his finger up, just once, to slow-roll the blades a little, pulling the bait no more than a foot off the bottom before letting it drop again. That's all it took. One of the bass latched onto it before the thing made it to the bottom. Using just his finger, Jim didn't get any kind of a hook-set so he didn't manage to put that fish in the boat, although it was a hoot to watch for a minute or two. Just the same, I had to think there was something to this spinner-bait business and first chance I got after we went home, I bought a half dozen of those things. I kept them hidden under some other stuff in the bottom of my tackle box though. I wasn't quite ready to let some of my other fishing buds know I had converted. A guy could get shunned as an outcast for committing a sacrilege such as that. Maybe even sentenced to a public stoning. After all, some of those guys still fished with water-dogs.

There was something of an odd phenomenon with bass fishing in those days though. You could catch boatloads of them but they all seemed to be in the same given age/year class at any particular time. On one trip you might catch nothing but pound-and-a-half-fish. Next time out, you might catch and release fifty in a day and none would be over three pounds or under two. Once in awhile, of course, you might catch the odd four- or five-pound fish but that would be an anomaly. And for all the bass caught at Powell over the years, I never caught what you might consider a real wall hanger. My all time best ever Green Bass came from Roosevelt Lake on Arizona's Salt River and weighed in a shade over ten pounds. And at other desert lakes I caught many in the seven- to eight-pound range. But my best ever Lake Powell bass was just a touch over six. Don't know why that is. Not sure I care either. Big bass are always a problem for me.

I dearly love to eat bass. They rank right up there behind walleye and crappie for me. But from my old man, who was something of a table fish connoisseur, I learned that while expedient, filleting a fish robbed you of a great deal of the fish's true flavor. For him, cooking a fish whole was the only way to truly enjoy it. So, having learned this from an early age and carrying it forward into adult years, cooking a fish that's too big to fit in a frying pan presents a dilemma for me. And therein lies the problem. What do you do with a big bass that's not exactly a wall hanger? There is but one answer of course: You release it, hard as that may be to do at times.

When I caught my best ever Powell bass, that's exactly the dilemma I was confronted with. I was fishing with John Hilliard, a good buddy who had never been to Powell before. He had recently bought a new boat, too, and wanted to try it out. It was one of the very early "Skeeters" with a hard chine and more engine than it reasonably needed, and rode like a backhoe on iron wheels. If the water wasn't dead flat it beat you to death. Well, with him being a Lake Powell Pilgrim, we of course had to do the obligatory trip up to Rainbow Bridge. So we put the boat in the water at Wahweap, loaded up our kit and busted off for Driftwood

Canyon where we made a poor camp near the mouth. We had to go through the Narrows of course, and even so, it took us no more than an hour and a half to get to our chosen campsite from the time we pushed the boat off the trailer. And by the time we made Driftwood Canyon my gums were bleeding and my back hurt so bad I wasn't sure I would ever walk upright again. I guess this is one of the reasons I'm still not a big fan of bass boats.

Some fine Lake Powell bass. P. Klocki photo

So anyway, we fished a little that evening before cooking supper. Caught a few, and bright and early the next morning we set off for Rainbow Bridge. This was during the week before Memorial Day in late May, and I think the year was around 1974, maybe '75. Maybe even a little later than that. On the day we went to see the bridge, half the population of the southwestern United States apparently had a similar notion. Everybody's cousin was running back and forth through Forbidding Canyon in all manner of boats, and even those new-fangled stand-up jet ski thingies with chainsaw engines. The water in the canyon was an absolute bathtub-sloshing disaster. There was no speed or trim angle that John could come up with that made sense. So, he just decided to go for it and get it over with. So he firewalls it and we go blasting through the canyon in an entirely unreasonable manner, flying off of one crest and slamming down onto the next, dumping tackle and rods all over the floor, turning over the cooler, and generally making a total mess out of the boat, not to mention our own personal discomfort.

After we got done with the hike to the bridge and back, we turned left at the junction of Bridge and Forbidding Canyons and went all the way back up into the end of Forbidding Canyon where we could fish in peace and in flat water. Had it to ourselves and we just slayed 'em. Kept the boat in the sun, fished the shade, and released a couple of dozen bass all in the three-pound range. Great day. We were both fishing those old "Crème" floating worms and having a ball.

Around noon or one o'clock, the bass turned off. We had kept two or three bleeders that weren't going to make it and I told John I'd cook these up for our supper. In the meantime, we might as well head back to Driftwood because it looked like we had worn this canyon out. I was temporarily out of the action anyway. I had done a stupid thing, trying to reach a nice looking piece of rock shelf with a long cast and had overthrown it. I was fishing Texas-rigged worms with a very light bullet weight that really wasn't suited to long casts anyway, and when my worm hit the canyon wall instead of the water, my reel overran and gave me a truly hideous backlash. It would take a long time to fix the mess. I deserved it.

So both of us rummaged around in the cooler and found the water-logged tuna sandwiches I had fixed up for our lunch that morning and we motored off back down Forbidding Canyon, headed for the main river channel. When we got past the wakeless zone at the marina, all hell broke loose again on the water. It was an impossible situation. I'm trying to pick apart my bird's nest with a tuna sandwich mashed between my knees while John is trying to somehow manage the boat with one hand on the wheel and the other clutching his own sandwich in a death-grip. The boat is slamming and rocking and pitching, and boats are everywhere. What's happening here is that it is impossible to maintain planing speeds and everybody is running bow up and hull-down at around 10mph and throwing up maximum wakes in the process. There was no other way to do it. But of course it was just making matters worse.

Coming at us is a pimple-festooned brat with a "Howdy-Doody" grin on his face and riding a stand-up chainsaw. He's on the wrong side of the waterway zig-zagging through opposing traffic. He passes between our boat and another and misses our gunwale by no more than four feet. John was a type-A man. His tuna sandwich hits the kid square in the chest as he flashes by. I can't deal with anymore of this. I want my sandwich. I'm hungry. I'm not about to throw it at somebody.

About a half mile shy of the canyon mouth there's a little inlet on the right side going out that leads to a cozy little hidden lagoon. Most of you know the place. I tell John to duck in there for awhile so I can pick apart my bird's nest and eat my sandwich while it's holding still. He does that. And it's like dying and going to heaven. You turn in on a narrow neck behind "Way High Rock," and you find yourself in a quiet, shallow water sanctuary where the water is undisturbed while the rest of the world is thrashing by no more than three hundred yards away. You can hear them out there, revving up, revving down, and shouting ugly stuff at each other.

John shuts down the engine and we drift in toward a sandy bottom pocket just a few feet deep. He raids the cooler to find another sandwich and a couple of Cokes while I go to work on my reel. It's nice, a welcome respite from the madness out there. As I clear loops from the reel, three or four feet at a time, I let the salvaged line trail in the water to keep it from under foot. This line has a floating, motor-oil colored worm on it with a smaller hook, two ounces maybe. Can't remember. But anyway, the setup is light enough so as the salvaged line goes in the water, the sliding sinker lies on the bottom and the worm is able to float slowly to the surface. I'm on my second sandwich, picking away at the reel, mumbling to myself, and completely engrossed in what I'm doing.

John says, "HEY! You need to set a hook! Something just scarfed your worm right off the top!"

I looked up and sure enough, my line was moving through the water and the floating coils on the surface were straightening out one by one. It was that terrible old early Stren mono—the stuff that had all the attributes and properties of 16-gauge electrical wire. I ignored it. How many two-pound bass does a guy need to release in a day? Besides, I figured whatever ate that worm would be spitting it out in short order anyway. So I just kept on working the backlash between bites of soggy tuna and paid that fish no mind whatsoever.

There was about twenty-five or thirty feet of slack line in the water and eventually the fish made off with all of it. When he did, the rod that was clamped between my knees almost went into the lake. I caught it just in time and as I did, it bent double over the gunwale and for a moment I thought it would surely snap in two. Hook-set or no, I was into a thumper. And now I had a real problem, or better said, a "reel" problem.

I have maybe thirty feet of line to work with at best. The spool was still all bound up and wouldn't turn, so drag didn't really enter into it and the reel would not free-spool either. With no more than thirty feet of line and the rod's power, I was in a real jammed-up fix. I could not reel line in over the mess and the only alternative was to strip-line with my left hand like I had a fly rod. The fish dove under the boat, pulling the rod tip straight down into the water, and broke out with an aerial show on the other side of the boat. I didn't see it, but John did.

"HOLY JUMPED UP CURLY HEADED JOSEPH! WAIT TILL YOU SEE THIS HOG!"

I discovered one of the advantages of a bass boat about then. Despite its other perceived drawbacks, it does allow one to leap out of the cockpit well, run up onto the casting deck on one side and back down the other, jump down again to start another circuit, and otherwise chase a determined bass all over the place. Somehow, after a spate of adrenalin-fueled profanity and ten minutes of telling the Lord how sorry I was for my indiscretions, John managed to get a net under the thing and dump it on the floor. The worm was spinning around about three feet up the line and the hook was nowhere to be seen. The line disappeared straight down the fish's gullet. No way it could be retrieved without killing the fish. So here came the dilemma. What do you do with a six-pound bass? Same thing. It's not a wall hanger and it's too big for the frying pan. And it is too noble a fish to fillet. It had to go back in the water.

"You can't release it with that hook buried in its gut," John said. "It won't make it anyway."

Well, I decided that I would give it that chance. If it didn't make it, nature would deal with it and the ravens might get lucky. After hanging it on a spring scale for a shade over six pound reading, I snipped the mono off just inside the lip line and hoped that the hook would in time dissolve. I didn't know what else to do. And I eased that hog back into the water.

"Uh, Pete? Didn't you want a picture of that fish?"

In the excitement of the moment, I never even gave it a thought. But I didn't feel all that badly about it. I had better bass than that one behind me and of course at the time I had no way of knowing that was to be my all time best ever Lake Powell bass. So in that regard, I suppose it is a loss. In hindsight, yeah, I could kick myself for missing that photo-op. But then, too, I really didn't even deserve that fish. You know what I mean? I did absolutely nothing smart or skillful to catch that fish. The fish basically caught itself. It would almost be like having a picture of some fish you found floating belly up on the lake. So you have this picture and you show it off to somebody, and you say what to them?

"Yeah, I was there that day when this fish caught itself."

After that, just about every time I had occasion to run in to Forbidding Canyon for one reason or another, I would duck into that quiet little side canyon and toss a few. Just in case Elmer still might be at home back in there. And ya know what? I've never gotten so much as a nudge in there since. A lot of the old "Honey-Holes" of the 60's and 70's don't produce much anymore either, for that matter. We know of course that green bass are not nearly as abundant now as they used to be, but there may be other reasons we don't seem to catch fish as well we used to beside that.

In those years we had none of the bells and whistles we enjoy today and would consider ourselves severely handicapped if forced to do without. We had no electronics worth mentioning, for example. The first sorry excuse I saw for a sonar unit was a rotary flasher the size of a computer monitor that was available at Radio Shack. If you turned the gain up enough to make out a blip that may or may not be a fish, you would get a double-bottom return that would sear your eyeballs. We had one of those on the IMP and never bothered to turn it on.

Somewhere around 1970 a few cheesy electric trolling motors were popping up here and there, but they were little transom mounts better suited to whipping up pancake batter than pushing a boat around. Our lines were crude, our rods were crude, our reels were jokes and so was much of our terminal tackle. We certainly didn't have any GPS units to tell us where we were either. Somehow we had to make do with landmarks, shore points, and maps. When I look back on it I have to wonder how we managed to catch any fish at all. The difference was that instead of relying on all the goodies we have today, if a guy was serious about catching bass, it was necessary to think like a fish. I mean really get inside their little fish brains and works things out the same way they would. So you paid attention to things that mattered to a fish and tried to get in sync with them, like thinking, for example:

"Is it time to make love? Or is it time to eat? Or can I do both? Am I happy with this wind? If I am, where would I want to be in order to enjoy it most? Am I cold? Am I hot? Am I sleepy? If the cows are bedded down does that mean I should be too? The mesquite buds are opening. Is it time to get on the nest then? Do I feel like chasing shad today, or should I just grub around for crawdads? With a sky this bright, shouldn't I hang out in some shade? Do I really want to eat a bluegill that big? After all, those dorsal spikes are murder. It rained yesterday and I felt great, but today I'm a slug—wonder why? These are my offspring—should I protect them, or should I just eat them? The days seem to be shorter. I should eat while I am still able to catch something for lunch. I can't see squat for a half hour after the sun hits my world. Wonder why that is so? What is that thing? I saw one last week and the next thing I knew, Bob was gone. I don't miss him though—he was always muscling in on my nest. If I stay down here it's cooler and I like that part, but I need to get a little higher so I can breathe better. I wish being a fish wasn't so darned complicated. Think I'll just hang out behind this rock and see what comes by."

When we turned on the electronics and quit worrying about what the fish were thinking, I think we lost something in the sport. I'm wondering now if we are still fishermen, or are we just technicians.

◆   ◆   ◆

As a family, we ate an awful lot of fish in those days. It made sense to. The more fish you had on the menu the less meat and other perishables you were obliged to haul along and this was an important advantage in a number of ways. Space was at a premium on our small boats and the elimination of a single ice chest might make all the difference in the world. But there were other considerations to keep in mind. Spoilage was always a concern. On a four- to five-day summer outing, the ice situation usually got a little iffy beyond day-three. Keeping uncooked beef or chicken longer than that was playing the odds against getting seriously sick. And if we became disabled by some gastrointestinal ailment 70 miles or so up the lake we could find ourselves in a pretty dangerous predicament.

So pre-trip menu planning became something of an art form. Patty and I would get our heads together and it would go something like this: Okay, Wednesday night we grill split chickens. That gets them out of the way. Thursday night we burn the steaks. Friday we do fish. Saturday we do fish. Sunday we can do hotdogs. Those won't spoil. And that's how it went. That gave us a couple of days to harvest enough fish to carry us over to hotdog night. Not being able to catch enough fish to feed a family of five for two days never entered into it. It wasn't even a concern. It was a given. Ten or twelve nice bass would cover the menu and providing that number was usually accomplished by default. What I mean by that is that on any given decent day you were likely to boat at least two-dozen nice bass and often times double that number.

Over the course of the day, and certainly over two days, when catching fish in that quantity you were bound to damage a few. "Bleeders," we called them. Those were fish who in the course of battle suffered a puncture, cut, or other damage to their gills. Fish very rarely survive such wounds, so those were the fish that wound up in our frying pans.

Sometimes I might have an off-day for one reason or another. Maybe I would have something else to do that interfered with fishing, like a hike up some mysterious canyon or an exploration of a ruin we had not seen before. When that happened I would simply set the Muppets up to catch bluegill for us. This served a dual purpose.

"Look, girls," I would tell them. "It's up to you whether we eat or starve. If you can't catch enough fish for us we will have to go home early."

This put fishing in a whole different category for them. No longer was it a novelty occupation that could be pursued or abandoned on a young whim. It was now serious business and this made them feel *extremely* important. You might read between the lines here to see the numerous other benefits to building young character that comes along with this. Getting them set up for bluegill involved nothing more than simple, uncomplicated tackle that avoided frustration, and tying on a white Miller or a small hook baited with salmon eggs was all it took. That, and a word of instruction advising them that fish smaller than the flat of the hand were to be tossed back in the lake *unless they were damaged.* In such a case, the fish was to be kept regardless of size.

They were assuming the heavy responsibility of providing food for our family while developing an ethic at the same time. Not only was Lake Powell providing incredible recreational opportunities for a young family, it was also a marvelous natural University where young people could discover much about life's most basic and fundamental institutions. In this regard, one would be obliged to search long and hard for its equal.

Largemouth bass may have been king in the 70's, but they were by no means the end of Lake Powell's fisheries story. The abundance and quality of the crappie population was astonishing. Seventy to a hundred crappies per day per angler experiences were entirely common. And with no bag limits back then, what sort of day you wound up with was dictated by your arm endurance.

Smallmouth bass had not been introduced yet and were not a factor. But the lake held other surprises besides healthy catfish numbers as well. I brought a fish to boat-side one day and before slipping a net under it I thought I had caught a snake. It was about eighteen inches long and no bigger in girth than a baseball bat. I'm glad I didn't try to lip it. It was a Northern pike and where it came from I know not. The lake may have held walleye back then or it may not have. I don't know. I did not start to catch walleye from Lake Powell until well into the 90's, and even then, only sporadically. It may be that my limited success with that species has something to do with the fact that I really don't know how to target and catch them on purpose. It's too bad, really, because without a doubt it is my favorite table-fish. Those few that I manage to catch now and then are entirely accidental by-products of bass fishing.

Patty and my girls were the cat fishermen in our family. None of them ever took an interest in bass fishing because they considered it too much work. Passive bait fishing was their thing. They could read the latest issue of Vogue while a chunk of something rested on the bottom out there somewhere and be perfectly content. Catfish were never really my thing. Live-bait hunting big flatheads with old Slim was one thing, but sitting around and waiting for something to come by and tug on a chunk of hotdog didn't do it for me. And besides that, getting the nasty things table-ready requires FAR too much work. A guy can dress and peel a half-dozen crappie or bass in the time it takes to do a single cat.

In 1974 Lake Powell's fishery began to change dramatically. Striped bass were introduced into the lake, and at the same time, trout stocking ended. Within a couple of years the trout fishery declined precipitously, and by 1978 you couldn't buy a trout in Lake Powell. Oh, you might snag one up lake in a narrow, cold-water canyon now and then, but you actually had a better chance of catching a Northern pike than a rainbow trout. The last 'bow I caught was in dark waters within and near the mouth of Hidden Passage, of all places.

The end of trout stocking and the beginnings of a striped bass fishery came about, I am told, as a management decision based largely on economics. The two species are both voracious predators and having both in the lake at the same time probably would have had serious consequences regarding the forage base of threadfin shad. Moreover, the continued stocking of five-inch trout would, from a practical point of view, accomplish little except to provide the striper population with a tasty and convenient snack. In other words, money spent to stock trout would have vanished down the striper's gullets.

There was a water stratification issue to be considered as well. Rainbow trout favor much colder water than stripers do. This biological fundamental meant that the majority of the trout population in the lake was largely confined to the deep and colder waters of the river canyon near the dam and the nearby canyon of Wahweap Creek, all of which was within the borders of Arizona. Striped bass, on the other hand, would range freely throughout the lake and its tributary canyons. Since the two species were incompatible, it is easy to understand why the scales were tipped in favor of striped bass instead of rainbow trout. The stripers provided more bang for the buck and created a fishery that many, many more anglers could access and enjoy from one end of the lake to the other.

Some will view the striper introduction as a blessing, others a curse. In my opinion, and as much as I miss the trout, I have to agree that it was a wise decision. The largemouth bass and crappie fisheries declined rapidly after about 1980. This was largely the result of degrading habitat in the shallower waters these species depend on for spawning and foraging. Striped bass were little affected by this habitat alteration as they were better equipped to forage on free-water shad populations. The result was that as the bass and crappie fishing opportunities fell on hard times, the striper fishery boomed. Without the stripers then, there would have been little to keep a Lake Powell fisherman happy. To offset the decline of largemouth bass and crappie, smallmouth bass were introduced to the lake to provide a little spice and variety. Good call. The lake now has a little bit of something for everybody, no matter what your fishing preferences are.

As my little girls advanced in age, they were quick to remind me that there was more to life than fishing. I didn't know that. But I like to think I keep an open mind. So it soon became apparent that we would have to get into this whole water-skiing thing. And this in turn led to an evolution of our various boats over the years. We jumped from one to another and then the next in a three-decade search for the perfect Lake Powell boat. The result of that quest eventually came to yield the undeniable fact that there is no such thing as the *perfect* Lake Powell boat. In one respect or another, every boat is a compromise. The obvious answer to this dilemma is that you need more than one boat to get the job done, and in fact, the more boats you have, the closer you are to attaining your goal.

It is at times difficult to convince a wife that such a problem exists in the first place. It may be even *more difficult* to explain to her that you have arrived at a workable solution. Well, this matter has popped up before and has been addressed way back in the beginning of the series. A guy will get nowhere with any of this until he develops the required skills necessary to make the entire problem and its solution the wife's idea. I don't mean to brag or anything, but I had such skills. I had picked them up by observing the methods of my old man as he adroitly manipulated my Mom. The guy was a natural.

You must flash back now to remember that our first little 16-foot wood-hulled boat was Patty's idea, right? And I have to give her credit. It was a nice little boat that served well enough in the beginning, especially after she convinced me that an engine upgrade was necessary. The boost from forty to sixty-five horsepower made all the difference in the world. She was right on the mark with that one. But when we outgrew that little boat, and *she* determined an upgrade was required, she was the one that picked out the colors on that miserable Dorset. Now that boat had all sorts of drawbacks and problems. With 135hp it had plenty of snort to drag the kids around all day but aside from water skiing it had little going for it. To begin with, its original purpose as an all-weather winter fishing boat was rendered moot when I got involved with the IMP. And then somewhere in the early 1970's the old man decided he didn't want that boat anymore and because I couldn't swing the slip rental fees on my own, we decided to sell it. That left me with just the Dorset, which was a lousy bass-fishing boat, was too small to accommodate a family of five and two dogs, was difficult to get in and out of when beached, and which I generally despised. Moreover, as the trout fishery declined and winter trips were seldom in the mix anymore, even its original purpose no longer made sense. But, after all, Patty had picked the colors. And since that more or less made it *her boat*, replacing it would require some creative thinking.

Meanwhile, in 1972 we had relocated from Phoenix and moved to Prescott, Arizona, and had purchased a home up in the pines at around 6100msl. I had grown up in the desert. Living in a mountain regime, and what that meant in wintertime was a brand new learning experience for me. Catching on to the freeze-thaw business took awhile.

The Dorset had a double bottom. The transom drain was *above* the inner floor level. There was about a two-inch air-gap between the outer hull and the inner membrane that was actually the floor. Somewhere along the way, the outer hull was compromised and the boat took on water. It was a small leak and a very gradual thing, but over time, the space between the outer hull and the inner membrane filled with water. I had no way of knowing this. It was not visible from inside the boat because the trapped water was beneath the floor. Had the boat been parked on a concrete drive when out of the water, it might have been possible to see water puddling under the boat as it seeped from the leak. But it wasn't parked on concrete. It lived on decomposed granite gravel. And if there was an externally visible drip, I never saw it.

So, over the winter months, and as one might suspect, the trapped water froze. When it did, it split the boat's bottom right down alongside the keel from the transom to about four feet forward. I discovered this state of affairs one fine spring morning when crawling under the rig to position an axle jack, and I noticed water dripping from the length of that crack. Bummer. It appeared that Patty's boat had been ruined. It was tough to break the news to her, but I really didn't have a choice. It was, after all, just about crappie time. I left that part out, of course, when I explained that we had suddenly become boat-less; emphasizing instead, how disappointed the girls would be to learn that their budding interest in water skiing would have to be cut short.

Ah, you see how these things work? Give the problem to the Mrs. and bless them, they seem to always be able to cut right to the core of the matter and offer a solution a guy likely would never have thought of himself. Patty was like that—a clear thinker. A black and white, matter-of-fact type. She at once recognized that including the girls in virtually everything we did had done wonders to create a fantastic family bond and that boating as a family had played a major role in that. We would need to replace the Dorset in order to maintain an important part of our family's traditions. Absolutely amazing. I don't know why I couldn't have thought of such an obvious solution.

I objected, of course. (Note that reasonable objection is part of the program). We really couldn't afford to buy another boat. I had started a new business when we moved to Prescott and it was not yet generating spare revenue. Hers was though. So she thought we probably could pull it off if we managed our budget carefully. Beautiful. Although there was a veiled message in there that didn't slip by me. I knew what "managing our budget carefully" meant. It would mean no new rifles, no new shotguns, no new rods and reels and no new manifolds, Carter AFB's, hi-lift cams or header sets for awhile. Okay, I could sacrifice as well as the next guy. And besides, it was spring; I was months away from needing a new rifle. So, the next order of business was to find our next boat. A perfect one. It would be a boat a guy could actually fish out of. And it would be big enough to haul a family of five, but still have enough speed to drag the Muppets around.

That boat turned out to be a 19-foot Glaspar SeaFair Sedan. Patty picked the colors—red and white. It was powered by a little 4-cylinder Chevy "Iron Duke" that put out 120hp and drove through a Mercruiser outdrive. That boat was *not* perfect. In many regards it was even worse than the Dorset. I hated it. And I don't know why I let Patty talk me into it. But I was like putty in her hands and so found myself stuck with yet another loser. With fold-down sleeper seats and the intrusion of the engine cover into the cockpit, it had no more net useable floor space than the Dorset had. The thing had a convertible canvas top that eliminated the need for a bimini, but it was so low that headroom was ridiculous. And with that top up, there was no way to get out of the boat at all unless you just fell over the side. Fishing from it wasn't all that great either. The girls liked it though. It had enough torque to make deep-water starts a snap for them. Which meant, of course, that I was stuck with it. But once again, the hand of Providence stepped in to bail me out.

Apparently I had learned nothing about freezing winters. The Mercruiser had a captive cooling system with a heat exchanger. That meant that water remained inside the engine block unless the system was drained. And, based on vague language in the owner's manual for this setup, I led myself to believe that plain water was a better coolant than an anti-freeze mix because plain water would exchange heat faster. Had I continued beyond that blurb a few lines I would have come to the part where a plain language caution recommended an ethylene-glycol mix to guard against freeze damage. So, you know what happened, right? One good hard freeze down around nine degrees and the block split open horizontally right down the cam-galley hump. Destroyed the engine. But as if that were not enough, I had also left the boat stored all winter outdoors with the lower drive unit tilted up so that multiple snow events filled the prop-shaft hub with water as the snow melted. This water managed to seep through the seals and enter the gear case housing where it of course froze and cracked that casting as well. So there we were, boat-less again.

The Glaspar. P. Klocki photo

We did, however, manage to get a couple of decent summers out of that boat. And if there was an upside to any of this, it was that I had acquired an in-depth education about the hazards of winters above 5000 feet. Moreover, I knew what the closest thing to the "Perfect Lake Powell boat" would look like. It would actually look pretty weird. But, man, it would be functional! I was fed up with boats that required you to turn sideways and squeeze through tight spaces and forced you to perform contortions to get in and out of it. I didn't want another boat that required an itsy-cutesy ladder to climb up on the bow or back down to the beach. I wanted to just be able to walk right off the thing and onto the sand. I also wanted a boat with enough under-deck storage to rival a Greyhound Bus luggage compartment. I had had it up to here with pitching tents too. I wanted a boat the whole family could sleep on. And while we were at it, one we could eat our meals on too, without the hassle of hauling charcoal and iron grates for cook fires. So that meant it would have to have a gas BBQ. I was pretty sick of the constant up-down-rig-the-bimini-top business also. I wanted a boat with a hard top. I didn't want to be throwing my back out of whack hauling eighty-pound ice chests around either. I wanted a boat with a built-in fridge or at the least, a built-in icebox. And of course it would have to be a boat I could fish with.

Except for the fish part, when I added up all the other things I wanted to see in our next boat, it sounded a lot like what I was thinking about was a *Houseboat*. Well, that's not what I had in mind at all, because besides the things I wanted, there were my Muppets to consider. The boat also had to be capable as a ski boat. So when you put it all together, it became abundantly clear that to wind up with a boat with all these attributes, I would probably have to build it myself, because at the time, nothing quite like what I had in mind even existed. The closet thing to my wish list would have been a pontoon boat. But while close, it lacked a few crucial elements. The under-deck storage was definitely out, which meant we would still be kicking stuff around above deck that was taking up valuable room.

What I really needed, of course, was a *deck boat,* but at the time, there was no such thing. I was pretty well bummed out over the whole thing. I knew what I wanted, but I didn't know how to get there. I had very little boat building experience. The only boat I ever built from scratch was a 12-foot long plywood flat-bottom I used for duck hunting, down on the river below the dam and on the Anderson Mesa pothole lakes near Flagstaff, and it was a pretty sorry affair. The boat I had in mind would have to be at least 20 feet in length with a fairly wide beam and I didn't even know where to begin with a project like that.

I sent away for boat-building plans from marine architects and wasted a lot of time and dollars in the process. I found nothing that was within my capabilities. There were no wood-hulled designs that filled the bill and I had no experience, equipment, or facility to build a Fiberglas-hulled boat. If I could have come up with a hull I could have taken it from there but without the ability to do so, I was dead in the water, so to speak. There were some other things to think about also—like money. We were in that joyous period of economic recession in the 70's with a prime rate crowding 21% and a wool-sweatered Jimmy Carter telling me that the country's problems were my fault. I was supposed to somehow shake the "malaise" that had settled over me. I would have loved to do just that. But the home building market was in the tank and in order to keep my guys busy I had bought a couple of 100-cord permits from the Forest Service and had the guys out with my trucks all day cutting shag-bark juniper for firewood. We were cutting fireplace-length, field splitting, loading it onto a Chevy C-60, delivering it, and stacking it for the homeowner, at the then-going market rate of $55 per cord. I ran the numbers on this and with truck and saw gas, busted chains, bar oil, tire repairs, and crew wages all accounted, it was costing me about $56 per cord to pull this off. So, not only did I need a new boat, I needed a bigger truck, too.

So one day down on Alamo Lake, fishing with an old fishing buddy named Harry Grant, I was pouring out my tale of woe about not having a decent boat to fish with, what I had in mind for a new boat, and how I couldn't even pull that off because I couldn't build a suitable hull, and on and on and on. We were fishing out of Harry's boat—a Larson similar to the one my Dad used to have up in Oregon.

"You like this boat for fishin' out of?" He asked, after I had run out my string of troubles.

"Well, sure. I guess so. Why?"

"Had to think about it first, didn't you? He said. "And you know why you didn't answer right off? It's because this boat ain't worth a damn to fish out of. That's why. I'll tell ya somethin'. You already got the best damned little fishin' boat a guy could ask for."

"What are you talking about?" I asked.

"You still got that little aluminum Jon boat don't you?" He was talking about a little 12-foot Jon I had that I used on Arizona's high-country cold-water lakes for trout. I didn't even count that one. It was a special-purpose boat that I could throw in the back of a 4x4 pickup and take off for Big Lake or Crescent Lake right after ice-out in early spring. That's all I ever used it for.

Harry pointed to the back of the cove we were standing off from. Water had flooded a salt cedar grove back in there and a guy was in the thick of it, fishing from a little tin boat.

"See that guy yonder? See what he's fishin' out of? He's been snaggin' bass out of there all morning. I can't get this boat back in there to reach the fish he can."

"So?"

"Point is, you have a boat that's even better than what he has. He has a V-bottom. Can't stand up in it to pee if he needs to. You take that little Jon of yours and paint it white, and you got yourself the best damned bass boat a guy could hope for."

"Paint it white? What's that all about?"

"For cryin' out loud, Pete. Thought you knew somethin' 'bout bassin'. A white boat don't spook fish near bad as a dark-hulled boat does. You fish out of a white boat and you get an advantage and ever little bit helps. Same with stayin' low. You keep a low profile and make longer casts. You do that and you will out-fish all those guys standin' up in fancy, dark-hulled boats every time. I kid you not. That little tin boat you got is a blessin' in disguise and you don't even know it. Wish I had one."

"Hmm … Never thought about that white-boat-stay-low business. Makes sense. You're just a regular wealth of information, Harry."

"Damned right I am. And I'll tell you somethin' else, too. I know right where you can find the kind of boat hull you're talkin' about. Ya can pick it up for chump change."

Harry was right. The hull I wanted was out there. And what he told me about white boats and low profiles got stuck behind my ear, too. My life was about to take a turn for the better and I didn't even know it yet. The hull I wanted was out in Chino Valley, sitting on a tandem-axle trailer that was worth more than the boat sitting on it. The guy wanted five hundred bucks for the whole pack-age—boat, motor, and trailer. I was looking at the goofiest boat I had ever seen in my life. Harry was right about the hull. That would work. But from the deck up, I was looking at something that would probably work well on the desert lakes as a floating ice cream, soda pop, ice, tamale, and taco stand. It was all I could do to keep myself from rolling on the ground and laughing out loud. But I held it back. And as seriously as I could make it sound, I asked the guy why he would want to part with such a masterpiece of ingenuity.

"Wonna git meself a regler bowt. Wountz wunna dem wiff a, a, whutcha call it, back end drive thangs."

"Stern drive?"

"Yup. Wonna dem."

"Hmm," says I. "I've got a boat like that, but it needs some work. It's got a cracked block and lower unit. Aside from those minor inconveniences, it's a pretty decent unit. Think you might be interested in a trade?"

"Well, I reckon Ah'd have ta see it first off."

So this sharp-trading urbanite jumps into my truck and I run him up to my place where he instantly falls head over heels in love with Patty's Glaspar, busted engine and all. I then hook up the trailer, drive him back out to Chino with his new treasure in tow, and then hook up to the ice cream boat.

"Now, y'all doan wanna be drivin' it o'er forty, ya know."

"Why not?"

"Thet dang roof mawt blow plum off."

When I pulled up in our driveway with it, Patty stuck her head out the door and asked a rather pointed, but valid, question: "What the hell is that?"

Fair enough. After all, that had pretty much been my own initial reaction. It was not until I looked beyond the obvious that I discovered the boat's remarkable potential. I could turn this thing into *EXACTLY* what I envisioned the perfect Lake Powell boat to be. It would take some work. But it was all do-able. First I had to explain to Patty what I could see, and she could not. She was looking at a 20-foot "Hydrodyne" flat-bottom ski boat with a tin roof over it and a fifty-horse "Homelite" four-stroke engine hanging on the transom. It had a pipe-rail control console with a wooden stool for a seat and a cage of one-inch square-tube railing around the deck to keep folks from falling overboard. That's *ALL* she could see.

"Does it float?" she asked.

"Probably. But if it doesn't, I can fix it."

"Does the engine run?"

"I don't know. Probably. But if it doesn't, I can fix it."

"And then what? Let's say it floats and runs. What do you propose we use it for? Night cruises only?"

"What do you mean by that?"

"You don't expect me to run around in that thing in the daylight, do you?"

I could see the way this thing was going to turn out. This boat would never be *Patty's* boat. This was going to be kind of like the dog thing—*"It's his boat! I had nothing to do with this!"*

I am not one of those "form-follows-function" type guys. Even in my architectural design work, my first concern is to create something that will still be standing well into the next century. If I can also make it pleasing to the eye, then that's a happy outcome—but it's not my first priority. This boat would *never* be pleasing to the eye. I understood that going in. But it was going to work, by golly. And the prospect of having folks pointing while holding their sides and rolling on the ground didn't trouble me at all. If this boat accomplished what I hoped it would, the joke would be on them. It did that. It was even better than I thought it would be, and this boat would serve us admirably all the way through to 2002 when we turned the page on a new chapter in our boating history. If you were paying attention to the math, you may have noticed that this meant that the goofiest boat on the lake served us for nearly twenty-five years! That has to be some kind of a record for being laughed at and loving it.

The transformation from a floating taco stand to a functional deck boat began almost immediately. It was a "start at the bottom work your way up" plan. The boat had a full eight-foot beam width with no taper to it aft of the bow-flare. This feature gave it nearly 15 full feet of wide, flat, useable deck space—plenty to work with. Below that deck, the interior of the hull was cavernous, tri-sected longitudinally by two stout glass reinforced stringers that were founded on the hull bottom, and rose to support the deck's full length. This design created a three-foot wide central alleyway between the two stringers and a large void outboard of the stringers on either side. These voids were each injected with some 20 cubic feet of expanding poly-foam to render the boat virtually unsinkable.

The taco stand boat. P. Klocki photo

The deck had a two-foot square hatchway beneath the tube-formed control console. This provided access to that below deck alleyway that provided the out-of-sight storage area I wanted. To utilize that space efficiently, I installed three large, plastic crates on runners with a cable and pulley system so that the containers could be drawn toward the hatch and accessed without having to physically crawl down below. And while working on this system below decks, I installed a high-capacity bilge pump, a bilge blower, and a 20-gallon molded polymer fuel tank to replace the existing rusted out 10-gallon tank. The inclusion of a 10-gallon fresh water tank with integral pump, and a lake-water pump to boot while I was down there, finished up what needed to be done below deck.

Above deck, the next order of business was to build an L-shaped cabinet complex that enclosed the tube-framed console, concealed the through-deck hatch, and provided a work surface top with a galley sink, a small propane cook-top, and housed a built-in six cubic foot ice box. With that done, a five-foot long bench seat was constructed on both sides of the deck forward of the galley cabinets. These seats served multiple functions. They were essentially boxes with hinged tops that allowed for additional hidden storage beneath padded and upholstered seats and seat-backs.

Between the two seats that faced each other, a pedestal mounted table provided sit-down dining for as many as eight people. When that table was not used for that purpose, it could be removed from its pedestal and installed on lips to form a continuous bridge between the two seats. Thus positioned, it was padded by unsnapping the upholstered seat-backs which were then snapped onto the table-top to form a king-sized bed. When the table was not in use for either purpose, it was demounted and stored overhead, slung under the roof on a suspension system.

Which brings us to the roof: whoever cobbled that joke together more or less had the right idea, but just threw it together with flimsy material. It would flutter in a mild breeze. Reconstruction with stronger materials did little for appearance, but did accomplish the goal of structural integrity. Fall-down bow, aft, and side-curtains were added to the roof's underside and hidden with a surrey-valance to provide the ability to close in the boat's interior during periods of bad weather. With its broad, flat bottom the boat had terrific shallow draft capabilities and best of all, low freeboard coupled with generous bow flare allowed one to step right off the bow deck onto a beach. Perfect! With the addition of an aft-mounted gas BBQ, a showerhead hose in-line with the lake water pump and a porta-potty, the creature-comfort specifications I had originally laid out were accomplished. The final order of business would now involve an engine upgrade.

The old Homelite actually ran pretty good but with the added weight of the various improvements the boat was only marginal at best for dragging the Muppets around. Deep-water starts on a single ski were impossible for my oldest daughter who was now a young adult with legs like wharf pilings and the strength of two men. This was a girl who was really into the sport and could ski non-stop for 30 miles without dropping off. She deserved something better than a slug-boat with a top speed of 23 miles per hour.

That lack of performance didn't make things any easier for my youngest daughter, either. Although she was small enough and light enough to pull it off, the arm strength required to work with a slug-boat wasn't quite there yet. Time and again she would almost but not quite make it up until I hit upon a solution that allowed her to succeed with but one attempt. I positioned her in the water and straightened the tow rope for her successful emergence right in front of, and in full view of, a group of boys of similar age on a wide, flat beach that had an unobstructed view of the lake. Worked like a charm. And she actually looked pretty good once she was on top, too.

The replacement engine involved a lot of work and modification. A control panel had to be built into the back of the galley cabinet to accommodate instrumentation and rigging the control cables below deck was no walk in the park either, but eventually it came together. A 115hp Merc hanging on the transom finished the boat off nicely, and gave it a top speed of just a smidge over 35mph. Perfect. It turned out to be a really great ski boat, with its flat bottom throwing off an ideal wake for interesting slalom work. Moreover, we now had a fully self-contained boat that could run from Wahweap to Dangling Rope in an hour. I at last had the perfect Lake Powell boat. Almost. There was one thing missing: You could fish from this boat fairly well. With a bow-mount electric motor and a folding chair on the foredeck it wasn't bad at all. If there was a downside, it was in the fact that the boat was just a bit too big for my fishing style. It wouldn't quite go everywhere I wanted it to go. This had something to do why this boat was christened: "FATSO." Ah, but there was that bit of advice I had picked up from Harry Grant—stay low, stay small, and fish from a white boat.

The next step then was to transform that little Jon boat into something that made sense for bass fishing. And of course the first thing I did along those lines was to paint it white. With that behind me, I carefully studied the thing and decided what I would need in order to turn something so modest into a functional fishing machine. The flat, metal cross-seats that also served to brace the hull laterally, were removed and alternate bracing was provided. With the flat seats removed, epoxy reinforced plywood floor panels were installed to provide a non-slip, flat, stand-up surface. Next came the installation of a poly-formed livewell unit mounted about near the center of gravity, two boxed pedestal seats, kept as low in the boat as possible, a Humminbird sonar unit with a portable side-scan feature, a 42lb thrust Motorguide trolling motor, a forward mounted high-capacity 12V battery, a bilge pump, a 12V aux-equipment port, and finally, of course, a bimini top.

"Fatso." P. Klocki photo

Fishing with this setup turned out to be an absolute joy! And towing it behind *FATSO,* I had everything I could ever have hoped for. I fish with it yet today, although it is now towed behind a houseboat and does double duty as a tender. The hull draws three inches and I need no more than ten inches to clear the motor's skeg. You can sit hidden atop a barely submerged rock reef and fool smallmouth lurking just below the far edge, staying completely invisible to the fish in sparkling clear water. And this little boat will squirm its way up any slot canyon four feet wide and work its way through stick-ups and brush that a larger boat is obliged to forego. In rough water it rides the waves like a cockleshell and can deal with two-foot whitecaps bow-on and seas twice that size running downwind. I can stand up in it without any problem owing to the benefit of its flat bottom, and when it comes right down to it, I wouldn't trade it for anything. I'll admit that early on the little boat had a deficiency. When used on high-country waters restricted to engine size, the boat sported a 7.5hp Merc that would barely plane the boat. That was fine on confined waters. But on Powell it needed a bit more speed and snort. Old Harry Grant had a solution for that, too. He sold me a 20hp Merc for two-hundred bucks.

The first time I ran the boat with that engine I nearly scared myself to death. Try to imagine what 20hp does for a 12-foot aluminum flat-bottom and you will understand what I'm talking about. Thirty miles per hour in a sixteen-foot or larger boat is one thing, but attaining that speed in a Jon boat with your butt just a few inches above the water will satisfy any "need-for-speed" thrills you are searching for in short order. I didn't have a death wish. I hung a 15hp Merc on it instead. Twenty-five miles per hour is fast enough for that boat. By the time I had the entire package modified and complete, and all tinkering had finally come to an end, all my Muppets had attained adulthood and had gotten themselves married off as young women are wont to do. Well, you do the best you can to give them the guidance in their formative years that you think they will need to become good, productive citizens with a decent work ethic and a strong value base. After that, you let them fly on their own wings and mind your own business. And now you can *REALLY* enjoy Lake Powell with a boat like *Fatso*. And boy, did we ever.

Fatso at full tilt. P. Klocki photo

We now had a long-ranger with the speed to make up-lake trips to just about anywhere the water was deep enough to float a boat feasible. There were no limits put on us because we didn't have the right boat or enough boat. Of course the boat still looked like it could do double duty dispensing beer, ice, and tacos, but this never troubled us in the least. And to reinforce the notion that we were not the only crazy people on the lake, a guy once walked up to me while tied up at the gas dock at Halls, and offered to buy the boat on the spot for ten thousand bucks. When I hesitated to answer, obviously giving some thought to his proposal, Patty put a hand on my arm and shook her head.

"Thank you for that," she said to the guy. "But *MY* boat isn't for sale."

Am I good, or what? The old man would have been proud of me.

◆   ◆   ◆

When the lake topped off in the 80's, the cuffs were off. We ran "Fatso" up the San Juan until we ran out of skeg clearance. We ran it up the Escalante until we ran out of skeg clearance. And we ran it up to the skeg limits below Cataract Canyon in the Colorado. We had the extraordinary good fortune to be able to say we saw, boated, and experienced all that Lake Powell had to offer from the year it began to flood Glen Canyon until it reached its maximum elevation. Running as far up the Colorado as a boat from below could possibly go ranks high on our list of memories. All told, that particular trip had us on the lake for seventeen straight days with one adventurous discovery after another.

The most memorable highlight of that particular trip came about shortly after we had encountered the floating sign in the river channel that advised down-lake boaters, who might venture beyond, that camping on sandy beaches upstream should be avoided as they would be needed by river runners emerging from Cataract Canyon. We had no problem honoring that request. By this time in our lives we had run rivers ourselves and understood the need for a viable campsite at the end of an exhausting day on the river. Moreover, since we now had our self-contained *perfect* Lake Powell boat, we had no real need of a sandy beach anyway. A patch of sand large enough to rest the bow on was all that was required, and failing that, dropping anchor in the back of some quiet and protected cove served just as well.

On this particular day we did exactly that, allowing the boat to drift back downstream on the river's current to the mouth of Dark Canyon. And that alone: *drifting,* on the river's back, was an experience to remember in itself. I never thought that would even be possible. When on a similar voyage toward ground-out in the upper San Juan, we had observed no suggestion of a current. The same with the Escalante, although one could see ripples on the surface ahead and had we not been stuck fast, perhaps some current might have carried us a short distance.

Making the turn to the east to enter Narrow Canyon at the mouth of the Dirty Devil, you enter a quite different geological regime almost as soon as you pass under the bridge that carries Highway-95 over the river. The sandstone formations typical down lake give way to a terraced, granitic look in the upper canyons. Vegetation changes as well. Juniper and pinyon pine become common, as does considerable scrub brush. Anchoring at the extreme end of Dark Canyon, we were entirely alone in country we had not seen before and suspected that few others had seen it either. At least from the lake. This was Butch Cassidy and The Sundance Kid country. They didn't choose it for its civic and cultural opportunities.

I am a hopelessly incurable, curious snoop. Given the history of the surrounding country I decided to hike up the canyon in the morning to see what I might be able to find. Who knows what might be up there? What if I ran across some tumbled down shack that Cassidy and the Kid once hid out in? Might have an old sardine can in it, bottle of Laudanum, whatever. I didn't find anything at all, except country that looked like it would be too tough to tackle in the hour or two I felt I could reasonably spare. Canyons cut in from left and right and soon it became difficult to figure out whether or not I was still in the canyon I started in. I decided to gain a little altitude to see if I could get a better grip on the geography but even that was beyond me. More than once I made it up onto a promising terrace to find myself at a dead end and unable to go any further forward, or any higher up.

During one such attempt, I heard a clatter of rocks just below me and I moved to the edge to see what had caused it, thinking perhaps I was on some iffy ground that was threatening to give way. When I looked over the lip of the terrace I saw two young bighorn sheep directly below my position and not more than ten yards away. One, an immature ram, was wearing an ear-tag, so I guessed, correctly as it turned out, that they were recent plants and had not started life there. I had time to snap one quick photo before they scampered off and out of sight up into the twists and turns of the canyon. There was no time to focus the lens or adjust for poor light. It was just point and shoot, hope for the best, or get nothing at all. When I returned to the boat, anxious to tell Patty what I had seen, she beat me to it.

"Guess what?" she said. "Some guy in a weird looking boat with a TV-looking antennae thing on top of it came by a while ago and asked me if we had seen any bighorn sheep."

She explained that the guy was trying to track a radio collar and was having problems with the signal fading out sporadically. Something like a dozen animals had recently been planted farther up the canyon and they were having a hard time monitoring them and any information about sightings would be extremely helpful. I asked Patty if the guy was State of Utah or Federal Fish and Wildlife but she didn't know. I asked too if she saw which way the guy went when he left Dark Canyon. Up river or down? She didn't know that either because I don't believe she could have seen him leave the canyon from our boat's location.

I had to assume the guy would have gone *down* river because unless he was jet-drive equipped he couldn't go far enough up river to make it worthwhile. And since we were planning on leaving that morning anyway, I figured we could just head back down and keep an eye out for him. There was only one other canyon downstream between us and the bridge and we would be able to see the back of it as we passed. I didn't think we would be able to miss him. There's really no place to hide in Narrow Canyon.

So we did a rush tidy-up-the-boat job, got under way, and beat cheeks down river looking for a big, flat-bottom work boat with a TV antennae on top of it. As Patty described it, I figured it would stick out like a sore thumb. We made it all the way back down to the bridge without seeing *any* kind of a boat. The canyon was deserted. Okay. So I figured I must have guessed wrong. The guy must have gone up the river from Dark Canyon after all. I asked Patty if she could tell if the work boat had a jet drive or not, but of course she couldn't, and it wasn't a fair question anyway. Unless she could see the lower unit it would have looked no different than a prop-drive.

Well, I thought the sighting of the pair of youngsters I had seen up in the canyon was probably something that the guy would want to know. So I took off up the river again as fast as Fatso would run. Nosed in briefly at Sheep Canyon on the way to make sure I hadn't missed him in there, and I had not, so continued charging on. Ran back into Dark Canyon again, too. Nothing. Shortly thereafter we ran past the floating beach camping advisory and a minute or two after that I folded the ears on our prop. Absolutely wiped it. All righty then. Stuff happens. That's why we haul around spare props. I have a son-in-law that buys them by the six-pack.

Changing out this prop is not going to be a big deal. After all, I can stand up in the river behind the boat to get this job done. I had to put the anchor down first though, in order to keep the boat from drifting downstream. I could have worked it from shore instead, but I figured, nope, the mission was to track down that biologist first, and since I was pretty sure he was on the river above us, sooner or later he would be coming back down. A goofy looking boat standing dead in the middle of the river was certainly going to catch his attention. If nothing else, I thought the guy would probably slide right up alongside and order two hot-dogs. One with kraut and one without.

I was right about a lot of things. The prop job was an easy fix, the guy defi-nitely was on the river upstream, and as I had guessed, his boat had a jet-drive. What I was wrong about, though, was the hot dogs. The guy came around an easy bend in the river with a full head of steam on and blew right past us. I tried to wave him down but he looked neither left nor right as he ripped by at around 30mph. I stood there in knee-deep water with a mangled prop in one hand and just watched in disbelief as he blasted right on past Dark Canyon. My first thought as I saw him go by was that he was hot on the trail of those two bighorns I had seen earlier. The little ram had been wearing an ear tag but the ewe didn't have one. So I thought the ram might have been the one with the radio collar, although I didn't remember seeing one. But had he been after that pair, he would likely have turned into Dark Canyon where the signal would have been strongest. He didn't. He just kept on tearing up the water until he rounded a bend and was lost to sight.

I finished up the prop job and we headed back down lake, watching for that boat with eyes peeled but we never saw it again. We stopped in to top off the tank at Hite and he wasn't there. I didn't go in at Bullfrog but I swung by Halls and didn't see him there either. I'm guessing he probably went in at Bullfrog. That made the most sense. By now it was mid-day and he probably hung it up to go eat lunch. I guessed too, right about then, that the guy was Federal. Two reasons: had he been a Utah State employee, he would not have passed a boater stuck in the middle of the river. And beyond that, you ever see a Fed skip lunch?

Our years on the lake with Fatso were some of our best. Not having to worry about finding a decent campsite added enormous flexibility to our travels. Any little cove or notch out of the wind would work, whether there was a sand beach or not. A lot of water had gone down the river though, and in the intervening years, both of our dogs went on their last hunt, the girls were off in California starting families of their own, friends and kin had passed on, and more and more frequently we found ourselves alone on our boating adventures. That wasn't all bad though. It enabled us to do our own trip planning and scheduling without the need to accommodate others, so we were essentially free to roam at will to wherever we pleased and whenever we wanted to. Still, that's a lot of "together-ness," and it's a wonder we weren't at each other's throats now and then. Maybe we would have been, I don't know, but I think part of the reason we weren't had something to do with the odd form of entertainment and companionship we had acquired after our dogs were gone.

You can tell by looking at our floating taco stand that we are not entirely nor-mal people. You know how some boats will turn heads because they are just downright pretty. Fatso turned a lot of heads. But for other reasons. Our boat pet turned a lot of heads too. And not because he was a good-looking dog. He drew attention because instead, you see, he was a good-looking *CAT*. Yep. We had us a "camp cat." He was probably the most incredible animal that ever adopted us. "Racky" was his name, a handle that got hung on him because as a kitten he had what resembled a raccoon's face.

Racky was no ordinary cat. In many respects his behavior was more dog-like. And when he wasn't acting like a dog, he was acting like a human, with an intel-ligence level that surpassed a couple of the guys I used to fish with. This cat was up for anything. Ride in a car all day, stretched out on the dash in the sun, snooz-ing. Ride in a boat all day. No problem. On a back-country ATV trail ride he would either ride on my shoulders or in the cargo basket. He didn't care. What-ever worked. That cat had done just about everything but fly, including *swim-ming!* Now admittedly, that was probably his least favorite thing to do, but when push came to shove and there was no way to get where he wanted to go, that cat would swim for it. That cat went everywhere we did and he did it without com-plaining. He was always up for a hike, tagging along behind or a few steps ahead. And when ahead of us, he would lead by no more than ten feet, turning to look back now and then to make sure he was leading us in the direction we wanted to go.

As a hunter, he had no equal. On those occasions when we had a shore-tie, any mouse that ventured up a line to board the boat was toast in short order. If there was a downside to this benefit, if his catch happened at two in the morning while we were sawing logs, he would drop his trophy on my chest as soon as he was done playing with it. He would carry this business a step further too. If there were no mice around that were dumb enough to invade his turf, he would get off the boat during the night and go find himself a couple. There was no dog on four legs this cat couldn't handle, either. I have seen him take on eighty-pounders and put an end to the argument with a quick right jab and fierce left hook to the nose bulb that left his adversary squealing. He would sit upright, seemingly uncon-cerned as a big dog approached. When the dog stuck its nose out to sniff this weird creature, Racky would throw those punches faster than the eye could follow. It was an amazing show. Unless, of course, it was your dog that just got smacked and was now headed elsewhere at a fast clip.

That cat loved Lake Powell as much as we did. No doubt in our minds. And his second favorite thing to do was go elk hunting, where he would have the opportunity to pursue the vicious mountain shrew, a much more worthy opponent than a common mouse. The rest of the time he would just hang around at home and mope. So in order to keep him entertained between trips a-field or afloat, we would just set him up on a TV tray in front of the TV and let him watch "Wild Kingdom" tapes or animated cartoons. He was something else. If he had any shortcoming at all, it was that he couldn't rewind his tapes. He never mastered the remote. He gave us fifteen years of wonderful memories before leaving us to go on to bigger and better things, chasing nerf-mice for the rest of eternity.

We moved on to bigger and better things also, I think. By 2001 we had pretty well worn out old Fatso. I was having a hard time keeping up with repairs and it was getting more difficult all the time to keep the old taco stand seaworthy. Patty and I were approaching "run-out" too. She did the triple by-pass thing and my lungs were about shot. If we were to continue to enjoy Lake Powell we would have to find a better way to do it. Heating in winter and AC in summer was starting to sound pretty good to us. So did hot showers and an honest bed. It was time to start thinking about a houseboat.

We had numerous occasions to rent houseboats over the years when the proposed head-count exceeded whatever capacity the current boat would handle. At one time or another we tried just about all of them, starting with the little 34-footers that Art Greene offered back in the 60's, to Aramark's "Admiral" class of 50-whatevers in recent years. So we were no stranger to houseboating on Lake Powell. And, in addition to our own four-decade long string of boats, just about everybody else in our family owns a boat as well. We are a somewhat nautical bunch, you might say.

Patty's brother has a nice little Sea Ray ski boat, one of my Sons-In-Law has a bigger Sea Ray, and my other Son-In-Law has a late model Skeeter bass boat, to name a few, and I've driven them all. And when coupled with the boats of our own in the past, we had enough boating history behind us to know what we liked or disliked in a boat, and what our true needs were by the time we reached the long side of sixty years old, and by the time we had to retire "Fatso."

Fishing was covered. My little flat bottom was all the fishing boat I ever wanted. And beating the water at more than 60mph in my Son-In-Law's Skeeter had not swayed me in the direction of a bass boat at all. I was happy with what I had. The focus on our next boat then would be confined to creature comfort. Neither of us was into skiing anymore, so that aspect didn't enter into it either. What mattered now was climate control to deal with Lake Powell's extremes, a full bathroom, a full galley, a comfortable bed, and a little elbow room. We toyed briefly with the idea of another cruiser type. But I knew that finding one to suit our needs would not be easy. Remembering the miniaturization of creature-features in that old I.M.P. made me realize that in order to meet the needs of our want list, a cruiser-type hull would have to be substantially larger than what a 23-footer would offer. But that posed a problem too. There would only be the two of us geezers to manage whatever boat we wound up with and the last thing we needed was more hassle at this stage in our lives. A cruiser in the 30- to 38-foot range would probably max us out.

A 34-foot Tolleycraft slipped at Wahweap became available, and Patty and I drove up to look it over. It was an older boat and consequently it was very affordable, so I was pretty keen on giving it as much benefit of the doubt as I could. But once we climbed aboard, both of us realized at once that a cruiser type would not be in the cards for us. It was the same old problem. Even at 34 feet, the boat was still plagued with miniaturization. We needed to be looking at a big Silverton or something like that in a 40-foot minimum length in order to get the living conditions we were hoping for. But we knew *that* was out. You don't beach boats like that, and properly anchoring a boat of that size in the water was going to be beyond our physical capabilities. Bringing a boat like that to dock-side for fuel or pump-out with Patty alone to handle the lines would be expecting too much as well. They are just too hard to get on and off of and the last thing we needed was a busted ankle or worse.

And then of course, and as always, there was the money thing. We had an absolute budget cap for whatever this boat was going to be of $50,000. Now the only 40-foot cruiser-types you can look at with $50K have been in the water since Harry Truman was a Corporal, have a few *decades* on the Hobbs meter, an engine manufactured by Studebaker, have a belly full of water, a 15-degree list to port and would have been abandoned by the rats long ago. Our next boat was obviously going to have to be a houseboat.

Two of the same concerns involving cruiser-types still lingered though: Money, number one, and size, number two. Same thing—how much houseboat does $50K buy, and how much houseboat can two old geezers handle alone? The answer to both questions is the same: *not much.* Tackling the size issue first, I really didn't want a houseboat over 43 feet in length. Two people had no real burning need for an ability to sleep ten or twelve people and the more houseboat you are playing with, the more sail you are carrying when the wind starts peppering you with blow-sand or shoving you toward a dock you have no intention of mooring to. So with the size limit established, we started looking at what Tracker Marine, Myacht, and some other entry-level models had to offer. As it turned out, we couldn't afford any of those either, but it didn't matter all that much because we didn't *like* any of those.

There was a two or three month period in there when I was completely bummed out over the whole deal because it looked like we would not be able to pull off a houseboat of any decent sort with our budget limitations. Fifty thousand dollars doesn't get you to first base. So I'm sitting around moping about it one day and happened to turn to the classified section of the Arizona Republic. Eyes opened wide when I read this:

"Houseboat on buoy at Lake Powell for sale. Runs. $15K obo." The ad had a phone number with a Colorado area code and I didn't bother to call it for three days. I could just imagine what a $15,000 houseboat looked like. But Patty thought otherwise.

"We could always go take a look, right? Just look, you know, for educational purposes. Let's just see what that kind of money buys."

The $12,000 houseboat. P. Klocki photo

So I made the call, got permission to board, unlock, and inspect the boat, and even got a $3,000 discount offer during the course of the conversation without even asking for it. Well, that had my interest, but something kept nagging at me. A twelve-thousand-dollar-houseboat? This can't be right. I had a picture in my mind's eye of what a 12K houseboat would look like, and it sure wasn't pretty.

We drove up to the lake with my little boat in tow and motored out to the buoy this prize was tethered to. The picture in my mind's eye turned out to be generous. When we slid up along side I didn't even want to board the thing. It was not simply a matter of not being *"PRETTY."* I had seen boats in the bone yard at Port Hueneme that had made it through the War in The Pacific and had been lying on the beach for over fifty years that looked better than this. This boat wasn't just ugly, it was criminal. I thought I knew now why the guy was so quick to lop three-grand off the asking price. I figured NPS had given him notice to remove the thing from Lake Powell within 90 days or risk civil penalty. It *had* to be leaching toxic waste into the lake.

"You know," Patty said, "it's kind of cute in a way."

"Get outta here. You're putting me on, right?"

"No. Come on, let's check it out."

"You mean, like, get on it?"

"Yeah, come on. Get us over there."

"I'm afraid we'll catch something."

So we get on the boat and the rear sliding glass door has a hasp and padlock on it. The guy had given me the lock's combination and as I am fiddling around with it, the hasp falls off in my hand. Inside, the boat looks even worse than it did from the outside. It is an absolute disaster. Patty takes a quick walk through from back to front, turns to face me, and says: "We can do this."

"WHAT?!"

"Look," she says, "you give the guy the twelve-grand and that leaves thirty-eight in the budget. You know what we can do to this boat with that kind of money?"

"Yeah, sink it."

"No, no, no. Now be sensible. A good cleanup, some elbow grease and some paint, some decent carpeting, get rid of this, fix that, add this to that over there, change this a little, and we have ourselves exactly the kind of boat we've been talking about."

I thought she was pulling my leg. This sounded like me talking her into the taco-boat years ago. She was getting even after all this time. She had to be doing a number on me!

"Do you have any idea how long it would take us to turn this into a boat?" I asked.

"Yeah. About two years. So let's get home and make this deal before somebody buys it out from under us."

"Hey, we could *walk* home and not have to worry about somebody beating us out of this hulk."

We bought the boat in August, 2002. The price was right, and the boat's dimensions were right. It is a 1979 Kayot—not a Boatel—while very similar in many respects, is not identical, having a significantly different pontoon sectional profile. The boat started life as a 36-footer, which is ideal for our two-geezer purposes, and was once a part of the Del E. Webb Corporation's rental fleet. Upon close examination beneath the boat, I was pleasantly surprised to find the horizontal "C-channels" that frame the deck were all in good shape. That's rare for a boat of that many years. Over the course of its service life with the Webb Corporation the boat was no doubt removed and returned to the water many, many times, and there is a risk of C-channel damage every time a boat like this is loaded onto a trailer.

The boat's roof was in water-tight condition despite peeling coats of paint, as were the fiberglass reinforced deck panels. The siding didn't have any major dents, nor did the bow's spray skirts, the glass was all good, and all in all, ugly as the critter was, it seemed to have pretty good "bones." But that fairly well summed up the good news. Patty's estimate of two years to turn it into a finished product stretched to fifty months. The last nine months of that period involved some unexpected problems with one of the new engines, so in fairness, I guess you could say that the actual restoration phase only took forty-one months. But somehow that doesn't make me feel a lot better. Her suggestion to eliminate this and move that to there and to fix this and replace that and apply a little elbow grease, paint, and carpeting proved somewhat conservative in the long run. There was a bit more to it than that.

The boat had a slight list, which of course meant that one or more pontoon compartments had taken on some water. The nose of the starboard pontoon had been treated badly by someone as well. And, both of the hulls had grown a multi-year coat of fur that gave them the appearance of viable, breathing life forms. So, the first order of business was to pull the boat out and go to work on the pontoons and other metal works. This was done in September and the boat spent the winter of 2002–03 in Page, where the pontoons were grey-metal blasted, re-panned, re-formed and recoated. At the same time, steel rub-rails on both sides of the boat were replaced, the motor wells were re-built, and I had an expanded

metal deck added aft to increase the overall length to 41 feet but without changing anything else of the main deck configuration. I also had a small davit fabri-
cated and socket mounted on the aft deck so it could be re-positioned to either
side as need dictated.

The primary purpose of the davit was not to load jet skis or anything like that.
I wanted it for the express purpose of pulling the old engines off and hanging new
ones in case I decided to undertake that chore myself. And failing that, they could
always be used as a tilt-assist in the event a smashed prop change became necessary. As it eventually turned out, I've never used it. I didn't smack any props on
the old OMC engines and I didn't do the engine R&R myself. And since the new
engines have power tilt, I don't suppose I will ever use that davit. But then again,
one never knows.

The expanded metal deck is not a swim platform. We are past that, too. It is
rather, intended as a utility platform to provide side-by-side access to both
engines, and to provide a really great place to clean fish. An auxiliary lake water
pump aft with hose and nozzle attached allows for quick hose downs and water
falls right through the expanded metal instead of pooling on a hard deck. With
the metal work completed and the boat back in the water early in 2003, the
housework began. The original range-oven was restored instead of replaced
because it had that rare advantage of an over-range configuration that is pretty
tough to find today given the dimensions we had to work with. Just about all else
was replaced though, including the refrigerator, the head, the water heater, and
virtually the entire plumbing system. Small, low starting-amp through-wall AC
units were added fore and aft; and a small, 3.5KW generator installed atop the
roof in a hinged, weather-proof cabinet was set up to run them. Those are the
only appliances served by the generator. The rest of the boat is a pure 12-volt system that is fed by a bank of four deep-cycle batteries.

Normally, the only time we run the AC units is during the humid monsoon
periods of late July and August and they have proved a blessing at such times.
Besides cooling the air, unlike an evaporative unit, the AC units re-circulate and
de-humidify the air in the process. And on the hottest summer days when afternoon air temperatures push to 105 degrees or more, the two AC units will maintain an internal cabin temperature in the 70's. At night, with only the aft unit
operating, we are able to sleep under blankets! *THAT'S exactly what we were after!*

I installed a sonar unit and did away with the original fresh water tank, opting
instead to go with a filtration/purification system that allows us to use the eight or
ten million acre feet of water in the lake without the need to haul around a single
eight pound gallon of tanked water. All the lighting was replaced, the aft cabin

bunk beds were done away with and replaced by a conventional queen sized bed, and the forward cabin fold-out gauchos were re-foamed and re-upholstered. The heavy, dingy-looking dark wood cabinet doors were stripped to bare wood, re-finished in natural blond and multi-coated with polyurethane. All other dark cabinet stiles and wall paneling were coated in a pleasing off-white finish to brighten up the interior with a contemporary look. Sliding glass door hardware and rollers were replaced and new carpeting, radios, a sound system and a few gadgets completed the interior.

Outside, I built a sturdy, load-bearing aft roof extension to provide a shaded after deck, the cabin roof was stripped and re-coated with elastomeric polymer coatings, and cabin walls, railings, decks and trim were all repainted with contrasting graphics added. We had done almost all of this improvement work and were ready to install the new engines by October, 2005. Now came crunch time. I had literally spent months trying to decide what make and model of engine I would replace the old ones with. Originally I had considered either rebuilding the existing engines, buying re-manufactured power heads or any number of other less expensive methods of building some reliability into the engines to avoid the cost of new. But in the long run, none of my options seemed attractive. A new power head is not the same as a new engine. There are still bolt-on parts and accessories to consider, not to mention tired lower units. And some parts for those older 3-cylinder 70hp OMC's were harder to track down than a Packard tail light lens.

Warranty considerations were at play here too. So with all things considered, as NPR would say, the scales were tipped in favor of new engines. But that was only half of it. Okay, we go with new engines. *WHICH* new engines? What horsepower ratings? Two-stroke? Four-stroke, carbureted, oil injected, fuel injected, and direct injected, Mercury, Evinrude, Yamaha, Suzuki or what? You know why it takes you twenty minutes to buy an ice cream cone at Baskin-Robins, don't you? I mean look, you could be gone in sixty seconds if all they had was chocolate and vanilla. So I talk to people and I read stuff and I order factory brochures and specifications and go on-line to chase blog-sites and I read test results and side-by-side comparison results and I talk to more people and I become thoroughly confused. I just want vanilla.

I get really confused when I start discovering who makes what for whom and how all that stuff works. I find out that Yamaha manufactures certain big-block motors for Mercury who is in turn suing Yamaha for allegedly dumping Yamaha engines with the same block on the U.S. market for less money. I discover that Ficht hi-pressure injection systems can blow up or something and that Merc's low pressure system is more reliable, safer, and actually is supposed to atomize fuel better with a fraction of the pressure that the hi-pressure system utilizes. That, according to Mercury anyway, although the Bombardier folks had something different to say. I find out Suzuki only makes four-strokes that weigh a ton and that an outfit named Tohatsu makes all of Mercury Marine's 2-cylinder blocks and Yamaha's entire single cylinder block line and, HUH? Who the hell is *TOHATSU??*

Didn't exactly sound Irish and I'd not heard of the brand name before, or if I had, not in the context of marine products. It sounded like something connected with Pearl Harbor, which I'm still mad about. So I start digging into this Tohatsu stuff and came away pretty impressed. I find out they have been building outboard motors since the 1950's and have an unrivaled *International* reputation for reliability although nine and a half out ten U.S. boaters have never heard of them.

In Japan, China, Taiwan, Indonesia, New Zealand, and Australia where independent commercial fishing is a big deal, the go-to engine for these offshore fishermen is Tohatsu. Well, that sounded pretty good. I mean after all, if a guy is going out to sea by himself you would have to think making it back home again is high on his wish list. Referrals from a guy who makes his living catching fish is probably something a guy should pay attention to. These aren't, after all, guys that run around with brand-name logos sewed onto their shirts.

Then I start to notice the name *"Nissan"* popping up in connection with Tohatsu. So what's up with that? So here it gets a little confusing. I know Cabelas has been selling a Nissan branded engine for years—smaller ones. And I really had no need or occasion to think anything about that one way or another. Now you dig a little more to get the Nissan story or connection and you find that Nissan doesn't make squat when it comes to outboard motors. That whole deal is a marketing marriage of convenience that enables Tohatsu to take advantage of a product name well known in the United States. All they do is paint the engines a different color and slap a cowl on them that says, "Nissan" instead of "Tohatsu." Regardless of what it says on the outside, every one of these engines is a Tohatsu and it is manufactured in Japan.

The dealer support and distribution center is located in Texas and when you check out the two names independent of each other, you discover that everybody has the same phone, fax, and street address number and no matter which name you type in on-line, you wind up looking at the same web-page. I probably didn't even have to know all that stuff. All it did was serve to further confuse me. It's kind of like a Merc-Mariner deal. Same stuff, different name. Who cares?

I go low-tech and look in the yellow pages, and find out there is a Tohatsu dealer right here in Prescott. It's a small shop and the owner is one of those old-time legends in his own time. So I go pay him a visit to chat a little and pick his brain about these Tohatsu engines. The guy moved down here from Oregon a few years back. He's been in the marine sales and repair business since they closed the Santa Fe Trail, and he's an authorized dealer for not only Tohatsu, but Mercury as well, and had an OMC franchise too until that outfit stepped in snot.

"I'll sell you whatever you like," he says. "Merc or Tohatsu, and I can even get you an Evinrude if you would rather. Two stroke, four stroke, you name it. What are you going to put it on?"

I tell him, and he says that in that case, if I want to go four stroke it won't be a Tohatsu because they don't make larger four strokes. They tend to keep their product line small and concentrate on what works best rather than chasing the industry around in a horsepower contest. Their largest engine is a 115 and the line goes down to little one-bangers from there. He uses the term, *"Bullet-proof."* He also says they make the smallest direct injection two-stroke on the market with their 40hp model. He explains how direct injection works. Unlike carbureted or even oil injected engines, the fuel and the oil do not mix in the combustion chamber. Instead, oil is injected into the crankcase to lubricate cylinder walls and the lower end components, while straight fuel is injected directly into the dome of the combustion chamber. And also, they used a low-pressure system like Mercury instead of the iffy "Ficht," hi-pressure system. He was giving way more information than I really needed. So I cut to the chase.

"If you can sell all the name brands, sounds like you don't have a dog in the fight. Which one would you recommend?"

"Well, you would be doing me a favor if you bought a Merc. You would do yourself a favor if you went with Tohatsu. Selling engines of equal horsepower, I would make a couple of bucks more on the Tohatsu than the Merc. The problem though, is that I get a lot of warranty repair work off the Mercs. I've never done a warranty repair on a Nissan or Tohatsu engine."

I bought the Nissan branded Tohatsu direct-injected two strokes with the little "carb" compliance stars plastered on them. I bought 50's, much to Patty's concern. We were replacing 70's and she thought we might have an under-power issue. I didn't see it that way. Looking around, I noticed Aramark was pushing rental boats much bigger than our boat with 50hp Mercs. And I doubted that we would be under-powered. And besides, when you are talking about a seven or eight mph boat, how much money do you want to spend to gain a mile per hour? So I stuck to the 50's, saved around $3,000, and discovered we now had a 10mph boat! Tony Ferrando, the authorized Nissan dealer in Page, did the haul-out and install for me over the winter of 2005–06. And we were back in the water with new engines the following March.

The whole project had come in almost $10,000 under our original budget cap and I was happy as a clam. The engines sipped gas, ran strong, started with a key-turn every time without hesitation, ran faster without effort, and life was good. Our little boat was perfect for us. It was ultra-maneuverable, easy handling at the dock or beach for old geezers, and had all the living comforts we could have asked for. I figured we were good to go for at least three, maybe four years, when the pontoons would require maintenance again. I didn't get three years of happy, fun-filled, carefree operation out of the boat. I got exactly 38.5 hours out of it.

"Pattycake," the finished houseboat. P. Klocki photo

You know, that's not entirely correct. One of the engines failed at 38.5 hours, but that's not the whole story. Actually we had something like 150 running hours on the old engines over the span of those many months with several up-lake trips. When I scanned back it sounded like we were engaged in some sort of non-stop restoration marathon since 2002. That's not exactly how it went. There was plenty of fishing time for me and plenty of "play-house" time for Patty. And sometimes I think that's all it takes to keep her happy. I'm guessing that if we never took the boat out of its slip again it wouldn't trouble her all that much. She might be perfectly happy to become a regular "dock potato." Whether or not the boat is underway has become largely irrelevant to her, because she can *play* with the boat just as easily here as there, wherever that may be. She has already changed the new window coverings once. She may do so again. "Fussing" with her boat has become her recreation. And I'll not be troubled in the least with that. Because, you see, this one really is *HER* boat.

As for the failed engine, I have no real complaint with Nissan, Tohatsu, or whoever they are. After several unsuccessful attempts to correct a fuel injector problem on one of the cylinders of one engine, the company agreed willingly to send out a complete new, installed, replacement engine, from prop-shaft to cowl, at their expense. Not just a component or even a replacement power head, but an entire new engine. I was impressed with that. It was actually more and better treatment than I expected, given today's business climate.

I have built enough engines and twirled enough wrenches over the years to fully understand that anything screwed together by human hands can very easily be screwed *up* by human hands. Stuff happens. The man that can admit to that is a man that deserves respect. It is well and good for me to worry about such things as engines. That is not Patty's department. Our shipboard duties are well delineated. It is written. Somewhere. There is woman work. And there is man work. In between, make play.

This last word on matter. This meeting now adjourned.

Reflections

By Robert Wille

"A lake carries you into recesses of feeling otherwise impenetrable."

—William Wordsworth

The Beginning

I don't remember exactly how old I was when I started going to Lake Powell. I suppose I was about seven or eight. That would have made it about 1973 or 1974. One day, my Dad came home from work and said that we had a fair chunk of money to blow on a special summer vacation that year. There were several proposals that we voted on. I only remember two of them. One was a trip to Disneyland. The other was to purchase a boat and go to Lake Powell. I had never even heard of Lake Powell, had never been on a boat, and generally had no interest in boats. I really wanted that Disneyland trip. I was the fifth of six kids, and my older siblings were teenagers, so of course I got out-voted. I was bitterly disappointed.

We purchased a small open-bow boat with an inboard/outboard drive. It was probably a 16-footer with a four-banger in it. We filled that boat full of food and gear, hitched it up to the Suburban, and drove down to Lake Powell in the middle of the summer with no air conditioning. I thought I was going to die of heat exhaustion, and thought that going to Lake Powell had to be the stupidest idea in the world. Visions of Disneyland danced through my head while I endured the six-hour trip in what had to be at least a 120-degree car. I distinctly recall watching the cows standing in the shade of the power poles and thinking this must be the most desolate place on the planet.

For whatever reason, we didn't visit Southern Utah in those days. For vacations, we camped in the mountains where there were trees. We had gone to Yel-

121

lowstone a couple of times. This was my first exposure to Southern Utah and I wasn't impressed. I couldn't imagine going out in the middle of this barren wasteland to find a lake.

We had filled empty plastic saline bottles with water and had frozen them to provide ice for the trip. My parents allowed us to take one of the saline bottles out of the cooler to share. We were each given two minutes to melt as much ice as we could, which we could drink before passing it on to the next sibling. It was a love-hate kind of thing. You'd take that block of ice and get as much skin contact with it as possible. Most of your body was roasting, except a small patch on your stomach or between your thighs, which would be absolutely freezing by the end of two minutes. All that for a teaspoon of delicious, ice-cold water. The ice would come back around after about 20 minutes, and you'd go through the whole roasting/freezing cycle again for another teaspoon of water.

After an eternity we arrived at Bullfrog. I was amazed by what I saw, and thought that perhaps Lake Powell had some possibilities. I had no idea what was in store for me.

◆   ◆   ◆

The Early Years

For our first trip to the lake, we had eight people and a dog, and food and gear for about five or six days. We packed really light, but light is a relative term when you're talking about that many people and that small of a boat. We brought with us a small canopy, a small folding aluminum camp table, folding camp chairs, a white-gas camp stove, a few boxes of dry and canned food, a few coolers, several five-gallon jugs of water, several cases of sodas, sleeping bags, pillows, air mattresses, fishing gear and a porta-potty. That was about it. It was unbelievably primitive. Even so, we completely filled the boat with gear before we started to put people in. We all just kind of climbed on top of the stuff. We sat on the engine cover, the backs of seats, on piles of sleeping bags, the gunwales, anywhere we could find. There's no doubt we would be ticketed now, but back then nobody really cared.

The lake was still quite wild back then. It still is a pretty wild, harsh, and untamed place, but it was a lot less developed and a lot less crowded. Moki Canyon was our favorite place to camp. In the past, you might share the entire canyon with a couple other families. Today, Moki on a weekend looks like an interstate compared to what it used to be.

We did quite a few trips in our little boat. Believe it or not, we sometimes took friends. Some trips we might have had nine or ten people instead of eight. Those were the days! I think every young boy has an inner desire to live like a caveman. And live like a caveman I did. I would put on a pair of cut-offs at the lake, and wouldn't take them off until we got home a week later. I would burn to a crisp and peel my skin off in sheets. I don't know why, but I would lie to my Mom about having put on sunscreen. For some reason, having a scorching sunburn was some sort of perverted badge of honor. We never took tents or cots or anything like that, and our boat was much too small to sleep in. We'd just sleep on the beach. My sleeping bag would fill with sand and it would scratch my lobster-red sunburned skin. It didn't bother me. I was young!

I don't really have very many vivid memories of specific events at Lake Powell. Mostly I remember spending the days exploring, swimming, floating on air mattresses, gazing up at the stars at night, catching bluegill on snelled hooks tied to my toes, catching crayfish, water skiing behind my brothers as they pulled me as they ran up the slick rock, and just plain goofing off. When I think about going to Lake Powell as a kid, I mostly remember that kind of stuff. We did plenty of water skiing too, but to me at that age, it was secondary to the messing around part. I loved the lake. I spent every waking moment exploring, swimming, trying to catch to fish and lizards, searching for interesting rocks and all the other kinds of things that young active boys do. I think if I had connected any more deeply with the lake, I probably would have died of exposure.

I saw Rainbow Bridge and Hole in the Rock, but I hardly remember them. But, I will never forget eating lunches in the boat in the shade of half-filled amphitheaters, while catching carp on green grapes. Another thing that really sticks out in my mind was that every trip was very different. It was the same lake, the same time of year, frequently the same canyon, and sometimes even the same campsite. But, every trip was a unique experience, and I never got tired of it, and I still haven't.

I learned how to water ski at Lake Powell. I have yet to admit this to anyone, but back then water skiing rather frightened me. But, the peer pressure from my older siblings kept me doing it. Funny how it used to frighten me back then, and now that I'm old, slalom skiing is my passion. I've cracked ribs, and I've hit the water with my face so hard that I've ended up completely blind for a frighteningly long period of time (probably only 20 seconds, but that is an eternity when you're wondering if your eyeballs are floating around in the lake somewhere). But even so, I can't get enough of it. My love of the sport started when I didn't love it so much, and was so small that I had to wear my tennis shoes inside the bindings, which I would cinch up all the way, and I could ski at an idle.

I don't know how my Mom put up with it. She is very fair skinned and is incapable of tanning. She burns after just a few minutes in the hot Lake Powell sun. She never went anywhere without a wet towel. It was pretty standard fare to see my Mom in a hat, with a wet towel draped over her with just enough space under the brim of the hat to peek out through. If that weren't enough, she was responsible for six kids, plus often times some friends. She cooked and cleaned and kept us fed and kept all our gear in order. She did all this in extremely primitive conditions. When I ask her how she managed, she just shrugs her shoulders and says that it was no big deal. That's the kind of person she is.

When I think about how primitive our camps were, I'm rather surprised that somebody didn't die or at least get deathly ill. Just thinking about being the responsible party for a trip like the ones we made regularly makes my hair turn gray. But, I suppose that was a different era, and things were just different back then. When you don't know anything else, you make do with what you've got.

I owe a tremendous debt of gratitude to my parents. Those Powell trips are the happiest and clearest memories of my childhood. I believe those trips helped shape my character and instill in me a love of nature and the outdoors—and not a love of just seeing and knowing about it, but a love of being completely immersed in it.

Just so my Dad doesn't feel left out, he put up with a lot too. He was never much for water sports. He rarely got in the water, and I don't know how he survived the heat. He was content to drive us around in the boat all day (no bimini, of course). He didn't mind. He was doing this for his kids. I have to confess that I wouldn't endure so much for my kids with so little in it for me. My parents are great people.

◆   ◆   ◆

The Big Break

Things changed in 1978. My Dad received a call to be a mission president for the LDS church in Peru. I was almost twelve at the time. The three-year trip to Peru put our Lake Powell trips on hold, but the adventures didn't end. They were just different—very different. But, that is a story for another time.

We returned from Peru in 1981 and purchased another boat. This one was a little bigger. It was probably an 18- or 19-footer. We shared it with a co-worker of my Dad's, which was a bad idea. More than one outing was spoiled due to problems with the boat that were directly attributable to the carelessness of the other owner's kids. They used the boat far more than we did, and we were always the ones left with the mess. But, I really shouldn't get started on that, as it really isn't relevant to my story.

After returning from Peru, I went to Lake Powell several times with my family as a teenager. Those trips were very much like the ones when I was younger, so I won't really elaborate. The main difference was that I had grown up. I used sunscreen and I learned to slalom. I never actually learned to ski aggressively until I was almost 40, but I enjoyed myself, which seems to be the point of water skiing. I suppose I had as much fun as a teenager as I had had as a kid, but it was definitely different. The caveman days were over, but not the fun. It had just become a little more sophisticated.

In 1985, I left to serve my own mission in Mexico. My next older sibling is five years older than me, so when I left home, it was pretty much just my parents and my younger sister. The family trips to Lake Powell officially ended while I was gone. When I got back from my mission, my parents had gotten out of the boating business, and weren't interested in getting back in. I started college a month after I got back, and got married less than a year later. It would be over 10 years from the time that I left on my mission until I next set foot in any kind of boat, 16 years until I next visited Lake Powell, and nearly 20 years until I had a boat of my own. It's amazing the sacrifices we make to get an education and raise kids.

In 2001 my sister called to tell me that a neighbor was going to charter a trip to Lake Powell on his houseboat. He owned a share in an old houseboat and didn't want to pay his dues out of his own pocket, so we gave him $1200 and paid for his gas, and he took us to Lake Powell. He took care of all the many issues associated with a houseboat, and also took us water skiing in his ski boat. It was the deal of the century.

That trip turned out to be one of the most enjoyable trips of my life. We went in September, which is my favorite time to go, and the weather was perfect and the water was warm. I even got to go for my birthday. How cool is that, to go to Lake Powell for your birthday after 16 years? It was a wonderful trip and I fell in love with the lake all over again. More over, this time I didn't have sand in my sleeping bag, and I had a toilet and running water. I was hooked again.

The following year I just had to go back. I still didn't have a boat, and I didn't have much of a budget either. The trip the previous year was a once-in-a-lifetime sort of deal, and houseboat rentals were way too expensive. Also, because watercraft would need to be rented, I needed a high person-to-watercraft ratio. That meant that shuttling people and gear any kind of distance was pretty much infeasible. I didn't know how I was going to do it, but I definitely was going to make it happen. I did make it happen, but ended up wishing I hadn't.

◆   ◆   ◆

Lone Rock

I spent a fair amount of time trying to figure out how to get to Powell that year. There really weren't a lot of workable options, considering my tight budget and lack of watercraft. I needed to be able to drive within walking distance of the beach. I was planning on taking a moderately large group of people, so convenient access to water, ice, and gas was a high priority. Bathrooms would be a plus, but I could deal with reasonable access to a porta-potty dump station. Considering the number of times I had been to Lake Powell, I was surprisingly ignorant as to what the lake had to offer. The only thing I had ever known was launching at Bullfrog, camping up a nearby canyon, and going home when the food ran out.

I was discussing my dilemma with my sister-in-law when she offered me a solution. She told me about a place on the southern end of the lake that I had never heard of. Her family had been there a number of times and they really liked it. She told me that I could drive right to the beach, that it had bathrooms, and that water, ice, and gas were just a few minutes away. The place was called Lone Rock. It seemed like the perfect answer. I took the suggestion and ran with it. I knew that it wouldn't be what I was really after, but it was Lake Powell, and it seemed to be the only way, and so I was willing to overlook the negative aspects of it. I gave my sister-in-law a few hundred dollars for the use of her boat, arranged for jet ski rentals, invited a friend, a brother and a sister and their families, and we headed to Page, Arizona in early August.

I live near Provo, Utah, and it is definitely a much longer drive from there to Page than to Bullfrog. But, the drive near Kanab was amazing, and as we approached the lake, I felt that familiar thrill in my stomach. Pretty soon I could see water and could hardly wait to get there. Then we came over the crest of the hill and I could finally see our destination. I felt sick. The entire beach was bumper-to-bumper RV's. Some campsites were stacked two deep. I couldn't believe I had driven all that way to claim 20 feet of beach in the middle of the crowds. Worse yet, I felt terrible that I had talked so many people into shelling out good money to come with me.

Camping out at Lone Rock Beach. R. Wille photo

Looking back on it, it was awfully naive of me not to realize that Lone Rock would be so crowded. I knew I would be sharing the beach with other campers, but I had no idea how many, and more particularly, how densely they would be crammed onto the beach. I had not seen that many people at Lake Powell ever in my life. What I didn't realize when I planned the trip was that my sister-in-law goes to Lone Rock because her family likes to go bowling, to restaurants, and to movies in the evenings. They put up with the crowds because it gives them access to that kind of stuff. One big reason why I go to Lake Powell is to get away from that. I do see the appeal. It just doesn't appeal to me.

I should have just turned around and gone home and reimbursed everyone for their gas. But, we forged ahead. We started to head down to the beach and promptly got all of our vehicles stuck in the sand. Some Good Samaritans pulled us out (isn't there always a Good Samaritan at Lake Powell when you need one?), and showed us how to avoid the deep sand and get down to the beach. We made it down to the water, and managed to stake our claim of beachfront property. We set up our canopies, camp chef, and Coleman stove. We were ready, or so we thought.

Of course the kids went right to the water. It didn't take long before a sand-war started and one of my nephews ended up with sand in his eye that required a visit to the emergency room the next day. He had some minor scratches on his cornea and needed antibiotic eye drops. That was just the beginning of the fun.

We didn't take tents or RVs. None of us owned an RV, and we all figured it would be too hot to sleep in a tent anyway. We'd slept on the beach tons of times before. What we didn't realize was that the canyons we used to camp in provided shelter from the wind. But at Lone Rock, the wind blew 22 hours a day, every day. We spent all night, every night, with sand blowing in our eyes and faces. We had to flush our eyes in the middle of the night. My daughter got so frustrated with her hair during the night she got up and plastered it down with sunscreen. My sister would wake up every morning with her lips so swollen she could look down and see them without the benefits of a mirror.

To make the nights even more enjoyable, there was always plenty of drinking and carousing going on at all hours of the night, with no tent or RV to help muffle the sound. We also had some wonderful drunk neighbor who thought it was fun to go four-wheeling in the wee hours of the morning in the deep sand next to our little campsite. Not only was it one of the most annoying and inconsiderate things I've ever experienced in my entire life, but he was also four-wheeling so close that I was afraid for our lives. The scumbag was lucky I didn't own a shotgun. Going to jail would have been a small price to pay for peace and quiet. Well, for as much peace and quiet as you can get at Lone Rock. As a backup plan to using public restrooms, we brought two porta-potties and a tent. It was a very good thing we did, because the public bathrooms filled up very quickly, and back then NPS wasn't very quick to pump them out for some reason. We had only been at Lone Rock for a couple of days when we were forced to use our porta-potties.

We set up the tent and put the porta-potties in it. We had way too many people, and the porta-potties got full rather quickly. As a matter of fact, they over flowed a few times. My brother had the dubious honor of hauling those things up to the dump station to empty them. Not wanting to put them inside his Jeep, he would transport them on the roof. It was quite a sight to see him driving up to the top of the beach with a porta-potty proudly displayed on the roof. It was something like 107 degrees every day that we were there, and that tent got pretty darn hot. You can imagine the smell of a nice, hot, overflowing porta-potty in a confined space.

The tent we brought was a standard tent for sleeping in. It wasn't one of those tents that is specifically designed for bathroom usage that has no bottom. When it was time to go, I just rolled up my tent and tossed it in the dumpster. There was no way I was going to clean that thing, and even less chance that I would ever use it again if I did.

The trip pretty much went downhill from there. The water had dropped big time that summer, and it was a long hike through deep sand to the bathrooms. My nephew used to comment that when you started thinking that sometime you should start thinking about going to the bathroom, you'd better start hiking. My wife had recently finished physical therapy on her knees. After a day of hiking back and forth through the sand, her knees were hot and swollen, and it was clear that she couldn't stay. I took her to a motel in Page, and returned to Lone Rock to take care of my kids and continue to function as the group coordinator.

We struggled with dehydration that trip. We had all the water anyone could possibly drink, but still ended up with problems. Three people got so dehydrated that they threw up. Sometime in the middle of the trip my youngest daughter, who was eight years old at the time, started throwing up. She couldn't stop, so I took her to the motel to be with my wife and returned to take care of what was left of my family.

My wife called the next morning and told me she had spent the night at the emergency room. Our daughter had needed IV fluids, and they also gave her some medication to try to control the vomiting. She continued to throw up, so they ran some tests and said that in addition to the dehydration, she might also be suffering from appendicitis. It was fairly early in the morning when she called to tell me her fun story. I hadn't had breakfast yet, I was weak from exposure and from being up all night worrying, and when my wife told me what had happened, I just collapsed on the sand and rolled under my brother's Jeep.

I rested for a minute in the shade of the Jeep, then got up and had some breakfast and water. I felt better, so I went to go see my wife and daughter. My daughter had been released from the hospital, but was still throwing up some, but it was definitely subsiding. I spent some time with them, watched Animal Planet, bought them some food, and made sure they were going to be all right before heading back to Lone Rock to check on the rest of my family. When I got back, I found that my oldest daughter had water skied for the first time in her life, and I had missed it. I was very pleased that she had gotten brave enough to try, but it would have been nice to been there.

As a brief aside, I think parents are detrimental to kids overcoming their fears. My oldest daughter learning to water ski in my absence is one such example. Here's another: before we bought a boat, my youngest daughter was terrified of them. My sister-in-law took us boating one evening, and my daughter wasn't going to have anything to do with it. She was probably about six at the time. My sister-in-law picked her up off the dock, dropped her in the boat, and took off. We heard the screams trailing off into the distance as they idled out of the harbor, and wondered how she would fare. She came back all smiles. I doubt that would have been the case if we had been with her in the boat.

Before I move on to the trip home, I should describe some of the interesting and unexpected things I found at Lone Rock. Usually I would wake up early in the morning, long before most of our crew got up. I'd take the opportunity to walk along the beach when it was peaceful and quiet. Lone Rock may be one giant party at night, but in the mornings everyone is dead to the world, most likely a direct result of the parties the night before.

One interesting thing I noticed was that while Lone Rock is located in Arizona, and is a stone's throw from Utah, it is 99% inhabited by Californians. As I'd walk along the beach, all the license plates were from California, with only an occasional Nevada or Arizona plate. I think we were probably the only Utahns. Our neighbors were, by and large, quite rich—or perhaps very deeply in debt. There was easily a hundred million dollars worth of equipment on that little beach.

It was also interesting to see what people did to make themselves at home. People brought trampolines (and not just the water ones), ping-pong tables, carpets and real furniture. They brought enormously huge canopies. They staked out their turf with tiki torches, which I have to admit is one thing that I really liked. What they didn't bring, they made out of sand. People made couches and La-Z-Boys out of sand, complete with drink holders. They built swimming pools, made sand sculptures and incredible sand castles. Some people put up hummingbird feeders. And they got visitors. I never would have thought that hummingbirds could survive at Lake Powell.

But the thing that totally blew me away was that many of our neighbors had either been there for a month or more, or had plans to stay that long. I love Lake Powell as much as the next person, but I cannot imagine spending a month even at the most serene and secluded spot on the lake under the most pleasant of weather conditions. I can only imagine the gas bill these people racked up running their generators, boats, and jet skis all day long for a solid month. But then again, money didn't seem to be an issue for these people.

I have already complained loudly about the inconsiderate jerks we encountered. But there were plenty of decent, friendly people as well. It seems that boating brings out the best in people. Camping seems to do the same. I find it interesting that most of the people you run into when boating or camping just seem to be nicer, friendlier people than what you usually encounter at the store, the movies, etc. Unfortunately, boating and camping also seems to have the opposite effect on a few.

Eventually it was time to go home. Words cannot express how happy I was to be leaving. Usually people want to do that last ski trip before leaving. Nobody was in the mood to do anything, not even the kids. We woke up around 7:00am and just started packing. I collected the rest of my family at the hotel, and we went to a restaurant to get a bite to eat before taking off.

We left the restaurant around 11:00am, and that's when a new wave of fun began. We were about five miles from Kanab when I noticed billowing clouds of smoke coming out of my engine. I stopped and found that transmission fluid was leaking on to the exhaust manifold. It looked like it was coming out slowly enough that we would be able to make it to Kanab, so we went on. We found a mechanic, who put the van on his lift and told me that the main seal was leaking and that he could fix it next week. I opted to buy a bunch of transmission fluid and take my chances.

Unfortunately, my sister's car was also having problems. Whenever she stopped, her fuel pump would quit working and she'd have to wait about an hour for it to cool down. I know if sounds weird, and it is, but that really was the problem. Anyway, I had to stop every half hour or so to add more transmission fluid. My sister didn't dare leave us in case the transmission died altogether, but if she stopped then she'd be stuck. Her car died more than once on the way home, and we managed to limp along, leap-frogging each other most of the way home. The constant smell of burning transmission fluid didn't help much either, and some of my passengers felt rather ill from its effects. Once it started to get dark and cooled off a bit, our problems largely went away. My sister's fuel pump would stay cool and I stopped leaking transmission fluid. In the end it took us 17 hours to get from Page to just south of Provo.

In the morning, I expected to see a pool of transmission fluid under my van, but there wasn't a drop. I took the van to the mechanic, who told me that I had simply overheated my transmission and that it had been venting fluid. I don't know whether to be grateful or annoyed that it vented on to the exhaust manifold. On the one hand, it was miserable having the smoke seep up through the floor. On the other hand, I could have permanently damaged my transmission if I hadn't known I was losing fluid.

All in all, it was the most miserable vacation of my entire life. I spent the vast majority of the trip worrying, not sleeping, not skiing, not relaxing and not having fun. I did get to water ski a little bit, but the water was almost always too choppy for that to be very enjoyable. What I mostly accomplished on that trip was to put my family's health and well-being in jeopardy.

The co-pay for the hospital visit ended up being more than our gas and rental expenses. The motel wasn't cheap either. I tried to go on a budget, but I would have been better off to have spent more money and to have gone in comfort, than to have spent all my money on hospitals and motels. Well, you know what they say: hindsight is 20/20. On a positive note, nobody died or was permanently harmed, and we didn't have any expensive mechanical problems, just inconvenient ones. I know that others have not been so lucky, so I do need to count my blessings.

After that trip, I'm somewhat surprised that in all my prior trips to the lake, even under very primitive circumstances, we never had a single problem with dehydration. I attribute our dehydration problems at Lone Rock to the wind. The canyons we used to camp in protected us from the constant wind. We didn't have that hot, dry wind blowing on us night and day.

In order to be fair, I need to say that if we hadn't had all of the many problems we had, I would have been glad that we went to Lone Rock, even though it wasn't what I had hoped for. I got to see the dam, which was very cool, and I got to see another side of Lake Powell that I had never seen before. Even after going through all that, if I were to move to Page, I would probably camp at Lone Rock from time to time in the off-season to go fishing. However, camping with a thousand other people in the smallest possible space is not my cup of tea, so I probably wouldn't go there in the summer even if it were in my back yard.

And, it wasn't all that bad. My oldest daughter learned how to water ski. My son loves to fish, and we caught a number of good-sized catfish from the beach. My youngest daughter worked out a little more of her fear of boats. I had a friend that came with us, whose family pretty much escaped unscathed, and he still admits that he had a good time. Needless to say, I did not visit Lake Powell the following year. I had had quite enough, and my boat situation was unchanged. However, the boat situation was to change dramatically the following year.

◆   ◆   ◆

The Reunion

My parents decided that they wanted to have a family reunion in 2004. By this point in time, my five siblings and I were scattered across three states, and my parents had something like 17 grandchildren. They had recently served several missions for the LDS church and it was definitely time to get everyone together. My parents offered to plunk down a pretty generous sum of money to pull together a reunion. We debated numerous possibilities, voted, and it was no surprise that Lake Powell won by a considerable margin.

Putting together that trip largely fell on my shoulders. It turned out to be quite a challenge. Even though the budget was quite generous, it was still difficult to get that many people to the lake in comfort. This time, I wasn't going to cut important corners and end up with another Lone Rock trip. I was determined to make it happen, especially for one of my older brothers. My brother, who is as big of a fan of Lake Powell as you'll ever meet, has had severe medical problems most of his adult life. He had recently had kidney and pancreas transplants, and was in better health than he had been in for years. He was actually well enough to be able to go to the lake. We didn't know how long that might be the case, so he were determined to get him there, even if we all had to ante up.

I ended up making a reservation for a houseboat rental that was going to run us about $5000 for a week. It wasn't a fancy boat, but we could get by with it. The houseboat definitely wouldn't provide us with enough living space, but it would provide us with a bathroom, a kitchen, a clean place to sleep, etc. We figured we could make it work by bringing a large canopy, extra tables and chairs and other camping gear so that we could extend our camp on to the beach during the day, and crowd together at night.

I mentioned my plans to a friend at work, and he told me that he wanted to get out of his houseboat share, and would be willing to sell it to me for $5000. It was very comparable in size and amenities, so I jumped at the offer. I canceled my reservation and bought my friend's share. None of my siblings were interested in houseboat ownership, so I became the proud owner of a houseboat share.

Now I just needed to arrange for toys. My sister-in-law was willing to let us take her boat again, but this time she refused to take any money, so that worked out very nicely (thank you Joyce). My sister arranged to rent jet skis in Logan, which she was able to get for a fraction of what they would cost at Bullfrog or Provo. I figured I still needed a second ski boat. There are six kids in my family, and most of us are water skiing enthusiasts, and most of us have kids. One ski boat just wouldn't cut it.

At this point in my life, it was starting to look like a small ski boat would be within the realms of possibility for my family. Our financial plans called for getting one a couple years down the road. Since our plans didn't include a ski boat before the family reunion, I started looking into rentals. The rentals were a lot of money, and it seemed ridiculous to plunk down a few grand only to turn around and buy my own boat a year or two later. So, we decided to put what we would have spent on a rental toward purchasing a boat. In order to avoid wasting money on rentals, my parents chipped in more than they should have, and they split the cost of a boat with me.

The family houseboat, the "Last Resort." R. Wille photo

I bought a nice, used 19-foot Caravelle Fish and Ski. It was exactly what I wanted. It was about seven years old, but it had only been used one year and had been in storage the rest of its life. The previous owners had left it in storage in Colorado without winterizing it and had moved back east. They couldn't afford to ship it or fix it and just let it sit for all those years. Eventually, the owner's brother paid off her loan, replaced the engine and put it up for sale. A potential buyer took it out for a test drive, hit a concrete block and severely damaged the outdrive. The outdrive was rebuilt, and then I bought the boat. I had what amounted to an almost new boat, with a rebuilt outdrive and an engine with four hours on it for half the cost of a new one. In a period of a few months, I went from no boat ownership to owning two. Things were great.

As a side note, getting the title to the boat left me a nervous wreck. The guy who took over ownership of the boat from his sister lived in Missouri, and it was registered there. Unfortunately, the VIN was wrong on the title. In particular, the real VIN has an I in it (in a spot where a letter is required), but the title had a 1 on it. To make matters worse, I's are not allowed in automobile titles, so nobody wanted to believe that it was an I. I had to have the VIN inspected numerous times, and to add to the fun, the VIN also has a 1 in it, and the I and the 1 that are stamped on the hull are identical. So, everybody that inspected it would claim that it was a 1, and not an I. If you think it's hard to work with a DMV, try getting the DMVs in two different states to cooperate. I eventually got it straightened out, but not before I had the chief detective over automobile theft over all of Utah County out to my home. Even then, I had to explain the I/1 issue to him. In the end, I spent about two months without a title, while some guy I had never met in Missouri had my money. It made for a lot of sleepless nights.

The houseboat is no Taj Mahal. It has no air conditioning or even evaporative cooling, and it always has electrical problems. But, it provides me with a bathroom, drinking water, ice, and a clean, flat, level place to roll out my sleeping bag. That's all I really need.

My ski boat is tiny compared to most of the boats you see at Lake Powell, but I love it. It fits my family just fine, is economical to own and operate, and does what I need it to do. Again, it's all I really need. And, that boat has taken really good care of me. It has spent about a month at Lake Powell, and other than a dead battery, has been completely reliable. What more could I ask for?

The reunion went reasonably well. We had the sorts of issues that you'd expect from a 20+ year-old houseboat, but nothing that couldn't be fixed or worked around. We had a lot of gear to load on the houseboat, so I sent my brother in my ski boat to go search for a place to camp while we loaded up. He took his daughter and a nephew with him. He found a spot, left the kids and came back to get us, but couldn't find where we were loading up. I had no radio in my boat, and my brother had forgotten to take a walkie-talkie, so there was no way for us to communicate. He looked around for us for a while until it became too dark. He tied up my boat at the courtesy dock near the Bullfrog launch ramp and spent the night at the top of the ramp on a picnic table. My niece and nephew spent the night in a crack in the sandstone.

It was cold that night. Even though it was mid-June, the temperature must have gotten down in the 50's. It was a miserable night for my niece and nephew. They had nothing but their swimsuits: not even a life jacket to help keep warm with. It couldn't have been much better for my brother. That night was a pretty anxious night for the rest of us. It's easy to let your imagination go wild in the night. In addition to worrying about family members being lost or stuck somewhere, I had visions of my new boat sunk at the bottom of the lake, or busted up on a submerged reef somewhere. In the morning we all found each other and all was well, and we had a new story to add to our collection of Lake Powell tales.

We had an impossibly large number of people for the size of houseboat we had bought. So, we had brought plenty of extra gear so that we could expand our camp on to the beach. It turned out that everyone would rather crowd into the houseboat than spread out on to the beach. So, we ended up causing ourselves extra work, plus we made everything even more cramped than it needed to be by bringing all the extra gear.

It took us about two days to put my sister-in-law's boat out of commission. We banged up the outdrive quite badly on some submerged rocks. It got used for a day and a half, but mostly we just towed it around. So, it largely turned out to be a liability. As for the rental jet skis, the spark plugs kept getting fouled, and so half the time they wouldn't run.

About halfway through the trip a few people in our crew got sick with the barfies. We don't know if it was bad water, too much lake water, food poisoning or just a good-old flu virus somebody brought with them to share. There were a few in our crew who were not terribly enthusiastic about our reunion location, and one of my brothers had two-year-old twins, and watching them was getting old. So, we sent a group home mid-trip. Among those that chose to leave early were my three kids. They weren't sick or anything, but were a little freaked out about the illness going around and didn't want to risk getting sick. Memories of Lone Rock were still rather fresh back then.

I had very mixed feelings about my kids leaving. On the one hand, I really wanted my kids to enjoy Lake Powell and get to know the extended family better. I wanted to teach them how to water ski and to enjoy the lake the way I had when I was their age. On the other hand, if they got sick, I'd be pretty hard pressed to get them to come back. Sending them home pretty much guaranteed I had another shot at getting them to love the lake. Also, kids are a significant responsibility. My kids are really good kids, but no matter how well behaved or mature kids are, they are still kids and are a pretty heavy responsibility. And, as much as I love them, it was nice to have that responsibility gone, because heaven knows I had enough on my shoulders that trip. But the thing that I will always feel worst about is that my parents also left, and part of the reason why they left was so that they could take care of my kids. They paid for most of the trip and then left early, partially for my benefit, and I still feel badly about that. Having half the crew leave was a mixed situation. It was sad to break up the family, but for those who stayed, it was nice to have a little more elbow room and less competition for the water toys.

In spite of it all, we managed to have a good time. The few days we were all together were great. We're a pretty close family (you'd have to be to put up with that many people on that size of houseboat), and it was great to get us all together, and it definitely was a time to remember. Incidentally, none of my siblings went home early. Those who went home early were my parents, some of the spouses and some of the kids. A big bonus to the family reunion was that we ended up with a share in a houseboat, and I ended up owning a ski boat.

◆   ◆   ◆

Houseboating

Houseboating is a fairly new experience for us. Every time we go out, we learn something new. In 2005, which was our third pilgrimage to the lake in our houseboat, we learned quite a lot. That year I had taken my parents, my sister and her family, a neighbor family and a few miscellaneous other people. We had a really nice group. I enjoy taking people to the lake that have never been before: it's fun to re-discover the lake through the eyes of someone else. I also enjoy taking a mix of family and non-family. Having non-family members adds some spice to the mix. This year proved to be a really nice combination of people. We all got along really well, and everyone enjoyed making new friends. My neighbors weren't boat people, but they enjoyed the lake so much they went home and bought a pair of jet skis.

We found a nice place to camp that had marginal anchorage. The beach was slick rock, but had two pockets of sand conveniently located about 70 or 80 feet apart. We pulled up right in between the pockets of sand, set our anchors, and it appeared that the depth of the sand would be sufficient to keep us anchored.

The trouble started with the rising lake. This trip was in June of 2005, and the lake was still rising rapidly, and it eroded the pockets of sand that we had used to secured our anchors. The lake reclaimed one of them in its entirety. I reset those anchors in sand that was under a couple of feet of water, and all seemed to be fine. In fact, it seemed to be more secure than before.

The day before we were to go home we had a late afternoon storm kick up, and this was when the important lessons started. The wind kept tearing our anchors loose. To complicate matters, my sister and her family left early because her husband didn't have enough vacation time to spend the whole week with us. My neighbor left early (but his family stayed) because he had a speaking engagement. I found myself the only male between the ages of 12 and 75. I can still picture all the ladies pulling on the anchor ropes trying to get the houseboat straightened back out while I tried to get the anchors reset.

Moored beneath a massive sandstone wall. R. Wille photo

Eventually we lost the battle with the wind. All the anchors but one pulled free. The wind was blowing more or less away from shore, and the one remaining anchor was tied aft, so the houseboat flipped around with the bow pointing away from shore. With the houseboat blowing freely at the end of its tether, it presented a much smaller profile to the wind, and so was relatively secure. However, it was precarious enough that I really didn't want to spend the night unsecured, and we decided that the best anchorage would be our buoy back at Bullfrog. After all, we were planning on leaving the next day anyway. The challenge now was to figure out how to get free of the anchors.

The insurance and the by-laws are rather picky about who captains the houseboat. I'm a by-the-book kind of a guy, and always follow the letter-of-the-law, particularly where liability is concerned. In this case, I wasn't exactly sure what the letter-of-the-law was, so I was very conservative and very strict. I always captained the houseboat and had never let anyone else do it. So, I found myself in the situation of being the only one strong enough to haul around the anchors, and the only one with any experience captaining the houseboat. I couldn't do both at the same time.

I started by taking care of the three anchors that weren't doing any good. They were all sitting in about 12 feet of water, and when I tried to pull them in, they promptly dug into the sand and refused to move anywhere. I swam down to the bottom of the lake to pull each anchor free. With an anchor loose, it provided enough weight for me to stay down on the bottom of the lake. I could then walk on the bottom of the lake, Pirates-of-the-Caribbean style, until I was under the houseboat, where I would drop the anchor, swim to the surface, and then haul it up. I repeated this with each anchor. Now I just had to deal with the one anchor that was keeping us from blowing into the rocks across the canyon.

To get the last anchor out, I had my Dad captain the houseboat while I dealt with the anchor. I was a moron, probably due to the duress I was under, and my plan was to pull the anchor loose, and swim it over to the houseboat with a life jacket. My Dad had no experience with anything over about 18 feet and he hadn't done even that for almost 20 years. Add the wind he was working against, and there's no wonder he struggled with the houseboat. He would get some slack in the anchor line and I'd pull the anchor loose and then it would get jerked out of my hands and into deeper water. We tried this a few times until I was in about eight feet of water and decided to rethink my approach. I swam back to the houseboat, untied the anchor, and then pulled it up and tossed it in my ski boat. It's what I should have done to begin with, but eventually I did get it.

By the time we got back to Bullfrog, the storm had blown itself out, and we spent a peaceful night and got away the next morning without any further incidents. I was so exhausted that evening, I could have dropped dead. I spent the evening composing the advertisement to sell the houseboat share that I would place in the paper the very next day. But, as with most things, problems always look better in the morning, and this was no exception. It didn't take me too long to repent of having vowed to get rid of my share. I learned some valuable lessons. First, make sure you've got solid enough anchorage. Second, make sure all the able-bodied men don't go home. And finally, make sure you've got more than one experienced captain. Our next trip, we brought steel spikes for anchoring at beaches, I made my brother-in-law drive the whole time, and I made sure he didn't go home early.

Incidentally, the following year we motored past that campsite. The lake was even higher than before, and there was no sand or rocks at all, just slick rock, but there was a houseboat anchored there. They anchored by laying their anchors on the slick rock, (which sloped down to the water at a pretty good angle), and piling rocks and logs on their anchors. It looked like a slight breeze would blow them loose. I wonder what fun experiences they might have had and what important lessons they might have learned.

◆   ◆   ◆

Reflections

I have thoroughly enjoyed our houseboat and ski boat the past few years. We've been on our houseboat four times now. Our trips have been lots of fun and they have been great experiences for my kids. I believe that Lake Powell improves a person's character. It helps develop a sense of love, appreciation, and respect for nature and God's creations. It's nearly impossible to develop a deep feeling of that kind unless you've been totally immersed in an experience in which you really connect with natural beauty around you. Lake Powell is a great place to get that type of an experience, but it is definitely not the only place. Two years ago I spent a week with my son backpacking 50 miles across Utah's Uinta Mountains. That was another one of those types of experiences.

I feel that it's important for everyone to have had a deep connection with nature at least once in their lives, because it can be such an attitude-changing experience. It's a tragedy that some people never have the opportunity to have such an experience. Then there are those who do not want one. They won't leave their iPods, cell-phones, and PlayStations to have this type of an experience, and they are truly missing out. Finally, there are some who actually make it to Lake Powell, but their focus is so much on water sports, parties, or whatever, that they manage to miss the opportunity to really connect with nature. I don't quite know what to think about them. I'm not saying that the recreational aspect of the lake isn't a great reason to go. It is, but it's only half of the equation. If you don't get both sides of the spectrum, then you've missed out.

Unfortunately, this chapter in my life has also come to an end. My wife has gotten a little tired of going to Lake Powell every year and would like to do something else for a while. And, I have to admit, as much as I love Lake Powell, there are a few other things I'd like to do too. So, I've sold my houseboat share to my sister and we are going to do other things for a while. I can live with that. I have experienced the lake in ways that I doubt that many people have, particularly in those early years. Nobody can take that away from me. And, I'll be back some day. In the mean time, you have a pretty good chance of finding me at Yuba. There's no doubt that I'll be back to Lake Powell someday. And hopefully, I'll add another chapter to this story in a few years.

Growing Up on the Water

By Tiffany Mapel

"In sweet water there is a pleasure ungrudged by anyone."

—Ovid, 13 A.D.

When I was about eight or nine years old, we moved from Denver to Bailey, Colorado, and Mom and Dad were avid sailors. It was 1980. My parents raced their Hobie Cat in various regattas around the state, and even at Lake McConaughy in Nebraska. The big race was always at the end of the season, held on Lake Dillon, just below the Continental Divide in Summit County, Colorado. The weather was almost always horrible for that race. My Mom recalled the regatta with fondness:

"It was rated one of the top 10 treacherous sailing waters in the world! The Rocky Mountain Regatta was a two-day event there each year. All the Hobie clubs raced that one. It was the grand finale. One year it was so bad, there were 110 boats upside down. Almost everyone got hypothermia. I was black and blue from head to toe from being thrown against the hulls and dragged under the dolphin striker—while I was in the trapeze! I would not let the coast guard take us in as I wanted to finish the race!"

Their first boat was a Hobie 16—the "Tequila Sunrise" model, and their starter-boat. Later, they upgraded to a Hobie 18—the "Chunky Banana." Hobies were given model names according to the coloring of the sails. Finally, they upgraded to a Nacra 5.2, a super-sleek racing catamaran. Mom and Dad went to the factory in Santa Barbara, California to pick it up. They even sailed it on the ocean to try it out.

"The waves were huge. We went out, tacked a few times and came screaming back in. It was FAST! When we got to shore, all the guys on the beach said, 'we never sail in that weather!' They washed our boat for us! (We're not worthy!!) Ha—we impressed them. Guess all that Lake Dillon training was worth it."

Ah yes, the 1980's were good to us. My two younger sisters, my older brother, and I would hang out on the beach while Mom and Dad sailed, and when they weren't racing the wind, we'd get to go sailing too. We got good at watching the wind direction, tacking when we needed to change sides on the boat, pulling whatever line needed to be attended to for the sails, and watching that the swinging boom didn't wipe us off the trampoline. We knew all the parts on the boat, and what they did. We could rig a Hobie Cat in 20 minutes and have it ready to sail. Sometimes we were even allowed in the trapeze. There's nothing quite like hull-flying across the water with the wind in your face.

A few years later, my Dad brings home a Catalina 22 sailboat one day. He announced we'd be taking it on vacation to "Lake Powell"—a lake I had no idea about, but was excited to go somewhere new. We would be camping at Lake Powell for a week, and hopefully sailing around too. The Catalina had a sparkling white hull and white sails. It had a small cuddy below with sleeping quarters for two very cramped adults. It also had a heavy six-foot retractable keel that could be raised or lowered with a winch.

"You guys will be sleeping in tents while Mom and I get to sleep on the boat," Dad informed us.

So be it. We were just excited to go to a new lake with a new boat. The year was 1985, and I was 13 years old. Powell had recently filled to full pool with a water elevation of 3700 feet back in June of 1980. The drive to Powell was long from Bailey—about eight hours—so we left Bailey around 3:00am that morning in May. We arrived at a lonely place called Hite Marina later that morning. The stark reds and browns of the desert didn't look like much at first. I was used to green trees and sandy beaches wherever we went sailing. This place looked like inhospitable rock. The water was a murky brown (from spring runoff I would later find out. The north end of the lake was always that way in spring).

It took awhile to rig the sailboat, as it was our first time on it. We also brought along a metal fishing boat, my Mom's wind surfer, and a variety of water toys and fishing gear. Finally we got the Catalina launched, and headed down-lake. We motored on with the sails down since the wind was calm. I remember it was a small black motor—not sure of the make or horsepower—but that was the same motor that would fall off and sink to the depths of Lake McConaughy a year later because it was not bolted on properly. (We later got divers to go look for the motor, but they never reached the bottom of the lake due to "large white fish" that made them quickly ascend). Well, we never got our motor back, and had to buy a new one.

My family and I sat on the deck of the Catalina enjoying the day, slathering on sunscreen, and taking in the views of Lake Powell. The lake got more gorgeous the further down-lake you went. My Dad was looking at a map and told us that Bullfrog Marina was further down south, and it had a restaurant. He said we would all go one morning for blueberry pancakes. But I was too wrapped up in the landscape to think about pancakes. I was busy taking pictures with my cheapo pink 110-film camera. I couldn't believe the colors, and I could visualize how great these pictures were going to turn out. My friends would surely not believe this place.

I don't remember seeing any houseboats on our trip, and very few boats of other kinds. It seemed like we were the only ones on the water. It was like having the lake all to ourselves. I don't remember what canyon we first camped in, but Dad snugged the boat into a pretty narrow crack in the slick rock. You had to hike up about 15 feet to a small patch of sand, a fire pit, and a great campsite. My siblings and I pitched our tents and made camp.

Dad got in the fishing boat and took off with my brother. The rest of us spent the day exploring, chasing lizards, and swimming. Mom actually got to relax a bit, and go windsurfing. As we set off to explore the slick rock surroundings, I was hunting for interesting rocks for my sizeable rock collection (which I still have, much to the chagrin of my husband). One of my sisters floated around the water on a blow-up lounger. My other sister came upon a small hole in the sandstone not too far from our campsite, and called us all over. It was about the size of a tire, and it was filled with water and algae. There was a small tree growing out of a crack in the rock above the hole. When we looked closer, we could see the water was filled with ... POLLYWOGS! They were huge, fat, black tadpoles, and there were a lot of them. They would intermittently rise to breathe at the surface, then lazily descend into the algae. They must have been bullfrog tadpoles, for they were bigger than any tadpoles I had ever seen. Jenny ran back to camp to get a bucket. For the next hour, Jenny, Heather, and I sat gleefully catching tadpoles and adding them to the bucket of water. We soon had a full bucket, and didn't even get all of them out of the hole.

Meanwhile, back at camp, Dad and my brother, Rick, came back from fishing. They had a few small bass in the boat, but came back in for lunch. We showed them the bucket of tadpoles, and Dad got a gleam in his eye. I don't know how he convinced us to take our bucket of pets fishing, but he did. Later that afternoon, he returned to camp with a boat full of striped bass. They were just lying all over the floor of the boat. I had never seen so many fish at once—they were beautiful, shining silver. Dad and Rick had fun cleaning and gutting the fish, and we ate them for dinner that night. We gathered around the campfire, and Mom prepared the fish fillets with her special recipe: stuff them with apple and cheese slices, croutons and butter. Then she wrapped the fish in aluminum foil, and we cooked them in the coals on the fire. Boy, were they tasty. We also roasted copious amounts of marshmallows. It was a great end to our first day on Lake Powell.

As night fell, the day cooled. Stars were out in abundance. Crickets chirped, and frogs croaked. Then we noticed some furry little critters scampering around the rocks in the glow of the campfire. I made a mental note to make sure the tents were all zipped up tight when we finally went to sleep.

The family boat camp. T. Mapel photo

The next day, we headed further down-lake. We could see the Henry Mountains to the north, and they still had snow on the tops. Since it was the end of May, snow was still possible in the higher altitudes. And the water had not yet warmed to the usual summer temperature of 82 degrees, so swimming was a bit brisk. Spring could mean strong winds, rain or snow, or nice, calm weather. You just never knew what you were going to get. The wind never got strong enough to raise the sails, so the little motor powered us onward. When we made our next camp spot, Dad again took off in the fishing boat. Rick stayed behind, and we all went out to chase lizards and play in the water. We explored our new spot, but never found another pool with tadpoles.

I don't remember much of the food Mom had packed for a week on the lake, but I do remember the lunches. She brought a lot of frozen meals, so that's what we ate for lunch, and sometimes for dinner if Dad didn't happen to catch any fish. And here's the funny part—we brought the microwave with us, and a small generator. I remember being so embarrassed bringing a microwave to the lake. The sound of the generator was so annoying, and I was hoping no one would notice us. There the machines sat, out on the slick rock—the microwave humming along, and the generator to back it up, screaming louder. They both looked so oddly out of place. I would much rather have had peanut butter and jelly.

The afternoon slowly turned to evening, and we were treated to a blazing Lake Powell sunset. Dad was due to come back, but had not yet shown up. Finally it was dark. Mom was pacing. She got out the floodlight, and scanned the water. Nothing. We were all nervous, too. Where the heck was Dad? Was the fishing that good? Did he hook into a big one, and it towed him all over the lake? We had to eat our microwave meals for lunch and dinner that day. Where was Dad with his usual bounty of fish? Mom was getting madder by the minute. This was certainly a good time to have had walkie-talkies. But no, we didn't have those. We didn't have a marine radio, either. And of course, no cell phones. Not like they'd work where we were anyway. I don't think cell phones even existed back then.

Finally, Dad showed up, the metal fishing boat clanging on the rocks near shore, the small motor sputtering down. You could definitely tell he was frustrated. He told us he got lost—which is understandable, if you're unfamiliar with Lake Powell. It's very easy to get lost, especially in the dark. We were all relieved to have him back. It was sure quiet around the campfire that night, save for the rodents dancing on the rocks just beyond the glow of the fire.

The rest of the week we moved around a bit, always exploring our new camp. I even tried my Mom's windsurfer, but I was not strong enough to lift the sail. The whole thing seemed rather sketchy, and I knew right away I'd never make it in life as a windsurfer. I gave it up and went back to chasing lizards. Back on the beach, I was looking down into the shallows, and saw a large catfish swimming around. It seemed to be swimming in laps around some rocks in a certain pattern. Maybe it had babies nearby? I grabbed my fishing pole, and put a piece of leftover bacon on the hook. I lowered it so the catfish would run into it on its next lap. Sure enough, the catfish sucked up the bacon. I pulled it right out of the water, and it didn't even put up a fight. That was certainly the easiest fish I ever caught, or more accurately, that fish caught itself. I don't know why we didn't just throw it back in, but we kept it. Dad gutted it with his next batch of stripers, and we ate fish again that night.

Years after our family Powell trips, I asked my dad how in the world did he catch so many stripers each day? He told me he would take his net and scoop up the small bluegill fish that hung out in the shallows. Then he would put the hook through the back of the small fish, and cast out into deeper water. The stripers would go crazy with the wounded bluegill swimming against the hook. I wondered how he got the hooks into the tadpoles too. It all didn't paint a pretty picture in my mind, and besides, using live bait is illegal at Lake Powell. I don't think he knew that back then.

With all our camp spots that week, I don't remember seeing a lot of trash. The only thing we found was a deck chair that was sitting in the muck in a few feet of water. We pulled it out, cleaned it off, and took it home with us. We never made it to the Bullfrog restaurant for blueberry pancakes. By the end of the week, those blueberry pancakes were sounding pretty good. We also didn't get the chance to raise the sails that week—no wind. As we moved the sailboat around the lake, I was in charge of raising and lowering the keel. I got to crank on the winch until the keel locked into place. Knowing the lake today, with the fluctuating water level and where most of the underwater rocks are, I'm very surprised that we never struck anything under the water with that six-foot keel. We were very lucky, I guess, and we didn't even have a depth gauge. Maybe that's why we never see any sailboat regattas on Lake Powell?

Our vacation week on Lake Powell had come to a close, and we had to head back up to Hite Marina on our final day. That day dawned a bit cloudy, and it looked like maybe we'd have some wind to raise the sails too. We sadly packed our things and got ready to leave. This became standard on all our Powell trips—the last day was always sad, because we didn't want to leave. And the older I got, the re-entry into the "real world" got even more difficult.

We got the Catalina under way, as the sky grew more ominous. A steady breeze began to pick up. We took a chance and raised the sails, but that was only short-lived. We were able to tack a few times heading up-lake, but it was obvious that a huge storm was coming down on us very soon. The sails came back down, and we made sure that everything was tied or battened down. My two sisters stayed in the cuddy below, Mom and Dad stayed on deck; Dad at the motor, my brother was in charge of the fishing boat that we were towing behind, and I was positioned on the bow to hold the windsurfer in one arm and the anchor in the other. My job wasn't too difficult, as the windsurfer and anchor were already tied down. I just had to make sure they stayed there.

We were somewhere between Bullfrog and Hite, near Good Hope Bay when the storm hit full force. The water was instantly whipped into a frenzy of white-caps and enormous waves. I don't remember if it was raining, but we were all getting wet as the waves slammed against the hull. The little motor pushed us along at 3 or 4 miles per hour, and with the strength of the waves, it was hard to keep the boat on a straight course. I wrapped my legs in some lines that were on the deck, and I held tight to the windsurfer and anchor. I wasn't going anywhere. I also don't think I was wearing a life jacket. I can remember getting soaked through my clothes, but I wasn't cold. The water was warmer than the air at that point.

As the Catalina bucked on the waves, I scanned each distant shoreline. One was sheer cliff; the other was low slick rock that gradually ascended. I figured if the boat sank, I could definitely swim to the shore. Well, maybe. It was a long way to shore, and those were some pretty big waves. I just prayed we'd make it to the marina soon, and tried not to think of the boat sinking. We pushed on through the storm, inching our way toward Hite. I looked back at my parents, who had their rain jackets on. My brother was hunched over, watching the fishing boat that was being towed behind. It's amazing that the little boat did not take on water and sink.

Suddenly, a wave hit me. I was in waist-deep water as a huge wave washed over the bow of the boat. In the next second, the Catalina crested a wave, and I was looking down about ten feet toward the water. Then we sunk back into another trough, and I was in waist-deep water again. Those were the biggest waves I've ever seen on Powell, to this day. It was a good thing I was wrapped up in those lines, or I would have been washed right off the bow when that first wave hit me. We rode like that for a long time, and it seemed an eternity to get to Hite. It was like riding a bucking bronco in slow motion. I don't remember finally reaching the marina. I don't remember pulling the Catalina out of the water, or even the drive home. I'm sure once we reached Hite, I crawled into the car and slept the whole way home.

We went to Lake Powell for our week vacation each year, from 1985 to 1989. Our last family outing to the lake was in 1989—the same year I graduated from high school. On our way home from the lake, we stopped in Durango, Colorado to drop me off for my summer orientation session at Fort Lewis College. It's purely coincidental that I chose a college that was only a 3.5-hour drive away from Lake Powell. I actually chose Fort Lewis because of the skiing opportunities, and I liked the town of Durango. All academics came secondary.

I spent four years at Fort Lewis College, graduating in 1993. During that whole time, I never made it back to Lake Powell. I was too busy in the summer working three or four jobs just to pay my rent and bills, and I was also saving for tuition money. I didn't have any time for fun. But I loved Durango, and knew I wanted to stay there. Winters were my time for fun. I worked at Purgatory, had a ski pass, and skied a lot. I raced on the ski team throughout college, and independently for several years after graduation. Most of my friends worked at the ski area too, and we all had our summer jobs that passed time until winter came again. If only I had known I could have worked summers out at Lake Powell. I'm sure I would have loved it. I could have been a junior ranger, or helped with the rental houseboats. I could have done any job and been happy, because I'd be at my favorite place.

It was 1994 when I finally made it back to Lake Powell again. My ski buddy, Chuck, had a Larson ski boat, so eight of our friends went in on a houseboat rental out of Halls Crossing. It was a brown 44-foot Boatel, common on the rental fleet in those days. Earlier that summer, I had met Frank, who would become my husband nine years later. I took him to Lake Powell for the first time that year. Had he known back then how ravenous I would become for Lake Powell and my obsession with water and boats, he might have run away screaming. But no, he stuck with me. My hubby, the landlubber, who is ever-patient and accepting of me and my water addiction.

Houseboating was a whole new world for me. It was so exciting to have a bathroom and fridge aboard, and I felt truly spoiled. We would drag the mattresses to the roof and sleep under the stars each night. We explored the lake, fished, hiked, and water skied our brains out. We learned where all the canyons were, and knew landmarks all over the lake. We all loved Lake Powell so much, that we came back each year. We called our group the "Sourdawgs," and our annual summer vacation became an event not to be missed. In almost a decade of annual summer Powell trips, we were always really lucky and had great weather—until our trip in 2002. The wind blew so hard for three days, and it was all we could do to stay out of the blowing sand and keep our sanity. Moving the houseboat was so treacherous because of the huge waves. To top it all off, we even had engine trouble. Once we got the houseboat beached, we stayed there to ride out the wind. Tempers flared and all our limits were tested. That was our worst trip to Lake Powell, but even so, I still managed to enjoy it.

We continued to rent a houseboat each summer, not letting one incident of bad weather keep us away from the lake we loved. The trips have been good. We've gotten some great hiking and exploring in, and even a new sport for us—wakeboarding—my newest lake addiction. We continue to fish, but most of the time we just catch catfish. Stripers always seem to elude us. Sometimes we get really lucky, and find a striper boil. Then they're easy to catch.

The houseboat rentals improved over the years too. Some of the boats had slides off the back, ensuring that all the adults onboard became kids again by going off the slide. We had so much fun stopping in the middle of the channel, and jumping off the roof of the houseboat in deep water. We also noticed nicer houseboats on the lake. Some had winches to load jet skis from the water to the deck of the boat, some were three stories, and get this—some of the more elaborate boats had hot tubs, huge TV screens (with satellite TV service), and yes, built-in microwaves and generators! It brought back memories of our little microwave we took on our family vacation years earlier. So basically, you could have all the comforts of home on the water. But that seemed a bit too much for me. I like the basic houseboats with just enough to meet your needs. Who needs TV when you are surrounded by Lake Powell? What a waste.

Nowadays, I have several friends who have either their own houseboat or a timeshare. It's great to have so many opportunities to go to Lake Powell. The SHAD Rallies at Bullfrog each spring and fall lure me out to fish. A hike to write about for Lake Powell Magazine gets me out on the lake two or three times each year. All I need is a reason to get to Lake Powell, and I love to go. The only problem with being boatless is, I have to rely on other people to get me where I want to go, and I'm pretty much on their schedule.

Having a boat at Lake Powell represents freedom—freedom to explore and take your time. There are so many places on the lake that I have yet to "discover." I rarely get the chance to spend a few hours hiking a new canyon. If I had a boat, I could do just that. I wouldn't have to answer to anybody. Someday, I hope to have a boat of our own that is Powell-worthy—a good, sturdy, and reliable vessel for our family. I want to be able to introduce our baby daughter to everything I love about Powell. She will hopefully come to know and love the lake as I have. I can't wait to teach her how to water ski and wakeboard. I also want to be able to bring our dog, a black lab that really loves the water. For now, I'll take Lake Powell any way I can get it. Viva Lake Powell!

◆   ◆   ◆

The Ghost Ship

The year was 1995 or 1996, I can't be sure. The Sourdawgs were on their annual summer Lake Powell vacation trip. We always liked to beach the houseboat in our canyon of choice, Slick Rock Canyon. The water was up back then, and our little beach was almost directly beneath that small cave, high on the Navajo sandstone wall that overlooks a nook in the canyon. We were pretty much the only boat in the canyon that trip. Nowadays, Slick Rock is approaching Moki Canyon in terms of summer population. We avoid it now. When we go to Lake Powell, we go to get away from it all—we don't want neighbors. We want to hear the ravens, the silence, and the waves lapping on shore. We'd rather not hear other boats, their generators running into the night, and loud, obnoxious neighbors. With Lake Powell being so large, we never have trouble finding our perfect spot.

One calm night on our Slick Rock beach, we all gathered around our campfire, sipping libations of choice. The night was still, warm, and dark. Stars sparkled overhead, and I felt truly absorbed into the landscape. It was a perfect night. We were all quiet, enjoying the crackling of the fire, when a huge lit-up houseboat drifted silently into view. It had white lights strung all over it, and to top off this spectacle, it was blaring Lawrence Welk music. We didn't even hear it coming—how was that possible? It was as though it suddenly appeared. We all stared in awe, and some of us questioned what we were seeing and why. Why was a houseboat of that size moving in the dark? What were they thinking? Just as quickly as it appeared, it was gone. Silence again. We expected to hear it run aground, metal hulls screaming on rock. Nothing.

"Did we just see that?" we all asked each other. "What was *THAT*?" It was far too bizarre.

I'd also like to add that although we had just begun our evening libations, no one was impaired at that point. We all saw it, and laughed about it well into the night. The "Ghost Ship" never returned, but certainly went down in the books as one of the strangest things we've seen on Lake Powell.

◆   ◆   ◆

Trackin' Trash

Some of us live, eat, and breathe Lake Powell. Hello, my name is Tiffany Mapel, and I, quite frankly, have a Lake Powell obsession. There, I've admitted it. (Maybe I'm just a desert rat with a water addiction? Could that be it?) I fully blame my parents for this.

Being a Powell fanatic can be time consuming. I check the Powell websites and webcams daily. I follow all news that pertains to the lake. I plot and plan my trips to Powell with great fervor and anticipation. I fight the "drainers" who wish to see Lake Powell drained with my mighty pen (or keyboard) by sending letters to the various governmental agencies, like the BLM and Department of the Interior in support of Lake Powell. Yes, I can name several other worse obsessions to have, so a Lake Powell one doesn't seem so bad in the scheme of things. And I'm willing to bet that since you're reading this book, you're a Powell fan too. There's no greater place on earth, right?

In the spring of 2002, I found out that I could volunteer to spend a week at Lake Powell cleaning trash around the shore and in the water. I literally jumped at the chance. While cleaning other people's garbage really has no appeal for me, I was more than willing to pitch in to help keep my favorite place clean. Little did I know how hooked on cleaning trash at Lake Powell I would become.

Back in 1989, a fellow named Steve Ward started the Trash Tracker program at Glen Canyon National Recreation Area for Lake Powell. Steve happens to be an Aramark employee, and also the president of the Friends of Lake Powell, a non-profit organization dedicated to protecting and preserving the lake. With the NPS and Aramark sponsoring the Trash Tracker, the program has been successfully running each year since 1989. Volunteers spend either 5 or 7 days on the Trash Tracker, cleaning the water and shores of Lake Powell. And since Lake Powell has such a great climate, the trips run from April to November each year. There's also a volunteer boat dedicated to cleaning graffiti from the sandstone faces—"True GRIT"—(Graffiti Removal Intervention Team). Volunteers work hard to erase the illegal markings people foolishly put upon the beautiful sandstone each year.

My very first Trash Tracker trip went out of Bullfrog Marina in the summer of 2002. We had "Captain Ron" at the helm of the Trash Tracker houseboat, and five volunteers aboard, including myself. We headed down-lake toward the Rincon. When Captain Ron got the houseboat beached and secured, we all split up to scour the land for trash. And let me tell you, there was no shortage. I set out over a hill, and just as I did, two large German Shepherds came running and snarling up to me. I must have looked menacing with my big, black trash bag, so I just stood very still. Finally, their owner came over the hill and called them off. So I got back to business, and started filling my bag. We cleaned the entire Rincon area that day. Much was found—trash of all kinds, and a few useful things too, like a shovel and some buckets. As we bagged all the trash, the bags were kept on the trash barge, dubbed the "Eliminator."

We also got into Iceberg Canyon, and cleaned the entire canyon in a day. The biggest piece of "trash" we found was a boat—an actual abandoned boat. It was really old, made of blue fiberglass, and was about 12 feet long. It had been underwater, since it was coated with grime throughout. It was found floating near shore, tied to some rocks. It looked like someone had probably found it, cleaned it out, and decided it was more trouble than it was worth, so they just left it tied to the rocks. On shore nearby was the motor—an *old* one—and two wooden water skis. We cleaned everything up, and towed the boat back to the houseboat. One volunteer noticed that the propeller on the motor was made of bronze, so he quickly claimed that as his prize. I guess they don't make propellers out of bronze anymore.

Since the current drought hit the western U.S. in the past decade, Lake Powell's waters have been dropping. Consequently, the Trash Tracker has been especially busy. Sunken boats began popping up all over the lake. Reports came in with GPS locations, and we'd clean them up, or move the boats if we could. One small boat we were able to bust up with shovels and an axe we borrowed from a nearby houseboat. It was a lot easier to haul out pieces of the boat, since it was in no condition to float. We found so many boats one year that we gave them names, like "Guido," and "Jenny B." If only those boats could speak. Who knows how or why they sunk? Each boat surely had a tragic tale to tell. In 2005, many of the sunken boats we couldn't move were salvaged by Jim Cross of Cross Marine Projects Consulting Company. He graciously donated his time and resources to help clean up Lake Powell.

Perhaps the only good thing to come out of this drought is the fact that the Trash Trackers have been able to get a lot of junk out—literally *tons*. On some beaches, we found trash sticking up out of the sand, so we'd dig down to get it out. Usually it would yield bags upon bags of garbage. Back in the 60's and 70's before it was considered a bad thing to litter, people apparently had no trouble pitching trash out of their boats. Some bags we found were weighted down with rocks in them so they'd sink out of sight. One plastic bag we ripped open contained a mustard bottle—with mustard still in it—and foam egg cartons. The groceries were straight out of the 70's, judging by the labels. And they were remarkably well-preserved. One pit we excavated on a beach contained about 50 tin cans. They were all sharp and rusty, so we had to be careful bagging them up.

Another good place that always has trash is the fire pits. With gloves on, we dig through the ashes and find plenty of stuff that doesn't burn—like aluminum cans, glass bottles, and other scraps of metal. After removing the non-burning items, we collapse the rocks into the fire pit and bury it with sand. I wish people wouldn't put things into fire pits that don't actually burn. It would save us a lot of work.

I think the two biggest pet peeves of Trash Tracker volunteers are broken glass and fireworks. Stepping onto a nice, sandy beach only to cut your foot on sharp, broken glass can ruin a vacation quickly. I always wonder why people bring glass bottles or containers to a place like Lake Powell, and then *intentionally* break them and leave them on the beach for the next person. Some of the shards are so fine and sharp, that we have to sift through the sand with a kitty litter scooper to get it all out. It is tedious work.

Did you know that fireworks and firearms are both illegal at Lake Powell? Since GCNRA is governed by the National Park Service, visitors are not supposed to bring those items with them. Yet, each year the Trash Trackers find plenty of used fireworks strewn about. You'd think that if someone were going to break the rules, they'd clean up the evidence, but no. Sadly, we find fireworks everywhere—especially after the July 4th holiday. One trip, we found professional mortar launchers, so we turned those over to NPS officials. At night, we make note of where the fireworks displays are lighting up the dark sky, then we head over in daylight to clean their beach. We always hang our heads in disgust at the mess left behind. We tell visitors that fireworks are illegal. Most of them didn't know that. Some feign ignorance, and keep doing the light shows at night anyway.

One memorable Trash Tracking trip in 2003 took us to the Escalante, one of my favorite places on the lake. We were cleaning 50-Mile Canyon. Captains Bruce and Pat were aboard, a dedicated team. They had been Trash Tracker volunteers for years, even getting married aboard the Trash Tracker. The water was up, so we were able to get beyond the large dune. Bruce deftly piloted the Eliminator through the narrow canyon. About a half-mile beyond the dune, we came upon a burned-out houseboat on the left shore. It was just coming out of the water, and debris was everywhere on the steep, rocky hillside. We got to work picking up globs of glass and congealed metal. The rubber seals from the windows were still sticky, clinging to the wreckage. Kitchen utensils were everywhere—muffin tins, silverware, pans … The standard-sized oven was halfway sunk, and halfway covered in rocks, and rusted all over. It took four of us to wrestle it into the Eliminator. We even found the houseboat key, and the owner's manual, which was charred and open to the pages of "generator maintenance." It was like coming onto the scene of the crime.

Trash Trackers with the houseboat slide. T. Mapel photo

With all the evidence available, we found out the houseboat was a Boatel rental out of Bullfrog. Apparently, something had gone wrong with the generator, or maybe the stove caught fire, and everyone had to abandon ship. In any case, the boat was just left there. We could just barely see the rest of the houseboat wreckage under water. It was too deep to try to pull anything up, and probably too dangerous. With sharp wreckage, we didn't go that route. The next year as the water level dropped, we were able to clean more at the houseboat site. Still couldn't reach the wreckage under water. The following year when the water dropped more, we couldn't get beyond the dune, so we couldn't reach the burnt boat. I wondered how much more of it was exposed? To get to the wreck at low water, we'd have to get a helicopter to get us in and out of there. I have a feeling that boat wreckage will be there for a long time.

During a summer vacation of 2005, some friends and I discovered a house-boat slide in Llewellyn Gulch while we were on a hike. It was about two miles from where the water ended, near the old high water line. I made a mental note of its location, and two months later on our Trash Tracking trip, we went up and retrieved the slide. That was our big prize of the 2005 trip. Hiking a fairly heavy fiberglass houseboat slide two miles through thick tamarisk and cactus-clad cow trails in the summer heat was no picnic. But the Trash Trackers persevered, and the slide was brought down to the Eliminator with much fanfare. We ended up taking it to Bullfrog marina at the end of the trip, and putting it with the rest of the houseboat slides on the maintenance dock since it was in pretty good shape. Hopefully the Bullfrog boys can find a houseboat to put it on.

Of all the items we find on the Trash Tracker trips, the golf balls have to be the most plentiful. They are virtually everywhere. It's like an Easter egg hunt as you hike around. As the water dropped over the past few years, literally thousands of golf balls have been removed. I guess I don't understand the allure of hitting golf balls off the roof of a houseboat, only to watch it sink to the depths. Golf balls belong on immaculately groomed grass—not in the desert, and definitely not at Lake Powell. There are so many better things to do at Lake Powell than *golf!* If people insist on golfing on the lake, perhaps they could purchase the float-ing golf balls, so they can retrieve them and use them again. Like I said, there's better things to do …

Once on a small beach in Iceberg Canyon, we found a stash of golf clubs—several of them—and a large box full of balls. There were also two white plastic chairs. No one was around. The beach was too small to be a campsite. There were no boats or people nearby. We grabbed the contraband, and then turned it all over to the NPS at the end of the trip. At least we saved the lake from involuntarily swallowing up that box of balls.

Two thousand four was a big year for the Trash Tracker program. It had received a national award for outstanding volunteerism from Take Pride in America. The Trash Tracker team traveled to Washington D.C. to accept the award in September, 2004. Then-Secretary of the Interior, Gale Norton, and then-National Park Service Director, Fran Mainella, were heading up the award ceremony on the rooftop of the Department of the Interior Building that over-looks the stunning obelisk of the Washington Monument. In attendance repre-senting the Trash Tracker were Kitty Roberts, Superintendent of Glen Canyon

National Recreation Area; Steve Ward, who started the Trash Tracker in 1989; Lisa Dittman, then-volunteer coordinator for the Trash Tracker; and myself, the token volunteer. Out of hundreds of volunteers who selflessly give their time to clean Lake Powell, I was asked to go to Washington D.C. to represent our volunteers at the award ceremony. I was so honored to be chosen, and I was proud to help accept the award that the Trash Tracker so deserved. Around 20 groups from across the U.S. were there to accept their *Take Pride in America* awards—scout groups, church groups, volunteers—all dedicated to cleaning up and taking care of our nation's beautiful, scenic places.

Since my first Trash Tracker trip in 2002, I still don't enjoy cleaning other people's garbage, but there's something about cleaning trash at Lake Powell that I cannot get enough of. I would have to say that it's actually *fun*. You have to look at it as an adventure—you get to hike around and explore, and clean trash along the way.

Cleaning up Lake Powell has taken me into places I might not have gone into myself. You get to see so much of the area that you don't readily see from a boat. It's fun to come upon a new arch, or some ruins you didn't know were there. I still haven't seen the elusive desert bighorn sheep. I know they're out there, though. We've seen birds of all kinds, snakes, and coyotes too. In Reflection Canyon, we found a covey of Chukar quail—such beautiful birds. They didn't mind us cleaning their canyon.

From my first trip, we cleaned up a lot of aluminum cans. Over the years, I've noticed less and less cans to pick up. I think people are finally being more litter-conscious, at least I'd like to think that. Most of the cans we find now are really old ones that have been buried or sunk for years. Some of them have been downright antiques, as they've got the "rivets" up the side of the can, or an old pull-top. But on the downside, less cans being picked up somehow means more plastic bottles. And there's no shortage of those.

Some of the things I've found over the years, I've kept too. Like some nice fishing lures that still looked usable. Then there was the new life vest that was floating in Ribbon Canyon. I also got a nice rope that I really had to work hard for, that I found in Davis Gulch. It was high on a wall, and connected to a small arch. It looked like people had used the rope to climb out and up, so they could jump off into the water. I keep hoping to find a really nice anchor—one that I can use for my future boat. I've found old, beat up anchors before, but nothing that could be used again. I also found one of the strangest items ever found at Lake Powell before: a bowling pin. It was an AMF wooden pin, sticking up in the sand near the mouth of Llewellyn Gulch. We all signed it, and gave it to the Trash Tracker coordinator.

The Trash Tracker program has definitely grown in popularity, so much that as soon as the schedule for the new year of trips is posted online and applications are accepted, the trips fill up *THAT* day. And there's a good-sized waiting list for trip cancellations, too. I doubt if there will ever be a shortage of volunteers for the Trash Tracker. It's such a worthwhile way to volunteer, and I hope that if you've never tried it, maybe now you'd like to give it a chance. You'll have a lot of fun, and keep Lake Powell clean in the process. And remember, you don't have to be a Trash Tracker to help keep Lake Powell clean. You can always be a good steward by leaving your campsite cleaner than you found it. Pack out what you pack in. Together, we can all make a difference for Lake Powell!

Lake Life

By Andre Delgalvis

"If there is magic on the planet, it is contained in the water."

—Loren Eisley

For whatever reason, we had a number of encounters with wildlife on our last trip to the Lake. *Where you see the acronym "OMO," this title of distinction refers to the "Oh Mighty One," a title awarded at each SHAD Rally. The SHAD Rallies take place each spring and fall at Lake Powell—they're not fishing tournaments, but just an excuse to gather and fish with friends. The OMO is the one who catches the largest fish during the Rally.

◆　　◆　　◆

The Coyote

On our first day out, Mac McCarty (the OMO) and I had driven the Houseboat up-lake past Tapestry wall. I was in the little boat scouting locations to beach the houseboat. I found what looked like a good spot, when a coyote rounded a bend on shore and was headed in the direction of our landing spot. I returned to the houseboat, drove it to the spot and beached it. After landing, Mac was setting out one of the anchor lines, when suddenly the coyote came up behind him and leaped past onto a steeply inclined part of the shore. When it passed it was closer than five feet to Mac. Apparently it wanted to get to the other side of the strip of beach we were on, and because of the steep incline, having to pass Mac was the only way to do it. The coyote hung around for a few days and we fed it piles of striped bass entrails, which it and the ravens seemed to enjoy immensely. The fur

159

on the coyote was very scruffy. Mac thought it might be a female with a litter someplace nearby, and its hunt for food overcame its shyness to people.

◆   ◆   ◆

The Heron

The day after the coyote encounter, Mac and I were fishing large top-water Sammies at the very back end of Cedar Canyon. The heavy rains earlier in the week had generated massive thick floating debris piles. We were picking up some nice large mouth bass that were hanging near the piles. Mac was fishing in the bow; I was in the stern. A mature great blue heron came flying into the end of the canyon and landed on a floating debris pile close to where Mac was working the surface. After walking the dog back to the boat, he cast out to the same spot. An instant before the plug hit the water, the heron took off and flew right into Mac's line.

After realizing what happened, Mac open his bail hoping the lack of tension on the line might free his rig from the flying bird. Rapidly, the line was playing out and got to the point where he had no choice but to close the bail. We both watched in utter amazement as the line tensed. When it reached the end, the heron did a near summersault in mid air. Mac was now reeling him back in. I reached for my knife to cut the line, but the OMO said no. He intended to get the heron back to the boat and extract the hook which we now believed must be caught somewhere on its body.

I was not very comfortable with that idea. The heron fishes with his long sharp bill, often spearing fish with it. Powerful wings, long clawed legs and large size gave it additional defenses. Earlier in the summer, I recalled two instances where people were impaled in the chest by sting rays. This was rapidly deteriorating into a real dilemma. Should I listen to Mac, respect his altruistic motives to try to free the heron from the line and hooks? Or was this planned course of action a folly that could result in even greater injury to the bird and potentially to ourselves? Should I try to overrule the decision of an OMO (retired), fishing partner, and close friend?

A boat captain's first responsibility is the safety of his passengers, crew, and vessel. The decision was made. I started making my way to the bow, knife in hand. The OMO was reeling in what was perhaps the largest catch ever made on his rig. The heron was still frantically trying to fly off in one direction, probably not quite understanding why it was being pulled in another. Again, I tried to reason with Mac, but he would have none of it, the great bird must be freed of its burden. Then, the line went slack. Somehow in all of the commotion, the hooks and line worked loose from the heron. It flew off, never looking back. Mac and I looked at each other in utter amazement and giddy relief. When all of the line was reeled in, we found a few very small feather fragments on two of the hooks.

First cast of the day. A. Delgalvis photo

◆   ◆   ◆

The Grebe

The very next day after the heron encounter, Mac and I were jigging for stripers in a cove just off the main channel between Cedar and Knowles Canyons. A large school was in feeding mode right below the boat and we were pretty much pulling one up on almost every cast. As was our custom, Mac was working the bow, and I was in the stern.

After about 20 or 30 minutes of constant action, I noticed a lone grebe swimming into our cove. Probably curious about all of the commotion on the water, it began swimming directly toward the stern of the boat. When it was about three feet away from the motor, I commented to Mac that this was the closest I had ever seen a grebe come up to a boat. The OMO (retired) had his hands full pulling in another striper, and either did not hear, or was too busy to comment.

About that time, I hooked into one and commenced to pull it up. The grebe came in even closer and was now circling right next to my line, less than two feet from the boat. I boated the fish and prepared to drop the jig for a go at another striper. I swung the rod over the side, but before I released the line the grebe lunged for the jig, thinking it was a quick meal. I was able to jerk it out of the way before the grebe nailed it. The bird would not relent. It was so close to the boat, you could clearly see its every detail, including its very odd feet. Every time I tried to drop the jig, it would either lunge for it in mid air, or dive for it as soon as it hit the water.

Recalling the heron incident from the day before, I tried switching from the starboard to the port to drop my line. Within moments, the grebe followed suit. I switched sides again. So did the grebe. After several rounds of this, the grebe must have tired of the game because it started swimming toward the bow of the boat, where Mac was again busily hauling in another striper. At last, I was free of the bird and could again concentrate on catching fish.

"GET AWAY BIRD!"

"*#!*# IT, GET AWAY YOU #*!!*# BIRD" emanated from the front of the boat. After two more choruses of colorful language, everything got quiet.

"Hey Mac, what's going on up there?"

"That #*!!*# bird wouldn't let me fish. So I finally had to tap it on the head a couple of times with my rod tip to make it go away."

From that moment on, we never caught another fish the rest of day. That night, the coyote happily feasted on striper entrails left on shore by Mac. The grebe, I suspect, was nursing a sore noggin. And if they dream, it was possibly visualizing dangling striper jigs. The heron—well, I wouldn't be surprised if it was still a little bewildered, trying to puzzle out the events of the previous day.

◆   ◆   ◆

The Grebe (part 2)

Mac (OMO-retired) had left fish camp the previous Sunday. My wife, Susan, had taken a week's vacation time and arrived at the Lake the following Friday evening. Sunday morning we made a gas run to Bullfrog. On the way back, I noticed whom I thought might be Howard (the reigning OMO) fishing near the mouth of Lost Eden Canyon. As we got closer, sure enough, there was Howard taking a striper off the line, while his fishing buddy was at the helm.

We got to talking, and I told him the grebe story that had occurred the week before. Howard waited patiently as I finished my tale, then said he had a grebe story as well. Earlier in the week, he and his fishing buddy were night fishing at the covered slips in Bullfrog. They had hung a light and were fishing anchovies at 50 feet. Howard's fishing buddy got a hit and began reeling it up. He commented that it had a very strange feel to it. After battling it up to about 10 feet from the surface, they could finally see what was on the line—a grebe! At about that point, the bird either decided to spit out the anchovy, or was able to throw the hook. It then broke the surface and flew off.

After I got back from the Lake, I told Mac about Howard's grebe story. I was astonished that a grebe could actually dive to 50 feet below the surface. Mac said that he thought he had read somewhere that they have been recorded at depths in excess of 100 feet. Both of these grebe tales involved, or were witnessed by OMOs, so their credibility doubtlessly cannot be called into question.

◆   ◆   ◆

The Ringtail Cat

For the most part, we don't keep sweets or snack food around the house. I guess it's because both Susan and I have what might be considered addictive personalities. By that I mean if it's there we'll eat it—all of it. But, all of that changes when we are on the Lake. For whatever reason, dry roasted peanuts in the large-sized jars somehow seem to find their way onto the houseboat. If I had to guess, I'd attribute it to the subconscious need for salt in the high desert climate.

Last season, Susan discovered and bought a manual push sweeper for the boat. This handy little gadget works like a vacuum cleaner without electricity. Basically, it is a roller that you push that sweeps up loose debris from your carpet and deck. One evening we were beached in what I call Dream Canyon, which is between Slick Rock and Iceberg Canyons. We both had pigged out on the dry roasted peanuts the night before and Susan had used the push sweeper to clean up the mess. She swept the stern deck carpet last and left the sweeper just outside the sliding glass door to our bedroom. That night, I awoke to a thud outside the stern deck. I shined a flashlight outside and there was a ring-tailed cat. It had turned the sweeper upside down and was trying to get its paws into the debris holding chamber that held the remnants of spilled dry roasted peanuts.

The Ringtail Cat. A. Delgalvis photo

This was my first encounter with a ring-tailed cat. What impressed me were its huge eyes, large ears, immaculate coat, incredible tail, and obvious addiction to dry roasted peanuts. Even though I was shining a flashlight on it and later turned the overhead stern lights on, the cat would not abandon its efforts in trying to get to the peanuts in the sweeper. As fate would have it, just as we had the presence of mind to get the camera out, the cat left.

If the cat was anything like the mice that found their way on board, I figured it would be back the next night. In the evening we set out a pile of peanuts on the stern deck and kept a camera next to the bed. The next morning, we found the peanuts untouched. The next night at about 3:00am, I heard the familiar thump outside. The cat had eaten the pile of peanuts and was back trying to scavenge the last of the peanuts out of the sweeper. This time I was able to photograph our visitor.

◆   ◆   ◆

The Mule Deer

Over the years of exploring around the Lake, I've come across deer sign, but had never seen one. Three years ago I came upon a deer skull with antlers far up Bowns Canyon. Another time I saw a pair of antlers lying on the ground on top of Wilson Bench. Last October, my wife, Susan, and I went up the San Juan arm to hike up to Peek a Boo Arch.

After mooring the boat, we scrambled up to the first plateau. The angle of the sun produced a spectacular light show as it backlit massive cacti groves, reflecting brilliant light off of their needles. Small yellow daisies and Mormon Tea added to the visual delight. Eventually we neared the narrow cleft that would provide us an access route up the towering Navajo Sandstone wall. The cleft is much like that found at Hole in the Rock, only a bit wider and steeper in places. All manner of broken rocks, boulders and huge limestone blocks littered the path to the top. Susan named the trail up "The Olympian Way," because of its majestic bearing and requirement of athletic prowess to reach its God-like summit. (She is the more cerebral and imaginative one in the family).

As we approached the climb, Susan noticed movement about 3/4 of the way to the top. I missed it as I've developed the habit of usually looking down as I walk, a spinoff of too much track searching. A scan with her binoculars proved the movement to be four Mule deer descending the boulder field in the cleft. When they saw us, they stopped short and we all stood there staring at each other. After several minutes, they broke off running. One pair started back up to the top, the other two decided to make for the bottom.

To descend this steep boulder strewn rock fall, you or I would have to carefully calculate each step. This is a process of continually changing direction, twisting, turning, looking for hand holds for balance, and testing each successive rock for stability before weight bearing. The two descending deer were doing it at full bore. Through a combination of pogo stick-like hopping, slip sliding, leaps, and occasional stumbling, they sped down toward us. Navigating a rock field on level ground with two legs can be challenging; imagine having to coordinate four legs in a narrow, steeply pitched boulder field, strewn with sharp-edged, often unstable rocks, with different traction characteristics and doing it at full speed!

We were still at the base of the cleft where it was relatively wide watching the spectacle. The deer ran past to our left, hugging the side of the sandstone wall, keeping as much distance from us as possible. Finally, only an occasional bright flash of white tail remained as evidence of their passing. On our ascent of the cleft, I scanned the rocks for blood, fur or other sign of injury and found none. Once on top, numerous tracks and game trail traces seemed to indicate the cleft was regularly used as a route to access the lush plateau below and perhaps even the Lake.

◆   ◆   ◆

The Seagulls

I was fishing at the Rincon using a Sammy Lure. The stripers didn't seem to be around, but the small mouth bass partially made up for it. I had just cast out, when a seagull started circling right above the Sammy. As I started walking the dog, the gull swooped down, hovered inches above the water, then made a grab for the plug. I saw it coming, jerked the Sammy, and the gull missed it. Not about to be outmaneuvered out of a quick meal, the gull made a second lunge. I jerked again. The gull lunged again. This went on and on until the gull and the Sammy were within five feet of the boat. I cast out again. The same thing happened again.

I cast out again. This time the gull almost caught the Sammy in midair. I had to close the bail in mid cast. When the plug hit the water, the gull went right after it again. By now about six more gulls appeared on the scene. I tried throwing out in the opposite direction. All seven gulls swarmed in midair trying to grab some supper. This time all seven were trying for the Sammy as I reeled it in. It became a standoff. I wanted to fish; they wanted to eat my Sammy. I blinked. They won. I left.

◆   ◆   ◆

The Scorpion

I just returned from 12 days on the lake and had a couple of adventures to relate. My last morning there, I was digging up the last of the anchor lines. This one had been buried in the sand under a pile of rocks for about six days. After pushing away the rocks, I started scooping sand away with my bare hands. After several scoops, I felt a sharp pain just at the base of my ring and third fingers on the palm side. I looked down and didn't see anything except a piece of dried out Russian thistle stem with a few thorns on it. I assumed that was the source of the problem. Although I could not see a thorn or any blood from an entry wound, the pain in my hand got steadily worse. I was bitten by a hornet about two weeks earlier, the pain from this was 4–5 times more intense and if anything getting worse.

Since I was alone and the houseboat was no longer anchored to anything, I tried to ignore the discomfort and focus on getting the last rope coiled, anchor stowed, and the boat underway. After getting out into the main channel, I got some cortizone cream and spread it on my palm. After a few minutes, the pain started to ease up. After pumping out the tanks and getting the boat on the trailer at Bullfrog, I noticed that both my ring and middle fingers were starting to tingle their whole length.

As I still had to button up the houseboat and drive back to Grand Junction, I decided a visit to the clinic might be in order. I related the events to the P.A. there and asked if there was some type of toxin in Russian thistle that could explain these symptoms. She said she was not aware of any, but it sounded to her like I had been bitten by a scorpion. If no allergic reaction occurred within 1/2 hour after the sting, she said there was really no treatment for it. About two hours later, I was on the road home. My two fingers no longer tingled; they were completely numb, like they had been shot up with novacaine. There was no pain, no swelling only numb fingers. Next morning they were still numb, so I saw my doctor that afternoon. After doing some research, he also concluded it was probably a scorpion sting and no treatment was needed. As I write this it is 2 1/2 days since the incident and I am starting to get some feeling back in both fingers. As I think back on it, in the 13 years I have been going to the lake, I have only ever seen two rattlesnakes. Both times they were at the rock pile on top of my anchor line and both times first thing in the morning. From now on it will be gloves and a shovel when pulling up the lines.

◆   ◆   ◆

The Echo

From late fall through early spring the lake becomes a much quieter and peaceful place. A day or more can pass without seeing another boat or human being. One's awareness of sound seems to become more acute because of the quiet. In early March, I had parked the houseboat just inside the mouth of the Escalante arm. Directly across the channel from the stern loomed a massive curved wall of

Navajo Sandstone. The lake is quite wide at this point, resembling more of a bay than a river channel.

Mac and I were fishing a narrow side canyon in the little boat, landing an occasional striper or walleye. I heard what sounded like a bird in distress. It was the kind of cry you might associate with a young bird in the nest wailing for its mother. Or, perhaps of one that had fallen out of its nest, finding itself in unfamiliar and dire straits. The disquieting sound did not stop. It occurred to me that its constant cry would lead a hungry coyote to it if its mother didn't rescue it first.

Thinking back on it, I had heard a similar sound at the lake before. Once while hiking up Davis Gulch, and another time in a side canyon off of Annie's Canyon. Both of those times I tried to find the source without success. This time, I saw what looked like a young hawk in the distance in the general direction of the wailing. The cry continued for about another 20 minutes then stopped.

The next evening I was on the stern of the houseboat and heard the same wailing coming from the cliff face on the opposite shore. Using the binoculars, I finally spotted a ledge, 400 to 500 feet above the lake level that appeared to have a nest on it. The wailing continued on and off for quite a while. Even though the nest was a good distance from the boat, the acoustics of the curved cliff face coupled with the sound carrying qualities of the water amplified the disturbing cries.

Early the following morning, I noticed a small hawk fly near the boat and land on a boulder high above our side of the channel. Soon the same disturbing crying started, this time from the area of the boulder. After spotting it with the binoculars, I realized what I thought was a hawk was really a Peregrine Falcon. It sat on that boulder and emitted a wailing screech on and off for about a half an hour. A while after it flew off, two ravens landed near the same boulder. In short order they started calling too. This lasted for about another 20 minutes until they too flew off. Each of the next two mornings the same routine occurred with both sets of birds.

On the third morning, I began to pay closer attention. For the first time, I realized that each time one of the ravens would call out, an echo of that call was bouncing off the cliff face across the bay and coming back to the birds. To this day I haven't figured out whether they were doing it out of curiosity—perhaps thinking there was another bird calling back to them—or maybe they understood the echo phenomena and were doing it for pure entertainment.

◆   ◆   ◆

The Fighter Jet

I was photographing panoramas about 4/5ths of the way up the long steep rock-slide that is now the only access route into Bowns Canyon. I heard the deep rumble of a jet fighter in the area. I spotted it as it was beginning a slow loop in my direction. It was low; I'm guessing 800–900 feet above me. As it got closer to me in its loop, it turned completely vertical then seemed to hit its afterburners on. It completed its turn right in front of me. I could clearly see the flames coming out of its exhaust as it leveled back out and screamed away. Then the noise hit—full blast—it was so intense, I fell backward onto the ground taking my camera and tripod with me. What a rush!!! I don't know if the pilot or I enjoyed that experience more.

◆   ◆   ◆

Dinosaur Tracks

As I understand it, before the lake was filled, several studies were commissioned by the federal government to survey the areas that would be covered by the rising lake waters. I believe the vast bulk of the surveys centered around the anthropology of the area and attempted to document early occupation and to rescue/recover artifacts. Fewer resources were focused on Paleontology. It was a race to collect as much information as possible with limited resources and limited time.

The result was that not everything was uncovered or recovered before the lake filled. Now that the lake is at a level not seen in 30 years the opportunity to discover previously unnoticed items of interest is available. There is a slab at the visitor's center at the dam with dinosaur tracks, which were found and removed from Explorer Canyon before the water came up and covered the track site. Tracks were also found, I believe, around Warm Creek Bay but these were above the high water line. Also, there are some sort of tracks in a rock slab at the Rincon.

Several weeks ago while kayaking next to the shoreline, in an unnamed canyon, I noticed a rock slab just coming out of the water with odd markings on it. On closer inspection, there were two 3-toed footprints each about 12 inches long, 11 inches wide, and 21 inches apart. It appeared that the creature was standing still and the prints were of the right and left feet. If conditions were right for these tracks to be preserved here, it was possible that more tracks might be found in the area. After spending the better part of the day exploring the area, I came across seven or eight more probable tracks. To the best of my knowledge, this area has not previously been described as one containing tracks. So, when the fishing gets slow, as it was on this trip, there are a lot of interesting exploring opportunities that may not be encountered again once the lake rises again.

San Juan Flood

By David Nelson

"A lake is the landscape's most beautiful and expressive feature. It is earth's eye; looking into which the beholder measures the depth of his own nature."
—Henry David Thoreau

My friends, Mark, Bart, Lane, and myself were on our annual fall waterski trip to Lake Powell in early October 2006. We were camped on the San Juan River arm of Lake Powell between Great Bend and Neskahi Wash, tucked up under some cliffs, about 60 miles from Bullfrog. Not too many people go that far so we had the lake to ourselves, and skiing is usually spectacular! After noon on Thursday the 5th it rained a little and we saw some small waterfalls cascading over 300-foot vertical cliffs above us. We were a good 1000 feet down the talus slope from the point of impact, and the thirsty desert sand quickly absorbed the water, so it never made it close to us. We did notice and discuss the 5-foot deep, 10-foot wide ravine to one side of the camp spot where water could eventually flow in a big storm. I said it would be fun to see a storm that big, but recalling the weather forecast of a 30% chance of scattered afternoon showers, we didn't think it would be this trip. We'd been coming to Lake Powell for 10 years and never worried about anything more than whether the wind would make the water too rough for skiing.

We had a very nice little camp. There was a large, flat sandy area for tents, and a nice overhanging rock that kept the cooking fire out of the rain. Bart, who worries about his loud snoring disturbing us, was kindly 50 feet away on a smaller bench. He'd gone to take a nap, and we'd just taken him his dinner of a barbequed, bacon wrapped turkey kabob. Lane and Mark thought ours were undercooked so we put them back on the fire.

At this time, about an hour before sunset, Mark noticed a really menacing storm rolling down Navajo Mountain, ten miles to the southwest. It was pitch

171

black on top, but the underside was lit by sunlight. It was dazzlingly white and hard to take your eyes off of. It was so bright I doubted whether it was rain—I wondered more about snow or hail. Lane asked whether it was safe to be here. Neither Mark nor I said anything. I was enthralled with the unfolding scene, and a little paralyzed realizing how helpless we might be. I kept thinking about how much water that ravine could carry, and each time I concluded it must surely be able to handle the water. The storm reached us in about fifteen minutes, dumping a torrential sheet of rain and plenty of marble sized hail, but we continued to enjoy the view from under our canopy. Our dinner was safely barbequing under an overhanging rock. What more could you want?

A few minutes later, the small waterfalls we'd seen earlier were reforming. Soon, the largest of three waterfalls was sending a sheet of sand-reddened water several feet wide and a foot or so deep over the edge of the 300-foot cliffs. It hit the slope below with crash like continuous thunder. There the stream flowed around and under huge piles of 20-foot boulders on the talus slope. A few minutes later the stream made its way to the large boulders above us and quickly filled the ravine to overflowing! Then a new stream formed on the other side of the camp. For the moment it looked like the large boulder we camped behind would protect us. Mark was using a shovel to enlarge the newly forming ravine, to make sure the water didn't head toward our tents. I was feeling rather protected, and really enjoying the chaos all around—until the sound grew louder. I looked up: the main stream over the cliff was now at least 10 feet wide and 5 feet deep. The other two waterfalls combined carried half as much water, but they also flowed toward us. The combined stream cascaded *over* the tops of the 20-foot boulders, even moving some of them!

We suddenly realized our big boulder would not protect us much longer. We madly started moving ice chests and throwing gear across the stream into the tamarisk bushes we hoped would remain outside the path of the water. As we feared, the water soon came over our boulder and right through our camp. Instantly, half the ground under Lane's tent was washed away. He and Mark grabbed the tent to carry it across the torrent now about 15 feet wide and 2 feet deep, through a 5-foot deep gorge. They made it, then came back for more tents. Struggling against that much water, sand, and rock hurtling down a 45-degree slope, standing on sand that erodes underfoot, is quite an experience. Bart came out of his tent, and noticed he was in danger of being undercut from the stream on his side. He dragged his tent to safety and then helped us get the other gear across.

In the midst of saving gear, Mark focused my attention on my ski boat anchored 10 feet offshore—the silt, rock, and debris were quickly piling up under it. I knew I had to get it out of there before it got silted in, whereupon the torrent would just flow over it and bury it, stranding us! I ran down and untied anchor ropes while trying not to be swept under by the current and all the debris washing down. I managed to push the boat out, then climb aboard and get it started, only to have the engine die after just ten feet of travel. The current had swept the anchor rope back under the hull where the prop caught it and wrapped it around the shaft, making it impossible to operate. When I couldn't free it, I knew there was nothing I could do but stay with the boat and try to keep it out of the silt. The eddy currents would suck the boat back in and I'd get back into the stream to push it out. As soon as I'd get the boat away from shore where the water was deeper, I had to struggle to keep from being swept under by the current. After several attempts I got the boat away from the main flow and silt bar. I didn't want to risk swimming under the boat to cut away the rope, so Mark threw me the other anchor rope which I tied to the bow. He pulled the boat tight between the two ropes so it was safely out of danger, then set the anchor to hold it there, and I swam back to shore.

After fishing out a few floating pieces of gear from the lake, the only things lost were a shovel, tent stakes, a grill, and a mangled canopy. Oh, and the delicious bacon wrapped turkey kabobs we'd been barbequing. I remember seeing the charcoal and one kabob float by as I was throwing gear across the river. That was the worst moment during the whole event. It wasn't until later that I realized how much danger we'd been in.

We dragged our soggy tents and gear out of the tamarisk over to a new spot out of danger. We just threw big rocks on the tent corners to hold them down and hunkered down in sleeping bags to get warm. My sleeping bag was wet, as were all my clothes, but those high tech fabrics really do keep you warm even when wet, just as advertised. That night the lightning was almost continuous through two more heavy deluges—bigger than the first by the sound of the three crashing waterfalls. It thundered on for over two hours, then subsided to intermittent light rain and wind. I think we all slept pretty well at times, but I kept waking up over dreams about leaving the boat ignition on and having a dead battery in the morning. It was definitely a long night!

Shortly after a very overcast daybreak the rain stopped. We noticed the lake level was over a foot higher than the previous night when Mark had set the anchor. Mark and I took turns swimming under the boat to cut away the rope and debris from the prop. Then we hastily packed our gear and took off for Bullfrog—a two-hour trip. On the way, it rained hard and continuously. At times visibility was only a hundred feet. I couldn't see through the windshield, so I had to kneel on the seat, exposing my eyes to the rain driven by a headwind and the speed of the boat. It was critical to see, not just to navigate the channel, but because many logs had been washed into the lake, and hitting one would damage the prop and strand us. At times the wind and rain subsided to expose spectacular views. Every few hundred yards there was a waterfall, or waterslide cascading into the lake from heights as great as 500 feet. Some were crystal clear and others carried a lot of red sand. It was really an awe-inspiring sight. And not one of us had a camera! I've always taken a camera on these trips, and each year I'd come home with pictures that looked pretty much like all the rest, so I decided not to take one this year. My wife, Kary, asked me afterward if I had my cell phone. I said yes. She reminded me it has a camera built in. Duh! It never crossed our minds.

We made it safely to Bullfrog—with one stop along the way. The engine temperature had been gradually climbing for the first ten miles. When it started rising fast, past 180F, and with my heart in my throat, I stopped and dismantled the cooling system. It was crammed full of wood chips and debris we'd picked up along the way. The engine ran fine at 130F after that. Whew!

Driving out of Bullfrog Bay, every little dry gulch was filled with raging torrents. It was amazing! Water raged down dry gulches. Slot canyons were full. White water streams ran off slick rock domes. Valleys were flooded. Normally dry Trachyte Creek had standing waves 5 feet tall, and filled the width of the 50-foot wide gorge. The water was black from eroded Organ Pipe sandstone upstream. Dirty Devil River was huge! The current had ripped out most of the nasty, alien, Russian tamarisk bushes that clogged the channel. Part of highway 24—a part we could avoid, fortunately—was under 12 feet of water. Little Price River looked as big as the Green River.

It rained all the way from Bullfrog to Vail, Colorado. Upon returning home Friday, the news from KSL-TV in Salt Lake City called this the storm of the century for Utah. The most rain Hanksville, upstream from Lake Powell on the Dirty Devil River, had ever had in 24 hours was two inches in 1907. Thursday they had three inches, and almost as much Friday. Most of southeast Utah was under flash flood watch, and many parts did flood. By Friday evening, the lake rose two feet, three and a half by Sunday, and five feet over the next seven days as water poured in from surrounding areas. I'd always wanted to see Mother Nature like that. I'm glad I did—I'm thankful my friends and I survived!

Oh—and if you ever find a nice sandy beach at the end of a ravine, it was the alluvial fan from the last big storm, which rose from the lake when the level dropped. It will look so inviting, but before you camp there, keep in mind how it got there.

Lake Powell Epics

By Alan Silverstein

"No one can see their reflection in running water.
It is only in still water that we can see."

—Taoist proverb

Glen Canyon is for me a rich source of what I call "epic adventures." Of course they're not on the scale of climbing Mount Everest. These are personal experiences that stand out in my memory, are revisited years later while daydreaming, and evoke a sense of wonder that once upon a time, I actually "did that."

New to Lake Powell, Finding Ancient Ruins

I spent a week in 1989 visiting *Heaven* aboard the *Houseboat to Hell* ... But that's a larger story. Here I will tell you only about my first, magical evening and morning in Glen Canyon, when I "discovered" a hidden Anasazi homestead in Slick Rock Canyon. (This preceded most of the bizarre and unfortunate events that transpired in the following days, which do not bear repeating presently).

It was the fourth summer *The Alternative*, a Fort Collins singles group, arranged a weeklong houseboat trip to Lake Powell. I didn't have much idea what to expect, but joined 14 other people anyway. After dealing with some initial problems, we departed Bullfrog Marina unusually late on a hot Saturday afternoon in July on a crowded 60-foot private houseboat with only one working outboard motor (but two bathrooms).

Soon after launching, a few of the women in the crew—recall, this was a singles group—"gifted" me with a Speedo swimsuit. They insisted I put it on immediately, "or we'll put it on for you." I was embarrassed, but yielded to the unavoidable, found it surprisingly comfortable, and wore it the rest of the week.

We made it to Slick Rock Canyon and moored on a sandy beach at the shallow, muddy end of the water. The lake was fairly full at 3678 feet, so we were near full-pool, well beyond the major and well-known Anasazi ruins that I believe were already fenced off. The boat was anchored before dark, and the crew got in the vacation spirit ... "Party time!"

The Righteous Brothers boomed from a powerful speaker on the roof deck. I set out on a short solo hike up the river-left wall above the boat to a natural cave, as high as I could go below the cliffs. Then I perched there soaking in the unreal scenery, peering down on the "beehive" below, basking in the glow of it all. I remember the surreal feeling of the music reverberating off the canyon walls ... "You've lost that lovin' feeling ..."

I also noticed something odd, a little too angular, directly across the canyon, tucked into the left corner of a huge, shallow, domed overhang. What could it be? "Maybe I can check it out in the morning." That night I was too tired to stay awake, but too elated to sleep.

Sunday dawned, a sunny day. I took a lady with me to explore the river-right canyon wall and check out the oddity I'd noticed. We found Anasazi ruins in remarkable condition, straw and charred-looking timbers still on their roofs, dusty stone walls mostly intact. It was a bit of a scramble up the last twenty feet, so perhaps they were not frequently visited. Certainly they were not on any map I've seen since then.

What I didn't know then, of course, was that the next summer I would buy a share of that houseboat ... And that, through 2006 I would lead 36 vacation trips to the lake and spend 244 days and nights of my life exploring Glen Canyon ... That I would go with 18 people and three boats, or just three people and four boats, or with four people and five boats; at high water and low water; north to the bridges and south to Friendship Cove; in summer heat and Thanksgiving snow; and especially, on foot over many miles, up, down, and around, finding my own way ... That I would hike two miles to the dead-end plunge pool of Slick Rock Canyon three weeks after an intense fire created a fascinating moonscape, including people-sized holes in the sand where cottonwood trunks had burned out ... That I would lead other people to the same ruins in Slick Rock many times, before they were fenced off and interpretively-labeled, although without explanation, as the "Mistake Alcove ..." That I would visit many other well-known Anasazi sites in Glen Canyon, and discover for myself even more unmarked locations with pictographs, stone tools and flakes, metates, corn cobs, pottery sherds, charcoal, and/or Moki steps cut into the rock walls ...

But I would never again find anything like those "perfect" ruins in Slick Rock Canyon.

◆   ◆   ◆

A Famous Person at Aleson Arch
... by Way of the Iceberg Canyon Grand Tour, Part II

One pleasant evening in September 2002, at the tail end of a long, epic hike, I met two people at the Aleson Arch—formerly, informally, the "Flying Eagle" or "Kissing Elephants" Arch. This huge span is about 900 feet above the lake on the south side between the Rincon and Iceberg Canyon, with a mind-blowing view. Encountering people on foot high above Lake Powell is rare enough, but one of them turned out to be moderately famous. Therein lies a tale, but to tell it properly, I must back up many years ...

Once upon a time, in the early days long before my time, a friend exploring Lake Powell discovered what we still call "Dougs Cathedral" way up Iceberg Canyon. This impressive, mossy natural amphitheater, complete with a huge "altar stone" where the sun never shines, is 700 feet below the rim of the canyon, up the last right fork a mere 20-minute walk from full pool.

After many visits by the canyon floor to the Cathedral, Doug and I got the notion to try looking down into it from above. While it's 40 miles by water around to the Great Bend of the San Juan River, it's only 2.7 miles across by land. (I suspect that in future geologic time, the Colorado River is going to capture and reroute the San Juan by way of Iceberg).

After several explorations by boat and boot, and one failed attempt two days earlier in what turned out to be a dead-end ravine, we managed to do a difficult scramble up and out of an unnamed canyon off the north side of the Great Bend. We believe this is the ONLY non-technical route up-and-out of this area. Then in an eight-hour round trip, we did overlook his Cathedral from above ... Wow.

Somewhat later it occurred to me that the old jeep road up and out of the southeast side of the Rincon might be an easier way to get to the same spot. Use of a map and GPS was mandatory (and it turned out to take about three hours one-way), but sure enough, it was possible. So I formulated what I called the "Iceberg Canyon Grand Tour." And then on one houseboat trip, we moored in an icky, muddy spot in the upstream arm of the Rincon so I could attempt the hike with a few friends.

This outing lasted 14 hours, from sunrise until well after dark. We managed to "only" look down into Iceberg from five spots: northeast across from the Cathedral (the only good viewpoint), at the pour-off itself (hard to see much), and down the ends of what I call the left, middle, and right forks of the second right finger of Iceberg Canyon. Incidentally, the view straight down 700 feet from the end of the middle fork of the right finger is one of the most spectacular drops you'll find on this planet.

Back at home, I still wanted to finish the "Grand Tour," now "Part II." Thus in 2002, starting at 7:55am on a Monday morning, I took one friend back up the Rincon road to the middle fork overlook. Then we proceeded northwest (clockwise) from there. After seeing the right fork viewpoint, he peeled off at about 1:20pm and returned to the houseboat (with radio) while I continued north alone. Later that afternoon I got to look into the end of the first right finger of Iceberg for a second time—but that's yet another story.

Then, overhead and in sight of the houseboat on the east side of the Rincon at about 5:10pm, I was prepared to drop back down through the Wingate cliffs and ramps directly to "home." I called the crew on the radio. The ski boat owner suggested I might as well continue to the arch. So I thought, what the heck, why not? Knowing I'd be out of radio range, I arranged for a 6:45pm ski boat pickup at the lake beyond the arch, down in Flying Eagle Cove.

With all that as preface, now you can imagine me approaching the familiar Aleson Arch from the west. It was late in the day, about 5:30pm. I'd been out on foot for 9.5 hours already, alone for the last 4+ hours. I had a new schedule to keep, but I could finish the tour in style, and spend about 15 minutes at the arch on the way.

As I approached the arch, I saw two people! It's hard to imagine how remote this place is, and how amazing it was to encounter other people at all—never mind who they turned out to be. One of them, an older gentleman, told me he'd been to the arch before, but he couldn't recall how to get below and behind it. I was going to help him and/or the younger woman climb up and down over a big boulder into the arch base area if they wanted. I went over it first, but then he and the lady elected not to follow. He handed me his camera through the hole below the boulder (too small for a person), and asked me to take some pictures for him.

I noted it was a nice, expensive camera, and said "sure." I asked if I should start with a shot of him—it was a pretty image in that direction. He said, "No, I don't need MY picture taken, shoot the arch!"

"How many?"

"The rest of the roll!" He had 15 or so frames left. That was kind of unexpected! And the camera had an extremely wide-angle lens, 15mm I think.

So finally I said … "Hey, who are you, anyway?" I thought maybe he was Stan Jones, and I just didn't recognize him. When he replied, "David Muench," I was floored. And then it was clear what he wanted (grin). Some people I've asked know of him as a successful landscape photographer, and others don't—but I sure did. He was doing a book on Utah arches, along with his daughter, Zandria.

So I worked with him for about 20 minutes, waiting for the right sunlight and taking his directions. The wide-angle lens could capture the entire arch and the incredible view beyond, plus the light was fantastic. After handing back the camera and climbing out again, I wrote a release on the back of his daughter's business card allowing him to use the photos, hoping in fact he would do so.

"They are your photos, I followed your directions; I just pointed the camera and set the f-stop. If you like them, put your name on them."

Unfortunately it was now 6pm, and I had to leave fast to meet John and Cathie at Flying Eagle Cove as prearranged for pickup. I'd stayed 15 minutes longer than I'd planned, so I rushed down, including one short, nasty section of downclimbing, and was just in time. They brought me a swimsuit, towel, and shampoo like I'd asked (ahhhh), and then we towed John around the lake for skiing before dark!

◆   ◆   ◆

Finding an Arch Under Water

When is a grand stone span not an arch, but instead a mysterious pond? When it's almost completely underwater.

In the summer of 2003 we took our houseboat unusually far south for the first time—all the way from Bullfrog Marina to beyond Rock Creek Bay. This was about 57 river miles, or about 10 hours of houseboat driving. After one night beyond Friendship Cove, starting back upstream, we moored for the next night at the point of huge, northeast-facing, V-shaped valley on the east side of Rock Creek Bay.

The next morning was the last day of July. I knew we had to get the boat moving by noon or so to be home by the end of our week. I had just a few hours to explore. I took my little flatwater kayak for a short spin south along the shoreline. Before long I'd found not one, or even two, but THREE natural wonders.

The first marvel was an unusual pillar of stone, previously underwater, standing above the slick rock. The second item was what we call a "Jesus rock"—another isolated stone pillar, glowing lime green just below the water, where it was possible to stand ankle-deep and "walk on water." And the third wonder—well, that's the story I'll tell here.

Sitting in my kayak, I could see the slick rock "shoreline" dipped down to only about three feet above the water. Then there was some kind of depression behind it. I couldn't see into it or tell what it was, but it sure was unusual. I pulled up alongside of it and, with care, got myself out of the boat while hanging onto the bowline so it wouldn't float away. Standing atop the rock, I could see there was a strange, emerald-blue pond beyond the narrow isthmus where I'd landed. It was perhaps thirty to forty feet across, of unknown depth, and at the same level as the lake. Most of the way around was a sheer or overhanging wall, highest at the back. Hmm …

I wanted to explore the pond, but knew that if I got into it, I might not be able to get out again. However, I'd practiced climbing into my kayak in deep water. It wasn't easy, but it could be done. I had to rapidly pull myself into it from the rear without filling it with water. I had a life vest and whistle with me, and figured the houseboat crew would eventually find me by ski boat if I got stuck. So I studied the backside of the isthmus, and took a chance. I pulled the kayak up onto the rock with me, then lowered it into the "pond." Then I carefully slid into the "lakelet" myself … So far, so good. I didn't have a dive mask with me, but I could let go of the kayak—it couldn't get away—and swim around the hole marveling at its sheer walls and its bottomless depth.

Time to go back to the houseboat. Could I get out? There was no way I could directly climb the stone wall, even after exploring it for handholds and footholds. So I got myself into the kayak—wuff!—and then I was able to climb (carefully, again) out of the boat onto the rock—whew! I reversed the earlier process, dragging the boat up onto the stone isthmus, launching it on the lake-side, and getting back into it from shore.

I paddled back to the houseboat, and didn't tell anyone what I had seen. We pulled the anchors, and headed out. Then I announced mysteriously that we were going to pause and explore "three natural wonders." After trying to build some suspense, I showed the crew in turn the pillar, the Jesus rock, and then the weird pond, which was easy to see from the bow of the houseboat.

I decided to put the bow pontoons against the rock and try to anchor there temporarily. Fortunately it was a relatively calm day, with smooth water and little breeze to blow the boat around. There being no better solution, I did something

I've never done before or elsewhere. I tied an anchor line securely to a cleat, stepped off the bow onto the rock carrying the anchor, and gently lowered it into the pond on the far side. To my surprise, this had just enough weight and pull to hold the boat against the shoreline.

Rock Creek Arch filled with water. G. Adams photo

With this anchor line in place, the crew was free to walk off, circle uphill and downhill around the hole, then dive into it—including jumping off the high back wall. The one-inch line also provided a convenient, if strenuous, way for a body to climb out of the pool and back onto the rock without using a kayak.

I put on a mask and snorkel and took my depth-measuring line into the hole. I floated face-down and let out eighty feet without touching bottom. I could see fish, but nothing else. Weird! Finally I dove down the anchor line to see what might be out of sight. Epiphany! Perhaps fifteen or twenty feet below the lake's surface was the graceful bow of the top of an arch! That explained everything. After several good looks through the opening—of course not seeing anything other than the filtered glow of daylight through the span—I debated swimming through it. But my SCUBA training included a fair warning about "overhead environments ..."

I was pretty sure it would be easy to get through and then back to the surface. I'd previously swum through an underwater arch—the Alice J Arch near Annie's Canyon, which is submerged when the lake is very full. But it wasn't as deep as this one was on this particular summer day, so it was safer to explore to the half-way point before committing. I gave up on the idea. But before we departed I dove down on the outside too, thus seeing the top of the arch from both sides. Awesome! I couldn't talk anyone else in the crew into joining me. I wished I had an underwater camera, but no such luck.

The ongoing western US drought continued. By the next year the arch I discovered was well out of the water. Thus I've seen pictures of it that way, including from inside the chamber looking up through the circular "hole in the roof" that formed my "mysterious pond." According to someone at the Natural Arch and Bridge Society, this arch has no official name, nor even an unofficial name or designation. I call it just the "Rock Creek Bay Arch." However, there's another unnamed span, a "wall arch," high on the cliff across the bay to the southwest.

Two years later I returned to Rock Creek Bay when "my" arch was back underwater. I dove down to see it again, but it was a windier day. We had to run the motors to park there briefly, so once again I didn't try to pass through it. During that trip I hiked to, and stood on top of, that other unnamed arch—but that's another story.

◆   ◆   ◆

Diving to See the Gregory Natural Bridge

In 1969 the lake was still rising for the first time. That summer it submerged one of the world's largest natural spans, the Gregory Natural Bridge. Thirty-five years later I was possibly the first person since then to get a glimpse of the bridge. This stone span is a few turns up from the mouth of Fiftymile Creek off the Escalante River arm. For many years while boating in the area, I didn't know where it was. It didn't appear on any map I could find. I'd heard about it, and I was curious, but clueless. It didn't help that one of the pictures in Stan Jones's "Boat and Boot" book was of the wrong span, and the other was mirror-reversed!

A few years before I finally saw the bridge, I studied a topo map more closely and had a pretty good idea where it MUST be. Then when visiting, I started watching for signs of it being the right spot. In 2003, with a western US drought in full force, the lake dropped to a hundred feet below full pool for the first time in decades. In late November of that year we pulled up our houseboat to the large sandbar in Fiftymile. It was the "end of the water" for boating. Just downstream, an indentation in the sheer rock wall of a peninsula suggested what might lie below. The huge but stagnant continuation of the lake beyond the sandbar, going out of sight around the corner at the same water level, bore witness to the connecting window deep below the waves.

The lake gets pretty cold in November! I put on a short wetsuit over thermal underwear, plus a mask, snorkel, and SCUBA booties, and waded slowly into the lake. When I got up to my neck, I stood there a moment assessing … Too cold! Discretion was the better part of valor, and I canceled any snorkeling. Later I learned it would have been a waste of time anyway. The underside of the bridge was still fifty feet deep!

The next spring we returned to the same area. On May 18, 2004, we moored the houseboat on the same sandbar for a few hours before going elsewhere for the night. The drought had persisted, and the lake was about 16 feet lower than the previous November. I had a print of Stan Jones's old slide picture of the bridge, obtained from the Natural Arch and Bridge Society website. While we motored in, I was able to line up three or so key identifying features of the span (rock) above the bridge, and mark on my print the present water line at about 3585 feet. There were a lot of changes to the details while the bridge was underwater. The small pillar shown on top of the span no longer existed, and the rock surface was fuzzed out by dried algae scum. The depth gauge on the houseboat read 82 to 90 feet in the area near the bridge.

After studying the rock-face and the photo, I put on a wetsuit and took a kayak over from the houseboat to the downstream side of the bridge. I made about five "deep dives" with a mask and snorkel. I expected the underside of the bridge to be about 28 feet down at 3557 feet elevation, based on the NABS website, and that's a hard depth to reach. (Worse, their website actually said 3552 feet and I'd misremembered). My personal record was 37 feet, but that was using a weighted line for a fast descent. But on the last four of the five dives, I saw the top corner of the roof, and on the last two dives, I actually got my hand on the corner for a moment. (Reflecting on this later, with numbers I'll get to in a moment, I must have actually dived something like 32 feet down! It was a good day).

The rock above the opening sloped outward a lot. I had to follow it down and in, and then bump against it a few times coming back up. It was dim, dark, and cold down there! I knew the water didn't go down forever, but still, each time leaving the surface—and following the slope of the wall—felt kind of creepy.

Very little light came through the span, and I couldn't get deep enough to see straight through the bridge.

The top of the submerged Gregory Natural Bridge. A. Silverstein photo

On our following trip to the lake in August 2004, I went down to see the bridge again. Now the water level was even lower at 3577.5 feet (my best guess). We moored a few miles away the previous night. I hitched a ride with my kayak into Fiftymile on one of our ski boats, and then spent a couple of hours alone, exploring (carefully) while they went sightseeing. I dove four times to the underside roof and got a good measurement, 27-feet, 0 inches, plus or minus a few—but this was to the "upper roof" angling up from the true underside. I saw the latter, but I still could not get deep enough to see straight THROUGH it. (Must not have been as good a day as in May). This bridge is massive, whether submerged or not!

I took the measurement by tying a light, weighted line to the kayak, pulling it snug down at the edge of the roof, holding that spot until surfacing, tying a knot while floating, and later measuring it with a 100-foot tape. I adjusted for the small distance, about 5 inches, from the knot on the kayak to the water level. The line itself was at a slight angle, not vertical, since the roof of the span is concave. On the fourth dive I double-checked the knot, then forced myself a bit deeper below the sharp roof edge to see, and much to my chagrin the bridge roof itself was a bit lower still. I only had a moment. I surfaced gasping and a little dizzy. Remember, I was there all alone. I'd scared myself, so I quit diving at that point. Deducting 27 feet (or a smidge less) gave 3550.5 feet (or a bit more) for the underside of the sharp roof, even though the high point of the bridge itself was perhaps a little lower.

That day I also dragged the kayak up and down over the sandbar to the "back pool" (now connected only through the bridge) to dive a few times on the upstream side. I didn't even try to get deep enough to see through it. I just watched for signs of light, and I did see a glow on the second dive. The upstream side was slightly away from the sun, but also lacked any reference points for the location of the bridge, and it was even creepier diving down in the shaded water. While I was there, I checked the rock on both sides for a way to get to the top of the lintel … No joy. MAYBE you could do a long hike in from some other up-and-out point, but I didn't have time.

The upstream side of Gregory Natural Bridge. A. Silverstein photo

Later I received some pictures taken of the Gregory Natural Bridge just before it was submerged. From studying these, my best guess now is that my measurement was a bit long due to the angle of the measurement line. The corner I touched was at 3548.6 plus about 4, or 3552.5 feet, more or less. That would put it about 25 feet below the surface when I dove to it, not 27 feet. If so, the pitch of the wall above the corner would be about 68 degrees (22 degrees off vertical), and the horizontal offset was about 10 feet, which is believable. I also heard that the top of the lintel is at about 3661 feet—meaning you can boat over it when the lake is full—and I actually did this at least once, years before knowing where the bridge was. This would make the span just about 110 feet tall. That's the rock ABOVE the opening!

Since 2004, I've heard of other people snorkeling or SCUBA diving down to see the bridge while the lake was low. As of this writing in 2007, it's 50 feet back underwater. Who will be the next person to get a good look at it, and when?

◆   ◆   ◆

Many People, Big Bay, With Meteors

Floating in a vast bay on Lake Powell on a dark, warm summer night at the peak of a meteor show ... Does life get much better?

I own a one-twelfth share of a sixty-foot houseboat. Of course during my weeks I get to use all of it at once. The boat nominally sleeps 12 at most, including two on the pull-out couch. Some owners regularly take much larger crews, but I think seven or so is perfect and 10 is crowded. (A crew of just three people means a busier firedrill when anchoring, but oh is it quiet and roomy ...)

We not only have a floating boat, we also have an unusual arrangement of "floating" week selections. In 2004 I had a high pick in the first round. I noticed that the Perseid meteor shower, which peaks around August 11, would fall during a new moon in the middle of a week, a rare opportunity. I thought I was pretty clever to snag it. Apparently so did a lot of other people, because 17 of them asked to come along! Most trips I worry about having enough people. So this was a great problem to have ... I hated to say "no" to anyone.

Okay, I thought, let's go with a huge group for once. This should be "interesting ..." And it was. The trip went surprisingly well, people got along great, we never left anyone behind by accident, and actually it didn't feel that crowded. This was partly because some folks lived on the roof all week, others downstairs, and they were rarely all together in one spot at one time. I thought there would be backlogs in the bathrooms and the kitchen, but most often any interference was on the spiral stairs to and from the roof! And of course it was sleeping-room-only as we packed in every night, inches apart.

Despite a few illnesses and injuries (that I learned about well after the fact), people were in good spirits and got along great. Some folks even said they LIKED having the large group! While over-preparing to support the huge crew, I tried to think of everything that could go wrong. One weird notion came to me … So on the first afternoon, just before leaving Bullfrog Marina, I had everyone join me on the roof. Then very slowly we all walked to one side and leaned over the railing. If this would dangerously unbalance the houseboat, I needed to know about it before encountering a "tour boat wake" on the high seas. To my pleasant surprise, you could barely see the ship react to the weight shift. Nor did anyone label me a kook for my caution.

A few days later at the mouth of the San Juan River, I called a powwow to decide where we should go next. The fresh water tank seeming full and the holding tank empty enough, we continued 20 miles upstream to Piute Bay for a couple of nights. This is a very remote, quiet, beautiful pond, many hours of slow big-boat motoring from any marinas, unreachable by houseboats with too-small gas tanks.

Before sunset Wednesday evening we were perfectly positioned for an awesome celestial show. The nights were dark, the winds were relatively calm, and everyone seemed to be having a good time. A funny thing about that many people at a party, it's harder to keep track of them than counting cats. So I don't know how many were floating in the lake that night after dinner when they invited me to join them.

"And leave your swimsuit behind, you don't need it."

They were right of course, you could barely see your way from the bathroom to the back deck. It was absolutely delicious and memorable. (If any fish nipped at us, I don't remember that though.) Once adrift in the water amongst the scattered bodies, I had someone still on the swim deck toss me a life vest to use as a floating pillow. Ahhh … Sweet. I don't know how long we stayed out there. It probably wasn't many minutes, but it was timeless too. Bottomless black, warm soft water reflected crisp star-points in the many ripples. It was a mile or more across the transparent night air to distant silhouetted cliffs.

Someone once said the universe is neither benign nor malicious, merely indifferent. But on a warm summer night, in a place like Piute Bay, it feels welcoming and natural. It's vast and lonely, but you belong there anyway. You can actually sense the ball of rock below you, with the thin veneer of air above you, floating forever through the boundless star-speckled void. And at least once a minute, a bright Perseid meteor streaked across the infinite dome.

"Oh, wow, did you all see THAT one?"

Of course sometimes the universe, while not necessarily malicious, can be ironic, or even exact payback. Thus it was on the afternoon of the second day, too late to move the houseboat, when the septic smell got strong enough that I realized we did in fact have a serious problem. First thing the next morning, we motored all the way back out to the main channel. I sent a ski boat ahead to explore the pumpout station in Oak Bay ("your entry fees at work"), and heard on the radio that the manual sucker was impotent, don't go there. So it was late afternoon before we finally had the houseboat tied up to the sewage dock at Dangling Rope to do the necessary ... Sigh. Now that was a day I remember all too well, but would rather forget.

◆   ◆   ◆

Up-and-Out at Glen Canyon

It's been said that, "Life is like a maze where we all go around trying not to find an exit." This aphorism is wisely recalled when hiking or scrambling in rough terrain, such as that found above the lake in Glen Canyon.

"Watch out, that sheer cliff a few feet to your left is a sudden exit ..."

But it's also said that life is like a metaphor, or at least an irony, and sure enough, there's also a wonderfully positive point of view on exits. When you are down deep in a spectacular canyon—the main one, or any of its innumerable smaller side-chasms—it can be challenging and entertaining finding ways to get up-and-out above the cliffs, to gaze back down in wonderment at where you came from, and how you got there. The lake and your boat can take you into some amazing places. Then sometimes you can hoist yourself up from them to high above them. I call these special places "exits" too, but they are a good kind.

Of course there are human spiders who can climb just about anything (with or without ropes). Me, I don't count a route as an "exit" unless I can do it without a safety line and still have a good chance of reusing my body at the end of the day. But use of all four limbs and comfort on steep terrain is often essential. Ideally an "exit" is a rare and special accident of topography and erosion. You know you've found one when the sensation of exploring it is rather like threading a needle—or a long sequence of needles in a row—but (to mix a metaphor), you can pass all the way through the looking glass to Wonderland.

For example, there's that massive, well-known "exit" called the "Hole in the Rock." After scrambling up and down it several times over the years, I discovered that you can easily "connect it" to a huge slick rock slope above the Jackass Bench a half a mile upstream. A willing friend with a radio and a ski boat completes a memorable loop that I've done once in each direction.

Much more remote and unobvious is an anonymous, unnamed canyon pointing mostly north from the outer side of the Great Bend of the San Juan River. It's one of a series of easily overlooked channels downstream of Alcove Canyon … But it's the ONLY one with a barely-non-technical route through the Navajo sandstone cliffs. A steep friction walk with exposure leads to a blind crack—and then you are on top. From there you can walk all the way north to overlook Iceberg Canyon! It took several trips and a lot of exploring, including a long stroll to the beautiful but dead-end of Alcove, to find and confirm this unique passage. Not that I still recommend it … It's much easier to get to the same area using the road up the southeast side of the Rincon.

Once upon a time, we found the Alice J Arch tucked into its own "little" cove a bit upstream from Slick Rock Canyon. Somewhat later, moored at the base of this arch, I attempted and discovered a marvelous section of steep scrambling up the gully to its left. Would it go all the way? Yes! It didn't take long, maybe twenty minutes, and I was on top.

"Better make a careful note of where I popped out, so I can find my way back down!"

That's right, the "exit," once proven, is often but the beginning of the mystery tour. It's merely the gateway to whatever lies (well) beyond. Perhaps, as in this case, a local high point a mile distant.

Studying maps, we knew there must be a way out of Bowns Canyon. First though, we had to discover the rockfall route—with an improved trail through it—up from the lake, just beyond the fork with Long Canyon. Otherwise there's no start to this adventure when the water is down. Then we had to hike several miles up Bowns, watching the terrain, to find the "one and only place" we could ascend all the way to the rim. Sure enough it was special—witness the decayed stock gate left at the knickpoint by a long-ago cattle rancher. This particular exit gave access to a mile-plus meander across the rolling plateau, all the way to peer down the cliff at the Zane Grey Arch in Explorer Canyon! Use of a GPS unit helped a lot in finding our way to the overlook, and added peace of mind to the return hike.

The very top of the Rincon can only be reached by a very long series of barely-negotiable "exits," first up to the base of the Navajo sandstone bumps, then around and up (and sometimes down) through their cracks and gullies. In this case your destination is a flat high point where the only remaining exit is by death or helicopter.

Late one afternoon we moored on the north side of the southeast estuary of Good Hope Bay. I had "only" three hours until sunset … Might as well see what was up the boulder-strewn hill above the houseboat. I figured I'd be back all too soon, in time for dinner. Well, the first gully notch didn't pan out, but the second one I tried led me right through! There was complex terrain to navigate across some traverse hollows, leaving cairns to guide me back, before I emerged on sandy flats. Suddenly I needed all of my available daylight to make a fast round-trip several miles north. There I gazed down the cliffs into Popcorn Canyon. Incredible scenery from a thousand feet up! On this particular jaunt I especially had to watch the sunset clock. I knew that if I didn't return through the "eye of the needle" before dark, I'd be forced to spend the night up there. Which would merely be thirsty and unpleasant, not fatal, but at least embarrassing.

There's a way up and out of the far left end of Music Temple Canyon. Here you can get atop the cliff and soak in the scenery of the mouth of the San Juan River. But I can't recommend this route. I scared myself silly years ago descending the short, steepest section of the slick rock. I recall saying to myself, "I have the rest of my life to deal with this very carefully." There being no other way down, eventually I had to go for it and trust the force of friction … But nowadays when I boat past this junction, I enjoy looking up with binoculars wondering which of the little bumps on the rim is the cairn I built to prove I was there.

All of the above are but selected examples of the many lovely exits I've sought and discovered in Glen Canyon. Of course there are myriad others still pending exploration, or which "got away." For example, despite hopeful hints on the topo map, there's no up-and-out from either arm of Ribbon Canyon. I know this because I did a long solo hike to both ends to check. But in this general area, there's one more exit of which I am especially fond, and saved here for last.

Over the years, as opportunity presented itself, I explored the three half-mile-long, unnamed canyons upstream from Ribbon on the same side of the river. Each is deep-set east-northeast into Navajo sandstone, with lovely and varied scenery. The north one has a high rock shelf upon which perched for an unknown time a bizarre "walking rock" on three pillar-like legs. (Alas, now defunct, probably of natural causes). I dubbed that one the "Walking Rock Canyon." The south one I call "Twin Edens Canyon," for the two gardens at its ends. The middle one I now refer to as the "Middle Rib Canyon" because … Well, therein lies a tale.

When you walk into one of these canyons, or any like them, on a deer trail—if you are lucky enough to find that much—the chasm envelops you and becomes for a time your entire world. It's a vast, complex, intricate place you could explore all day—although you seldom have that much time. Yet from outside, passing by on the main channel, it's easy to not even notice the opening. Thus it was some years of twice-annual houseboat trips before I even entered Middle Rib for the first time. I enjoyed the deep, cool, cottonwood-shaded ravine on its south side. I found remnants of an Anasazi camp under a flying buttress that looked like an arch, but wasn't—yet—it's just a tiny little stone feature, until you stand below it and it looms over you. Plus I admired the enormous grandeur of the "middle rib" of smooth, rounded sandstone that descended perhaps five hundred feet from the cliffy rear wall. It aimed straight out at the canyon mouth, splitting the ravine in two huge, but unequal spaces.

"Middle Rib" Canyon hike. A. Silverstein photo

"Is it doable?" I went up it as far as I was comfortable. Hmm … Good friction, clean reddish-gold sandstone. There's one "crux" section, perhaps forty feet in length, where any steeper would be insane. You could ascend it easily enough, but would you slip and die coming down? I remembered Music Temple, and didn't go farther that day. A few years later when next it was feasible, I brought a friend and we aimed to find out. Most of an hour's hike from the boat brought us to the crux slope. He headed right up without hesitation. What could I do? I followed with trepidation, knowing we MUST return this way, but not until later. The route shallowed a bit while remaining quite arduously steep. It fanned out into alternatives at various points. Then we crossed a small notch and were above it all!

Clearly this up-and-out was known to the Anasazi. Masters of friction, they didn't deem it necessary to cut Moki steps into the ridge. But given its rarity, it had to be a major highway for them. It's the ONLY exit for ten miles on that side of the Colorado River! Way upstream around mile 72, there are perhaps seven gullies leading to very rough terrain well west of the Rincon ... Hardly a reason to climb out there other than to sightsee (or hunt). And way downstream at Cottonwood Canyon, well, that's where the Mormons finished their crossing of the river from the Hole in the Rock, enroute to establish Bluff.

This successful exploration gave us access to loop around to the right, above Twin Edens Canyon. Less than an hour later we stood on top of the recently-named Bell Tower Window! It was a very impressive, yet hidden, stone span at the heights of the sheer wall.

Later, coming down the rib was scary. I just HAD to crab-walk, using both feet and hands, to get more square inches onto the rock. I never slipped, but I slid a little, and I burned my palms on the hot stone surface.

Back home, often on a cold winter night, knowing now it was possible, I began to daydream about where that Middle Rib could lead me ... Hence on a lovely fall day, all by my lonesome, I walked over eight hours round-trip, up from the houseboat, up the middle rib again (with due caution but less fear), and out the notch on the top. I built up our previous cairn, took GPS readings and digital photos, and set out cross-country northeast for several miles—all the way to the Rincon!

This was a fabulous excursion across land that almost never sees humans. At the "Rincon" high point (actually southwest of the bowl itself), there were various "ancient" brass survey markers from the 1950's and early 60's. The wooden tripod had long ago blown down the east side of the steep hill leaving anchor pipes embedded in the rock. The panorama of the Waterpocket Fold and the southwest side of the Rincon was surreal. I stayed up there for over an hour. Then I continued down northeast to the very edge of the Rincon bowl ... And then back west over a mile to peer into the unnamed abyss upstream and across from the mouth of the Escalante ... And then over and up and down to the head of Walking Rock Canyon. As usual, route-finding on the huge pillows of fossil sand dunes required patience, and even a sense of humor.

Throughout all of this I was utterly alone, yet connected to the world by ham and marine radio channels. I checked in occasionally with my wife down on the houseboat. I tried to convey to her the simple yet epic nature of my ongoing experience. I also kept in touch with two crewmembers who ran their ski boat all the way to Wahweap and back for the day.

Eventually once more at the head of Middle Rib Canyon, I rested and gathered myself before praying my way down the "highway." No incidents—whew! Back to the boat—wow! Suddenly a big windstorm—uh oh!

◆   ◆   ◆

At Glen Canyon, up-and-out means—to exit the merely magnificent for the magical—and then to return for a refreshing cool-down dive into the lake. A day spent, or a week, exploring Glen Canyon—by boat, on foot, or simply sitting quietly with your senses wide-open means a brief exit from the rest of your existence. It's an excursion to the eternal.

The lake is ephemeral. The canyon itself is a passing snapshot in the geologic span of time. Yet both are so rich, so vast, so profound, that here you may connect in silence with their greater nature—and perhaps too your own. As your heart pounds with exertion, or simply with joy; as you bring home a bit of sand in your sandals, and sandstone sculpture in your soul; as you aim in vain to put it all in proportion, and to explain it with meager words and images to someone else; you know that, here, you are intimate with wonders beyond your comprehension.

Resources

We hope you enjoyed reading *Lake Powell Tales*, as much as we all enjoyed sharing our stories. Maybe someday we'll have another edition of *Lake Powell Tales* as more stories come to light. You can find us on the bulletin board over at Wayneswords.com.

Royalties from the sale of this book will benefit the Friends of Lake Powell. Thank you for your support! And please visit our favorite Lake Powell links online:

Friends of Lake Powell	www.lakepowell.org
Fishing and other information	www.wayneswords.com
Lake Powell Resorts & Marinas	www.lakepowell.com
GCNRA Webpage	www.nps.gov/glca
Glen Canyon Dam operations	www.usbr.gov/uc/water/crsp/cs/gcd.html
Lake Powell water level/records	http://lakepowell.water-data.com
Lake Powell Magazine	www.lakepowellmag.com
Lake Powell Yacht Club	www.lpyachtclub.org
John Wesley Powell Memorial Museum	www.powellmuseum.org
Glen Canyon Natural History Association	www.glencanyonnha.org
Natural Arch and Bridge Society	www.naturalarches.org
100th Meridian Initiative	www.100thmeridian.org

"Let your hook always be cast,
and in the pool where you least expect it,
you will find fish."

—*Ovid*

978-0-595-45126-5
0-595-45126-8

Printed in the United States
85811LV00005B/72/A

9 780595 451265